THE OFFICIAL ILLUSTRATED HISTORY OF

RAF SEARCH AND RESCUE

PAUL E EDEN

THE OFFICIAL ILLUSTRATED HISTORY OF

RAF SEARCH AND RESCUE

PAUL E EDEN

ADLARD COLES

LONDON · OXFORD · NEW YORK · NEW DELHI · SYDNEY

To Ben and Elisabeth, who both think planes are boring

ADLARD COLES
Bloomsbury Publishing Plc
50 Bedford Square, London, WC1B 3DP, UK

BLOOMSBURY, ADLARD COLES and the Adlard Coles logo are trademarks of
Bloomsbury Publishing Plc

First published in 2020

A catalogue record for this book is available from the British Library

Library of Congress Cataloguing-in-Publication data has been applied for

ISBN: HB: 978-1-4729-6090-0; ePub: 978-1-4729-6091-7; ePDF: 978-1-4729-6088-7

10 9 8 7 6 5 4 3 2 1

Typeset in Bulmer by Phillip Beresford
Printed and bound in India by Replika Press Pvt. Ltd.

FSC
www.fsc.org
MIX
Paper from
responsible sources
FSC® C016779

To find out more about our authors and books visit www.bloomsbury.com
and sign up for our newsletters

men and women of the Royal Air Force provided courageous, life-saving
scue services for 75 years, from the formation of the RAF Air Sea Rescue
service in February 1941, to the end of formal, large-scale RAF SAR
operations, in the Falkland Islands, in March 2016.

Born through the necessity of war, air-sea rescue employed marine craft
working in concert with supply-dropping aircraft and the legendary Walrus, a
sturdy amphibian regularly obliged to taxi home over the sea when the
additional weight of rescued personnel prevented it from reaching take-off
speed. Later, the Hudson and Warwick dropped airborne lifeboats with varying
degrees of success.

This combination of vessels and aircraft eventually served in every theatre
where RAF airmen were likely to be shot down or forced to abandon their
aircraft over water. There were many courageous rescues, but also heart-
breaking tragedy. Equipment and techniques were often inadequate for the
difficult job in hand and men who might have lived were lost, while the rescuers
themselves frequently succumbed to adverse weather, enemy fire, or both.

While the Walrus added relative speed and range to the Air Sea Rescue
Service's response, and could alight to recover casualties, it was vulnerable to
rough seas and limited in performance. Truly effective rescue from the air
required an aircraft that could stop, without landing, collect casualties and then
depart with them safely embarked.

Such a reality dawned in 1945, when the Royal Navy and Royal Air Force
began investigating the operational possibilities of the helicopter. The RAF's
first rescue helicopter, the Sycamore could barely lift its own crew and
equipment, although the latter initially extended to little more than a rope
ladder.

The more capable Whirlwind arrived during the mid-1950s and established the
fundamentals of RAF helicopter rescue – the new art of search and rescue –
including the bright yellow colour scheme that became synonymous with these
operations.

Many years later, I was privileged to train as an RAF Sea King pilot with what by then had become the Search and Rescue Force. Flying with 'C' Flight, 22 Squadron from RAF Valley and on detachment in the Falkland Islands, I saw at first hand the incredible courage, professionalism and teamwork of the RAF SAR crews.

During my three-year tour we flew missions to gas rigs, winched crewmen from ships and life rafts, and flew into the mountains to the aid of climbers and walkers in distress, often working alongside the volunteers of the Mountain Rescue Service. These were times and experiences that I will never forget.

This beautifully illustrated, carefully researched book is a fitting tribute to Royal Air Force search and rescue. I will always be immensely proud of my time with 22 Squadron and trust that this work will help preserve the memories and ethos of 75-years of RAF lifesaving and all those who served in it.

CHAPTER 1

LAUNCHES AND LYSANDERS

MARINE CRAFT SECTION

On 1 April 1918, the Royal Flying Corps (RFC) and Royal Naval Air Service (RNAS), the aerial branches of the British Army and Royal Navy respectively, merged to create the Royal Air Force (RAF). The change had come as a direct result of the need to defend Great Britain against attack by heavier-than-air bombers and airships. Such defence had proven complex and difficult to implement but placing responsibility for air power under a single organisation was seen as an important step in ensuring the safety of the British public in their homes.

There was a gradual transition to new rank structures and uniforms over the next 12 months or so, while the nascent RAF's leaders came to terms with a massive air arm – among the largest in the world at the end of World War I – that numbered a sizeable fleet of seaplanes among its equipment. With seaplanes came the need for tenders, small boats equipped to service aircraft

moored just offshore. The RNAS was replete with tenders and crews, these forming the nucleus of the RAF's Marine Craft Section (MCS), formed on 12 April 1918.

Under the MCS construct, Lieutenant Colonel GRA Holmes was appointed Senior Officer for Marine Equipment. It was therefore to Holmes and MCS colleague, Captain WEG Beauforte-Greenwood, that the task of assessing the MCS inventory fell later in 1919. Under constant harassment from senior British Army and Royal Navy officers, Major General Sir Hugh Trenchard had returned as Chief of the Air Staff on 11 April 1919, having resigned the post on 14 April 1918 after difficulties at the Air Ministry. Determined to establish the RAF as a permanent service, Trenchard called for a complete audit of personnel and equipment, reasoning that it was impossible to establish a separate service without knowing its complement.

It was no straightforward task. Some vessels, loaned to the RNAS by the Admiralty, were now Royal Navy property, while others now appeared to belong to the RAF

Curtiss H16 Large America N4060, is typical of those used by the Royal Naval Air Service against submarines and Zeppelins, and for air-sea rescue, between 1917 and 1918. Around 69 of these large flying boats passed to the RAF, of which approximately 39 were serviceable.

but were under Royal Navy control. With the audit underway, Holmes defined the RAF's post-war marine craft requirement as 73 seaplane tenders, including 32 capable of going to sea; 92 docking lighters; 18 aircraft ferries; six kite balloon craft; and a similar number of compass barges. He estimated a force of just fewer than 2,500 personnel would represent sufficient manning for the emerging MCS. There was no mention of vessels or men assigned for rescue duties.

Beauforte-Greenwood delivered the audit in autumn 1920, by which time a strength of 191 craft had been agreed upon. Primary responsibilities were seaplane handling and work in their take-off and alighting areas, moving personnel and equipment, checking for semi-submerged obstacles and other general duties. Responsibility for buoys and moorings was added subsequently.

More significantly, that same year, the Air Ministry issued an order including the following statement:

> At all units where large boat [flying boat] or seaplane flying is carried out, or at any other unit which is provided with motorboats where overseas flying is carried out, a motorboat will be detailed to stand-by in case of any accident occurring while flying is in progress. This boat will either be under

way in the flying area or standing by at the pier. If standing by at the pier, the engine will be run for a few minutes before flying starts and at least once every hour in the summer and every half-hour in the winter.

The seed that would germinate into the Air Sea Rescue Service in 1941, and eventually evolve into the Search and Rescue Force (SARF), had been sown.

By the mid-1920s, first-aid training had become a standard component for new recruits, but the suitability of existing MCS vessels for rescue work was becoming questionable. Their obsolescence became more obvious when the Marine Aircraft Experimental Establishment moved from the Isle of Grain to its new base at Felixstowe. It brought with it the latest aircraft, typically larger and or faster than their predecessors, and therefore requiring vessels of greater capacity and performance in support.

Meanwhile, the Schneider Trophy, a pre-war competition for seaplanes, had returned in 1919 and the RAF established its High-Speed Flight in 1927, with a primary focus on winning the trophy after a number of poor showings. Flying from the major RAF seaplane base at Calshot, the Flight demonstrated the speed of its optimised single-seat racing aircraft, while simultaneously highlighting the inability of the old MCS boats to reach an accident scene quickly and then to have the capacity to deal with it.

Three 54ft Thorneycroft coastal motorboats (CMBs) were borrowed from the Royal Navy as an interim measure. Capable of 35 knots in calm conditions, the CMBs had the performance for the job but lacked

Major General, later Marshal, of the Royal Air Force the Viscount, Trenchard, the first Chief of the Air Staff.

© Royal Air Force Museum

manoeuvrability and were difficult to slow down. Worse still, their engines had a tendency to catch fire on start-up, such an incident accounting for one of the RAF's borrowed trio. There remained clear need for a purpose-designed vessel.

In a peculiar twist, the push that finally convinced the Air Ministry that it ought to enter the boatbuilding business came from TE Lawrence, none other than Lawrence of Arabia. His connection with the RAF had begun in 1922 when close relationships with the Secretary of State for Air, Winston Churchill, and Trenchard, saw his entry into the service on dubious grounds. In 1927, he was posted

SUPERMARINE WALRUS

Today most readily associated with the Spitfire, Supermarine had based its aviation business on seaplanes, among them a series of single-engined biplane amphibians culminating in the Fleet Air Arm's Seagull Mk II. From this, Supermarine developed the Seagull Mk V, flying a prototype on 21 June 1933. Orders came from Australia and the RAF, the latter renaming the type Walrus in August 1935, long before its first example flew on 18 March 1936. With 285 Walruses completed, Supermarine gave production over to Saunders-Roe late in 1939, releasing factory space for building Spitfires.

The majority of aircraft delivered for RAF ASR were therefore Saunders-Roe built, production continuing into January 1944, by which time 746 aircraft had been completed. In October 1941, 275 and 278 Squadrons took the first ASR Walruses into RAF service, with 277 and 276 Squadrons following by January 1942. In RAF service the Walrus was habitually known as the 'Shagbat', a moniker for which no explanation can be found.

Number 283 Squadron debuted the Walrus in overseas ASR service at Algiers in April 1943. Initially covering the North African coast, it subsequently moved into Italy alongside 284 Squadron. Meanwhile, 294 Squadron began flying Shagbats over the Eastern Mediterranean and Persian Gulf in September 1943.

The Walrus reached the Far East in February 1944, when 292 Squadron began covering Burma from Jessore, just as 269 Squadron began covering the mid-Atlantic out of Lagens on the Azores. The latter served until March 1946, withdrawing shortly before the Sea Otter replaced the Walrus in the ASR squadrons during April.

••

SPECIFICATION

SUPERMARINE WALRUS MK II

Powerplant one 775hp Bristol Pegasus VI radial piston engine

Length 37ft 3in (11.37m)

Height 15ft 3in (4.66m)

Wingspan 45ft 10in (13.97m)

Wing area 610sq ft (55.67m²)

Maximum speed at 4,750ft 135mph (217km/h)

Range 600 miles (965km)

Service ceiling 18,500ft (5,640m)

Armament one 0.303in Vickers K or Lewis machine gun in the bow, plus one or two similar weapons in the midships position for self defence

This Walrus is believed to have been serving either 276 or 277 Squadron. It was photographed at Warmwell, Dorset, on 8 January 1944.

to Karachi, returning to Britain, after an epic military campaign, in January 1929.

Still with Trenchard's ear, Lawrence found his way to Calshot, where he joined the MCS crews on rescue duties. Attending a Blackburn Iris crash on 4 February 1931, he assisted in the rescue of six casualties by diving into Plymouth Sound, but six others died in the incident. Lawrence was quick to pass his observations up the chain of command. His thoughts, added to those of Wing Commander Sydney Smith, the Officer Commanding RAF Mount Batten, where Lawrence was based, and Beauforte-Greenwood, both of whom had been pressuring the Air Ministry, finally forced change for the better.

The Air Ministry commissioned boat and aircraft designer Hubert Scott-Paine, at the British Power Boat Company, to develop a purpose-built launch. The first 200-class Royal Air Force Seaplane Tender (RAF 200) began sea trials on 19 February 1931, meeting with instant success. Eight more boats were ordered, but a fire destroyed all but ST 201, which became a training vessel. Production restarted with ST 202, an improved RAF 200 that became the basis for a variety of special-purpose craft including, from 1933, rescue.

Lawrence transferred to the Marine Aircraft Experimental Establishment (MAEE) at Felixstowe on 28 February and remained intimately involved in the design of high-speed rescue launches for the MCS. Two years later, he left the RAF and just a few weeks after that died as the result of injuries sustained in a motorcycle accident. His legacy to the MCS was as a vociferous supporter and promoter of new technology, and his influence helped steer the unit into a new era, long after his passing.

Still the pace of aircraft development was outstripping the capabilities of the MCS fleet, however. RAF 200 proved triumphant, remaining in production until ST 324 was completed in 1940, but further designs were needed to suit the larger, heavier flying boats that were emerging.

In 1936, therefore, plans were made for a new 64ft high-speed launch (HSL), capable of accommodating a crew with living and workspace, and suitable for tender and rescue use. In the event, the RAF 100-class was an adaptation of a Royal Navy motor torpedo boat (MTB) evolved from a design developed by Beauforte-Greenwood, Lawrence and Scott-Paine and put to industry by the Admiralty, on the RAF's behalf, in June 1935. A triple-engined craft capable of 35 knots, it accommodated a crew of eight and had space for a sick bay. The resulting HSL prototype for the RAF was launched in May 1936, departing for sea trials on 23 May.

The Air Ministry ordered numbers 101 to 114 for delivery in 1937, adding 115 and 116 in

Seaplane Tender Mark I ST201 speeds down the Cattewater, passing a 10 Squadron, Royal Australian Air Force Sunderland moored at Mount Batten, Devon, in late 1940. Aircraftman Shaw, in reality TE Lawrence, used ST201 to train RAF coxswains during 1931.

1938, and 117 to 132 in 1939. In fact, production ceased at 121, the final 11 craft being completed in 1941 to a revised standard.

INADEQUATE SERVICE

Terror had been visited upon the British public during World War I, as airships and giant bombers delivered their weapons against what were very often the wrong targets – navigation was difficult and bombing accuracy poor, generating random results that might hit a target of military or industrial value but might just as easily hit civilian housing.

Later, the Allies took the offensive to Germany, attacking industrial and military targets in the world's first properly planned strategic bombing campaign.

There was agreement among air warfare strategists that the bomber would be decisive in any future war and no doubt among senior officers at Royal Air Force Bomber Command that it would be sending bombers across the North Sea when it was called into action. Another theory, misguided as it turned out, was that the bomber would always get through, thanks to its combination of performance and defensive firepower.

Nonetheless, bombers were likely to be lost during a sustained campaign and some

HSLs 122 and 142 were British Power Boat Company HSL 100 Type Two craft, similar to the original HSL 100, but 1ft shorter and equipped with turreted armament as standard. Completed to an early standard and photographed on 7 April 1941 off Dover, Kent, these boats have single 0.303in Vickers guns in each of their turrets. The Type Twos were nicknamed Whalebacks for their cabin and hull shape.

means of recovering their crews from the North Sea was required. Aircrew were costly, time consuming to train and tended to be more motivated if they felt there was a sporting chance of rescue in the event of ditching. It should be remembered that casualty rates in peacetime were high, through navigational error, equipment failure and human factors. Even during wartime, training and non-operational accidents were often as lethal, if not more so, than the enemy.

In December 1938, therefore, Air Officer Commanding (AOC) Bomber Command, Air Chief Marshal Sir ER Ludlow Hewitt called a conference, at which the inadequacy of MCS rescue coverage was addressed. Just six HSLs covered the east coast from Donibristle and Tayport, Fife, in the north, to Calshot, Hampshire, in the south, with a seventh boat assigned to Pembroke Dock, Pembrokeshire. A further challenge emerged in 1939, when the need was identified for 13 HSLs to serve abroad; individual boats had reached Aden, Basra, Kalafrana (Malta) and Singapore by the outbreak of war in September.

It was an expanded HSL fleet that enabled the MCS to give a good account of itself during the Dunkirk evacuation, although not through aircrew rescues. Working from Malta, HSL 107 provided rescue cover for Hurricanes making the hazardous overwater flight to the beleaguered island, ironically recovering an Italian pilot from the sea but no British personnel, at least officially, until 12 June 1940.

Back home, the RAF was engaged in the Battle of Britain, with no less than the end of the British way of life at stake. History records that Fighter Command was successful against

LOCKHEED HUDSON

In June 1938, the British Purchasing Commission in the US ordered a military version of the Lockheed 14 Super Electra commercial transport as the Hudson. It was intended as a navigation trainer for the RAF. The first example flew on 10 December and featured a bomb bay as well as provision for a reasonable defensive armament, regardless of its proposed second-line role.

Powered by the 900hp Wright Cyclone R-1820-G102A, the initial Hudson Mk I aircraft arrived in Great Britain on 15 February 1939, by which time the type's training mission had been abandoned. Subsequent variants introduced revised powerplants, improved armament and performance increases. Although the Hudson was primarily a maritime reconnaissance and anti-shipping/anti-submarine type, some were also equipped to drop airborne lifeboats for ASR work.

At least two lifeboat-capable Hudsons served 251 Squadron from its Reykjavik base, while 269 Squadron operated similarly equipped Hudson Mk IIAs from the Azores between March and November 1944. Number 279 Squadron formed on the Hudson in 1941, operating Mk III, V and VI aircraft successively, and using them with airborne lifeboats from early 1943. Finally, the Hudson served 281 Squadron, alongside the Warwick, after its re-formation in November 1943. The RAF's final Hudson operator, 251 Squadron, withdrew its last Mk IIIs in August 1945.

....

SPECIFICATION

LOCKHEED HUDSON MK VI

Powerplant two 1,200hp Pratt & Whitney R-1830-S3C4-G Twin Wasp radial piston engines

Length 44ft 4in (13.53m)

Height 11ft 11in (3.63m)

Wingspan 65ft 6in (19.99m)

Wing area 551sq ft (51.19m²)

Maximum speed at 15,000ft 261mph (420km/h)

Range 2,160 miles (3,476km)

Service ceiling 27,000ft (8,230m)

Armament two 0.303in machine guns each in fixed forward positions and dorsal turret, plus one 0.303in machine gun in a ventral position. Provision for two similar additional weapons in beam positions; up to 1,000lb of bombs and other stores

This dramatic photograph was taken during the evacuation of the British Expeditionary Force from Dunkirk in June 1940. It shows a 220 Hudson over the beach, with burning oil tanks in the distance. A general reconnaissance unit, 220 added ASR to its duties later in the war.

Malta's air-sea rescue provision initially comprised only HSL 107, seen here moored in January 1941.

the odds, but at the cost of many fighter pilots, a large number of whom were lost in the English Channel and North Sea. Those who were rescued gave thanks to a motley selection of civilian craft, RAF HSLs and other boats, Royal Navy vessels and Royal National Lifeboat Institution (RNLI) lifeboats. The RAF contribution included just 13 HSLs, three of which were generally unserviceable or otherwise unavailable – engine problems were frequent – while only ten covered the Channel and North Sea.

In the last three weeks of July 1940 alone, 220 RAF aircrew went missing or were confirmed killed at sea, 260 more joining them by the end of October, at which time the Battle of Britain was transitioning into the Blitz. The losses and the country's inability to reach survivors were shocking. A Sea Rescue Organisation was established in August 1940 to coordinate rescues in the Channel and North Sea, much of the task falling to RAF Coastal Command.

Meanwhile, the Luftwaffe's air-sea rescue organisation was setting an exemplary example. Employing a useful mix of vessels and seaplanes, plus German navy E-boats, it also had fixed 'floats' at mid-Channel, moored to provide refuge and life-saving equipment at known locations towards which hapless pilots could steer before ditching. Interestingly, both sides worked hard throughout the war to rescue airmen, regardless of nationality.

Coastal Command quickly realised that providing a casualty with flotation equipment, rations, medical supplies and survival gear might dramatically improve their chances of survival. The so-called Thornaby bag was developed along these lines at Coastal Command's Thornaby base and is notable not only for its life-saving contribution but also the move towards delivering rescue, or at least part of a rescue, from the air. Air-sea rescue was evolving. Thornaby introduced its fabric bag in 1940 and RAF Bircham Newton followed with its 'barrel', produced from bomb parts and a cylindrical container, with similar contents.

At RAF Lindholme, the station commander, Group Captain Waring, and his team took the concept a stage further, incorporating a self-inflating dinghy into a 500lb bomb tail section and attaching it by ropes to four 250lb bomb sections containing other equipment and supplies. Pilots were expected to swim to the dinghy, and then haul in the other containers once safely inside. The crews of larger aircraft, bombers and Coastal Command patrol aircraft, enjoyed the slim comfort of knowing their aircraft carried a dinghy and other emergency equipment, but the Lindholme gear and any other help from the air were always reassuring.

But the air-sea rescue service in late 1940 lacked a key ingredient: coordination between RAF commands. No matter how many HSLs were available, there would be no real improvement in efficiency if their crews had little idea where they were needed.

In recognition of this fundamental problem, 24 January 1941 was set as the date for the appointment of a Director of Air Sea Rescue Services (ASRS). Since the organisation was schemed as a joint RAF/Royal Navy effort, its first director was Group Captain Croke of the RAF, while his second in command was Captain CL Howe of the Royal Navy. The ASRS directorate's headquarters were established alongside that of Coastal Command at Northwood, Middlesex.

Originally formed from Dutch personnel, 320 Squadron began flying the Hudson Mk I on ASR sorties early in 1941.

WESTLAND LYSANDER

Known without exception as 'Lizzie' to its crews, the Westland Lysander replaced the Hawker Hector biplane with the RAF's army cooperation squadrons, beginning with 16 Squadron in May 1938. The type had first flown on 15 June 1936, and served extensively in France with the British Expeditionary Force Air Component from September 1939.

Apart from their primary reconnaissance and artillery spotting missions, the Lysanders engaged advancing German troops in brave bombing attacks for which they were ill-equipped – 50 were shot down during the Battle of France. With France effectively lost, the surviving Lysanders were flown home during May, covering the Dunkirk evacuation beaches from stations in England.

The Lizzie continued on the front line at home and overseas, particularly with the 12 UK-based squadrons assigned anti-invasion patrol duties. These continued into December 1940, by which time the Lysander's home-based army cooperation role was drawing to a close. With Curtiss Tomahawks and North American Mustangs replacing it, the type was assigned air sea rescue, special duties and target-towing roles.

When Lysander production ceased in January 1942, some 1,366 machines had been completed, in several versions: Bristol Mercury XII-powered Mk I, Mk II (Bristol Perseus XII) and Mk III/IIIA (Mercury XX or XXX). Compared with the Mk III, the Mk IIIA introduced a twin-gun mount for the observer's defensive armament, and it was this variant that made its way to 275 and 278 Squadrons for ASR duties.

• •

SPECIFICATION
WESTLAND LYSANDER MK IIIA

Powerplant one 870hp Bristol Mercury XX or XXX radial piston engine
Length 30ft 6in (9.34m)
Height 14ft 6in (4.45m)
Wingspan 50ft (15.24m)
Wing area 260sq ft (24.15m^2)
Maximum speed at sea level 209mph (336km/h)
Range 600 miles (965km)
Service ceiling 21,500ft (6,400m)
Armament two fixed forward-firing 0.303in Browning machine guns with 500 rounds per gun, plus two similar weapons in the rear cockpit for self defence

RAF AIR SEA RESCUE SERVICE

On 6 February 1941, the Directorate of Air Sea Rescue Services (ASRS), which later became the RAF Air Sea Rescue Service, was assigned three primary tasks:

· To coordinate all sea rescue operations for aircraft and aircraft crews
· To provide equipment that could be dropped by aircraft at crash scenes in order to improve the air crews' chances of survival until the arrival of rescue craft
· To provide adequate marine craft, moored buoys and other aids to rescue.

Emphasising the requirement for cooperation, the directorate was attached to the Area Combined Headquarters of Coastal Command's 15, 16, 18 and 19 Groups, which effectively divided Great Britain into four areas of responsibility, with a directorate liaison officer working closely with each group. Within the areas of responsibility it was considered that any RAF station ought to provide air sea rescue (ASR) assistance as needed, although the RAF's Army Cooperation Command was already employing the Westland Lysander on such missions, especially in southern England. An extension of the aircraft's anti-invasion coastal

V9547/BA-E was a Lysander Mk IIIA of 277 Squadron. Seen here during preparations for a training sortie from Hawkinge, Kent, on 29 September 1942, it is equipped with M-Type dinghy containers on its stub wings and smoke floats on its rear fuselage bomb racks.

patrol task, the coverage extended from the Wash in East Anglia and all along the coast, out to 20 miles, until Milford Haven in Wales.

As well as defining practical means of rescue, the directorate also worked alongside the Ministry of Aircraft Production on methods to improve crew safety and provision of survival equipment. Techniques and procedures were also developed for safer ditching and safety drills devised for use post-crash. Later, actual incidents were written up and their descriptions circulated with notes on what crews had done well and areas in which they may have taken more successful courses of action. A crew well practised in survival procedures was far more likely to be rescued – by any means – than one simply hoping for the best.

More HSLs were being built, although not quite fast enough, while the newly developed airborne systems began showing their worth. In April 1941 an Armstrong Whitworth Whitley heavy bomber ditched, its crew surviving 72 hours before they were picked up, thanks to a Thornaby bag and a Lindholme kit. But there was still more to do.

Ditching after a raid on Germany in June 1941, a Handley Page Hampden crew survived eight days in their dinghy before a Hampden assigned ASR duty spotted them on 1 July. It dropped Lindholme equipment, which sustained the crew until an HSL arrived, but

86 SQUADRON

Two World War I attempts at forming an operational 86 Squadron failed, so that the unit only really became established on 6 December 1940. Flying Blenheim IVs within Coastal Command, it became operational in March 1941, adding ASR to its primary convoy escort role in June.

That same month, it began re-equipping with Beauforts, embarking on anti-shipping work in earnest from November. It continued its maritime strike role, latterly with the Liberator, and completed its time on transport flights to India from October 1945. It disbanded on 16 April 1946.

239 SQUADRON

Number 239 Squadron was established in the maritime role when a coastal reconnaissance outfit stationed at Torquay was given the number in August 1918; it disbanded on 15 May 1919. The number returned on 18 September 1940, applied to a new unit created through the amalgamation of sections of 16 and 225 Squadrons, equipped with Lysanders and nominally for army cooperation.

In fact, the Lysanders performed a number of support functions before moving on to army cooperation, but Curtiss Tomahawks arrived to replace them in June 1941, and they were instead employed on ASR duties out of Manston and Plymouth. The unit subsequently flew a variety of types, latterly the Mosquito, and fought a busy war before disbanding on 1 July 1945.

241 SQUADRON

Another of the RAF units established out of RNAS flights, 241 Squadron's origins were in a coastal patrol unit from which it formed in August 1918. It disbanded on 18 June 1919. On 25 September 1940, sections of 4 and 614 Squadrons combined into a new 241 Squadron, intended for army cooperation with the Westland Lysander.

The work began immediately, alongside the unit's original coastal patrol role. In April, an expanded mission set included ASR work from Bury St Edmunds, but re-equipment with Tomahawks saw a new emphasis on tactical reconnaissance.

This continued with the Hurricane and Spitfire, while the squadron moved to North Africa and then into Italy.

A reconnaissance specialist, 241 Squadron's particular skillset saw it return to ASR in a search capacity, from Bellaria and Treviso, flying the Spitfire Mk IXE. It disbanded in August 1945.

320 SQUADRON

Initially comprising Royal Netherlands Naval Air Service personnel, and eight Fokker T.VIIIW and one C.XIVW floatplanes freshly escaped from the German assault on the Netherlands, 320 Squadron flew anti-shipping patrols from 1 June 1940, before lack of spares grounded its aircraft.

Re-equipped with Ansons and Hudsons from October 1940, it took a number of crews from 321 Squadron, a fellow Dutch RAF unit, before flying its first operational Hudson mission, an ASR sortie, on 19 February 1941. It worked primarily on patrol and anti-submarine tasks until transferring to Bomber Command and the North American Mitchell from March 1943. It remained as a Mitchell unit until August 1945, when it transferred back to the Royal Netherlands Navy.

500 SQUADRON

The Special Reserve units were an important component in the pre-war build-up of RAF air power, albeit few were established before being absorbed into the Auxiliary Air Force. Number 500 Squadron was among the few created under the Special Reserve, standing up with a mix of regular and volunteer personnel at Manston on 16 March 1931. Initially equipped with the Vickers Virginia for night bombing, on 7 November 1938 it was assigned a new role as an Auxiliary unit for general reconnaissance with the Anson, receiving its first examples in 1939.

In fact, it undertook a variety of other roles too and, after re-equipping with the Blenheim, from 15 May 1941 added ASR to its work. The role steadily grew in importance and continued after the Hudson came on strength, although offensive missions soon became the priority. Anti-submarine missions now became its primary occupation, 500 Squadron moving to Gibraltar for the North African landings. The squadron remained in the Mediterranean theatre, replacing its Hudsons with Venturas in December 1943.

On 1 August 1944, 500 Squadron disbanded into a new 27 Squadron, South African Air Force, although some of its personnel remained to create a new Baltimore-equipped 500 Squadron. This transferred to Kenya in September 1945, where it disbanded by renumbering as 249 Squadron.

The Royal Auxiliary Air Force (RAuxAF) resurrected the Auxiliary and Reserve concepts post-war and 500 Squadron reformed at West Malling in June 1946, as a Mosquito night-fighter unit. From July 1948 it became a day-fighter squadron operating successive Meteor models until the Royal Auxiliary Air Force disbanded in 1957.

614 SQUADRON

Formed as an Auxiliary Air Force unit at Llandow on 1 June 1937, 614 Squadron initially received Hawker Hinds, but in late 1937 exchanged these for Hectors, which were more suited to its army cooperation role. It re-equipped with the Lysander at Odiham at the onset of war, subsequently beginning coastal patrol work over eastern Scotland. From November 1939, the emphasis was again on army cooperation, but in June the following year a detachment was sent to Tangmere for ASR. The Blenheim IV arrived to oust the Lysander in July 1940.

In August the Blenheim V came on strength and 614 Squadron took these into the North African campaign as bombers, before establishing base at Tafraoui in May 1943. It returned to patrol and other maritime duties on 6 June, once again taking on an ASR role.

The unit disbanded in February 1944, but stood up again on 3 March by the renumbering of 462 Squadron, a Halifax-equipped bomber unit stationed in Italy. 614 Squadron finished the war as a Liberator operator, on 27 July 1945. It reappeared under Royal Auxiliary Air Force on 10 May 1946, again at Llandow. It flew the Spitfire and Vampire, before disbanding again on 10 March 1957.

Some 57 years later, 614 (County of Glamorgan) Squadron re-formed in Cardiff as a Reserve general support squadron.

they were perhaps only hours from being lost. The incident demonstrated that even while more suitable equipment was arriving in quantity, the process of searching for survivors remained inadequate.

Army Cooperation Command units, exemplified by 239 and 241 Squadrons, had proven the Lysander's worth as an ASR asset, albeit too small an aircraft for Lindholme gear. Instead the Lysander carried dinghy packs on the erstwhile weapons pylons under its stub wings. Many other squadrons also contributed aircraft as and when required. Among them, 86 Squadron, Coastal Command, employed its Blenheims on secondary ASR duties from June 1941, while 500 Squadron, Auxiliary Air Force (AuxAF), had used the same type on ASR since May 1941. Another AuxAF unit, 614 Squadron, had been flying Lysanders on ASR out of Tangmere since June 1940, but latterly switched to Blenheims.

Most unusual among the squadrons listing ASR among various duties, 320 Squadron was manned by a majority of Dutch personnel, its initial cadre having escaped the Nazi invasion of their homeland by flying their Fokker floatplanes to Britain. Later taking Avro Ansons and Lockheed Hudsons, it flew an initial ASR Hudson sortie in February 1941.

But more specialised aircraft and dedicated ASR units were clearly the way forward. In particular, an aircraft that could alight on the water, recover survivors and then take off for home would in many cases remove much of the complication of having a spotter aircraft guide a vessel to the incident location.

The Royal Navy was already operating the Supermarine Walrus, a small flying boat ordered for naval and RAF use as early as

AVRO ANSON

Developed from the six-passenger Avro 652A airliner, the Anson satisfied an Air Ministry requirement for a twin-engined coastal reconnaissance landplane. First flown on 24 March 1935, the Anson delivered significant new technology into RAF service, for not only was it the first monoplane delivered under the interwar expansion schemes, but it also introduced the retractable undercarriage.

Initially retracted through a manually operated system, the aircraft's mainwheels moved forwards to sit semi-recessed in the engine cowling undersides, considerably reducing drag in flight. Flown as the Anson Mk I production aircraft for the first time on 31 December 1935, the type entered service with 48 Squadron on 6 March 1936.

Perhaps best remembered in its training and communications roles, the Anson was in fact the mainstay of Coastal Command's frontline strength at the outbreak of war. Early Lockheed Hudson deliveries meant that the type was slowly being replaced, yet the Anson was still serving Coastal Command late in 1942 and equipped 275, 276, 278, 280, 281 and 282 Squadrons in the ASR role.

The RAF took the last of 10,996 Ansons built on 27 May 1952 and finally retired the type from its communications role on 28 June 1968.

SPECIFICATION

AVRO ANSON MK I

Powerplant two 350hp Armstrong Siddeley Cheetah IX radial piston engines

Length 42ft 3in (12.89m)

Height 13ft 1in (3.99m)

Wingspan 56ft 5in (17.22m)

Wing area 410sq ft (38.09m^2)

Maximum speed at 7,000ft 188mph (303km/h)

Range 790 miles (1,271km)

Service ceiling 19,000ft (5,470m)

Armament one fixed forward-firing 0.303in Vickers machine gun, plus one similar weapon in a dorsal turret; up to 360lb of bombs or other stores

This 276 Squadron Anson Mk I was being packed with a dinghy and its supplies at Harrowbeer, Devon, on 20 March 1943.

May 1935, but the bulk of deliveries had gone to the Royal Navy. RAF requests for aircraft to be transferred for the ASR role initially fell on deaf ears, but six aircraft were reluctantly released. The Walrus was fully capable of alighting unless the sea state was too severe, and had limited payload capacity for survivors. Its arrival into RAF service proper during September 1941 coincided with the formation of 275, 276, 277 and 278 Squadrons, the Service's first dedicated flying ASR units.

There was still a vital role for marine craft, however, as statistics for early 1941 prove. A pilot down at sea prior to the ASRS's formation stood only a 20 per cent chance of rescue; between February and June 1941 this rose to 46 per cent. High-speed launch (HSL) production therefore continued, equipping units all around the British coast and overseas, especially following a 28 July 1941 announcement that the fleet was to be expanded to include an additional 64 HSLs and a large number of supporting vessels.

Cooperation between Walrus amphibians and surface craft remained a primary ASR technique until helicopter search and rescue became practical during the 1950s.

CHAPTER 2

SHAGBATS AND SPITFIRES

DIRECTORATE OF AIRCRAFT AND AIRCREW SAFETY

Further cooperation between established organisations was secured on 23 September 1941, when the Directorate of Aircraft and Aircrew Safety brought the Directorate of ASRS, Assistant Directorate of Regional Control and Directorate of Fighter Operations under a single commander. Among its more fundamental suggestions, the Directorate of Aircraft and Aircrew Safety recognised that differences in radio equipment and frequencies between ASR aircraft and HSLs was stifling communication during operations.

In the air, the Lysander had continued its ASR patrol work but, with the Walrus joining it, these sorties were to range 40 miles out to sea, doubling the existing provision. The first of the ASR squadrons also began forming: 278 Squadron standing up on 1 October 1941, 275 on 15 October and 276 on 21 October, while 279 Squadron formed on 16 November,

and 280 and 277 Squadrons on 10 and 22 December 1941, respectively.

Now fielding dedicated squadrons equipped with suitable aircraft, the RAF ASRS still faced the challenge of how to find stranded aircrew. Fighter Command operated an advanced early warning system comprising radar stations, reporting stations and visual observation, all integrated via telephone into its headquarters at Bentley Priory. It employed specialist radar operators and plotters, most of them from the Women's Auxiliary Air Force (WAAF). WAAF operators assigned to fighter communication might be in direct radio contact with formations and this, combined with the possibility of generating a radar fix for an aircraft's last known position, gave a reasonable start point for an ASR search.

However, the wind, tides and enemy action, either offensive or through picking up survivors, still complicated the rescue task and many men perished. Pilots flying single-seaters usually had only their Mae West lifejacket, but crews from larger machines had a sporting chance of boarding the aircraft's emergency dinghy. If this could be fitted with a radio, or beacon, then rescue would be simplified enormously.

Efforts to create a dinghy radio began in 1941 and by September, a prototype was ready. But a German NS2 radio was captured and, proving far better in design, became the basis for a reverse-engineered set. By January 1942, orders for the 'new' radio totalled 10,000 and while production ramped up, attention turned to producing a beacon as a temporary measure. Ultimately, the beacon proved too challenging, while the NS2 did eventually enter production but in the US and only to the extent of 1,000 units.

Another possibility resided with the RAF Pigeon Service. Its birds already routinely flew in Bomber Command's aircraft and other large aeroplanes, but refused to fly in fog or at night, and could not fly when wet through. They were housed as standard in waterproof containers but were usually killed if an aircraft crashed. A watertight, floating container, introduced in January 1942, gave the bird a chance of survival in a ditching. It proved its worth on 23 February 1942 after a Bristol Beaufort crashed, although the message-carrying bird was lost. Meanwhile its colleague, which had escaped, returned to the loft. Its arrival triggered a complex set of calculations and assumptions that launched a Catalina, a Hudson, HSLs and a Walrus into action. An HSL picked up all four survivors and pigeons became a standard addition to ditching drills. After a scheme to create a dinghy radar beacon also failed, they remained crews' only method of signalling their position at range.

Problems with the marine craft continued into 1942, with slow deliveries made good in part by loans from the Royal Navy. There were also efforts to equip the HSLs with gun turrets, not unlike those installed on RAF bombers, as a defence against the regular attacks their crews were suffering from Luftwaffe fighters and patrol aircraft. Another slow programme, it led to a compromise in which two individual weapons were mounted on HSLs likely to encounter the enemy.

In the air, two of the new ASR squadrons – 279 and 280 – were scheduled to bring their dedicated Hudsons into the fray. Capable of carrying a heavier payload over longer ranges than either the Lysander or Walrus, the Hudson could deliver Lindholme gear far out to sea, but a dearth of aircraft and aircrew delayed the formation of both squadrons so they only became properly operational early in 1942.

Even so, a proportion of Hudson production had been diverted to the Soviet Union, causing a switch in 280 Squadron's equipment from Hudson to Anson even before it had taken delivery of a single example of the Lockheed twin. An adequate patrol aircraft that had already demonstrated its usefulness in ASR, the Anson failed in as much as it was unable to carry Lindholme gear, although adaptations were soon undertaken to overcome the shortcoming.

The combined problems of vessel and aircraft supplies saw the happier rescue statistics of mid-1941 fall dramatically, to just 17 per cent in February 1942, offering somewhat worse odds than those faced by crews before the RAF ASRS had been formed. Against this grim backdrop, on 12 February 1942, British forces engaged German navy battlecruisers *Scharnhorst* and *Gneisenau*, heavy cruiser *Prinz Eugen* and other escorting ships.

RAF Bomber, Coastal and Fighter Commands and the Fleet Air Arm launched aircraft to attack as the vessels steamed through the English Channel on their way back to Germany from France, where they had suffered repeated air attack. The strikes were disastrous, with 44 aircraft shot down. Pre-warned, the RAF ASRS had HSLs and other boats in place. Various Royal Navy and other vessels were also ready to respond in the aftermath of battle and Fighter Command also contributed aircraft to the search effort.

The search continued into 13 February and extended to within 30 miles of the Netherlands, but only five aircrew were recovered and then by the Royal Navy. Once again, the ASRS had demonstrated its abject inadequacy.

Walrus, Sea Otter and Defiant

But change was in the air, quite literally. A new era began on 7 January 1942, when a 275 Squadron Walrus departed RAF Valley in search of a crashed Anson crew. The mission demonstrated both the excellence of the Walrus and its ability to set down and recover casualties, and its major shortcoming, a lack of power, which manifested itself in a limited payload, especially for operations off water. The aircraft alighted alongside the survivors' dinghy but had to make two trips since it could only manage to take two of the men at a time.

In the unit's next live ASR sortie, on 9 May, the same pilot, the Officer Commanding 275 Squadron, Flight Lieutenant RF Hamlyn, landed alongside the dinghy of another hapless Anson crew, effectively keeping them company until an HSL came on scene.

It was 277 Squadron's turn to complete an initial Walrus rescue on 1 June 1942, recovering the casualty from the Channel in two hours. On 3 June, it was back to the Channel, this

Contemporary images provide a dramatic comparison in HSL weaponry. The single-gun turret configuration was photographed on 7 April 1941, while Whaleback HSL 169, serving 27 ARS Unit at Dover in 1942, was equipped with the additional pair of twin Lewis guns.

190 SQUADRON

Number 190 Squadron served as a night-fighter training unit between 24 October 1917 and January 1919. It re-formed at Sullom Voe, Shetland, on 1 March 1943, employing surplus 210 Squadron Consolidated Catalinas on anti-submarine warfare (ASW) and MR tasks. These continued until 31 December 1943, when 190 Squadron disbanded.

It stood up again on 5 January 1944, as a transport squadron, flying the Short Stirling IV. The unit flew operations in support of the Special Operations Executive (SOE), but work-up for, and participation in, the Normandy landings were its most important task. Glider towing and supply drops, including participation in Operation Market, SOE work and bombing kept it busy into 1945, when it also began flying ASR sorties with the Stirling. Ultimately, 190 Squadron disbanded on 28 December 1945.

196 SQUADRON

There is considerable similarity between the histories of 190 and 196 Squadrons. Established on 7 November 1942, 196 Squadron was a Stirling-equipped bomber unit, but began transport and SOE supply drops early in 1944, in the run-up to D-Day.

Like 190 Squadron, it took part in the Normandy landing, its towed gliders and took part in the ill-fated Operation Market.

In October 1944, it returned to bombing and SOE re-supply, at the same time adding ASR to its regular tasking; the squadron also towed gliders during the Rhine crossing in 1945. Its transport role continued until 24 March 1946, when it disbanded, still as a Stirling operator.

220 SQUADRON

'C' Squadron, a general-purpose RNAS unit serving around Gallipoli, officially became 220 Squadron, RAF on 1 April 1918, but failed to take up its new designation until September. It disbanded in August 1919.

Not unlike 217 Squadron, it re-formed as an Anson GR unit at Bircham Newton in August 1936. It converted into the Hudson in September 1939, continuing with the type into December 1941, when in a peculiar development two

220 Squadrons existed briefly, one with the Hudson and the other a renumbered detachment of 90 Squadron on the Fortress I, in Egypt. On 1 January 1942, the Hudson section took on the remainder of 90 Squadron's aircraft at Polebrook, the two parts of the squadron coming together in February at Nutt's Corner, operating both types.

The Fortress proved more effective as an MR platform than as a bomber. The squadron began re-equipping with the Fortress IIA in July, adding ASR to its regular anti-submarine patrols. The work continued until December 1944, when conversion to the Liberator began. By March 1945, 220 Squadron was exclusively Liberator equipped, but U-boat targets had dried up it focused on ASR. In September it became a transport squadron, before disbanding on 25 May 1946.

Now equipped with the Shackleton, 220 Squadron re-formed at Kinloss on 24 September 1951, flying all three major MR variants before renumbering as 201 Squadron on 10 October 1958. In a final existence, 220 Squadron operated as a Thor inter-continental ballistic missile unit between 1959 and 1963.

248 SQUADRON

During August 1918, 404, 405 and 453 Flights, RNAS at Hornsea Mere re-formed into 248 Squadron, RAF. Flying anti-submarine patrols, the unit disbanded on 6 March 1919. It reappeared at Hendon on 30 October 1939 on the Blenheim, moving north under Coastal Command in February 1940.

It employed its Blenheims on a variety of reconnaissance and anti-shipping work, continuing with these as primary tasks when its attention turned to the Dutch coast from June 1941, but adding new missions, including ASR. Re-equipped with Beaufighters from July 1941, 248 Squadron focused on offensive and escort sorties, latterly to its own flight of Mosquito FBXVIII anti-shipping and coastal strike aircraft.

After VE-Day, 248 Squadron returned to ASR, employing the Mosquito FBVI, before renumbering as 36 Squadron on 1 October 1946.

254 SQUADRON

No fewer than five RNAS flights, 492, 515, 516, 517 and 518, combined at Prawle Point in August 1918 to create 254 Squadron, RAF, which disbanded from its coastal patrol role on 22 February 1919.

The unit returned in the fighter role on 30 October 1939, equipped with Blenheims and moving to Coastal Command duties the following January. After re-equipping with Beaufighters in June 1942, it added torpedo missions to its regular roster, losing several aircraft on operations and therefore supplying its own ASR cover.

Although the Beaufighter remained on strength to war's end, 254 Squadron added a few Mosquito FBXVIIIs in April 1945. Its final operational sortie involved six Beaufighters in an ASR sweep on 11 May 1945. It disbanded, by renumbering as 42 Squadron, on 1 October 1946.

Personnel and Anson (foreground), Spitfire (right) and Walrus aircraft of 276 Squadron arranged at Harrowbeer on 21 March 1943. The unit's commanding officer, Squadron Leader RF Hamlyn, standing in the foreground, had previously been a fighter pilot, with 13 confirmed victories.

275 SQUADRON

Formed at RAF Valley, Anglesey, on 15 October 1941, 275 Squadron was the first of the dedicated ASR squadrons, taking over a role that the army cooperation Lysander units had been performing since the evacuation from France. Initial equipment comprised the Lysander Mk IIIA and Walrus Mk II, with the Defiant coming on strength in 1942, followed by the Anson and Spitfire Mk VB in 1943.

The squadron provided cover over the Irish Sea from various stations until April 1944, when Warmwell, Dorset, became its new home. Well placed to recover casualties from the D-Day operation on 6 June 1944 and beyond, it flew from stations in Devon until disbanding at Harrowbeer on 15 February 1945.

The unit reformed at RAF Linton-on-Ouse, North Yorkshire, on 13 April 1953, initially on the Sycamore HR.Mk 13, before becoming a Sycamore HR.Mk 14 operator; it re-equipped with the Whirlwind HAR.Mk 4 in 1959. However, 275 Squadron renumbered as 228 Squadron at Leconfield on 1 September that year.

276 SQUADRON

Established at Harrowbeer on 21 October 1941, 276 Squadron employed the Lysander Mk IIIA and Walrus Mk II as its initial equipment. With detachments at Fairwood Common, Gower Peninsula (now Swansea Airport); Roborough, Devon; Perranporth, Cornwall; and Warmwell, Dorset, the unit took Hawker Hurricane Mk IIs soon after its formation, adding the Defiant and Spitfire Mk IIA in 1942. The Spitfire Mk VB and Anson came on strength in 1943, followed by the Sea Otter in early 1944 and the Vickers Warwick ASR.Mk I in April.

In September 1944 the squadron moved to Amiens-Glisy in France, covering the northern European coast until the end of the war in May 1945. It returned to Great Britain soon after for a brief stay at Andrews Field, a US Army Air Force base in Essex, now known as Saling Airfield, before deploying to Norway. There it remained until November, when it returned home to the UK again, this time disbanding at Dunsfold, Surrey, on 14 November 1945.

277 SQUADRON

Number 277 Squadron was established at Stapleford Tawney, Essex, on 22 December 1941. Its first missions were flown with the Lysander Mk IIIA and Walrus Mk II, but thereafter its equipment deviated somewhat from the norm.

The Defiant and Spitfire Mk IIA arrived in 1942, with the Sea Otter following in 1943. During 1944, the Spitfire Mk VB and Warwick ASR.Mk I came on strength. The unit maintained detachments at Hawkinge, Kent; Martlesham Heath, Suffolk; and Shoreham and Tangmere in West Sussex, ideal stations from which to cover the Channel and Thames Estuary. On 15 February 1945, the squadron disbanded at Hawkinge.

278 SQUADRON

Established at Matlaske, Norfolk, on 1 October 1941, 278 Squadron roamed the east coast from Sumburgh on the Shetland Isles to the north, down to Thorney Island, West Sussex. Initially equipped with the Lysander Mk IIIA and Walrus Mk II, it later took Defiants, with the Anson Mk I arriving in 1943, followed by the Warwick Mk I and Spitfire Mk VB in 1944. The Sea Otter came on strength in 1945. The unit disbanded at Thorney Island, on 14 October 1945.

279 SQUADRON

Number 279 Squadron formed at Bircham Newton, Norfolk, on 16 November 1941. Equipped with Hudsons, it undertook long-range missions over the North Sea, continuing the work with the Warwick ASR.Mk I, from November 1944.

In April 1945, it added Hurricane Mk IIC and Mk IV airframes to its complement, with Sea Otter Mk IIs coming on strength in July. The Lancaster ASR.Mk III arrived in September, replacing the Warwick and remaining as the only type on inventory when the squadron disbanded at Beccles, Suffolk, on 10 March 1946.

280 SQUADRON

Established at Thorney Island, West Sussex, on 10 December 1941, 280 Squadron flew Ansons until October 1943, when the Warwick arrived to replace them. From January 1946 it maintained Warwick detachments at Aldergrove, Lossiemouth, Reykjavik, St Eval and Thorney Island, before disbanding at Thornaby, on 21 June 1946.

281 SQUADRON

Unusual in forming on the Boulton Paul Defiant, 281 Squadron stood up at Ouston, County Durham, on 29 March 1942. It soon added the Walrus and Anson to its inventory, and moved to Drem, East Lothian, where it disbanded on 22 November 1943.

It re-formed immediately at Thornaby, North Yorkshire, on the Hudson and Warwick. In February 1945 it relocated to Tiree in the Inner Hebrides, from where it provided cover for the Northern Ireland and west Scotland coasts. By the time it disbanded at Ballykelly, County Londonderry, on 24 October 1945, it had also flown the Sea Otter and Vickers Wellington Mk XIV.

282 SQUADRON

Number 282 Squadron formed at Castletown, Isle of Man, on 1 January 1943, operating Walrus Mk II and Anson aircraft. It disbanded on 31 January 1944, re-forming at Davidstow Moor, Cornwall, on 1 February and serving on until 19 July 1945, flying the Sea Otter, Walrus and Warwick. It disbanded at St Eval, Cornwall.

Number 276 Squadron ground crew load a dinghy into Spitfire Mk IIA P8131/AQ-C at Warmwell, during a training exercise on 7 July 1942.

HAWKER HURRICANE

Less technologically advanced than the Spitfire, the Hurricane was nonetheless the only modern fighter available to the RAF in quantity at the outbreak of war. It served as the cornerstone of Fighter Command strength during the Battle of Britain, but towards the end of that turning point in history the Spitfire clearly represented the future in the air-to-air role.

But the rugged Hurricane was easily modified into a superb ground-attack aircraft, in variations of which role it served until war's end, managing to score many more kills in air combat along the way. As with the Spitfire, the Hurricane gained increasingly heavy gun armament and it was as the cannon-armed Hurricane Mk IIC that the aircraft first found its way on to the ASR squadrons.

Number 276 Squadron took its first Hurricanes in December 1941, with 279 and 283 Squadrons following. Among them, 279 Squadron was unique in operating the Hurricane Mk IV alongside the IIC, albeit only briefly between April and June 1945. For airmen adrift in the sea after ditching or bailing out, the presence of a cannon-armed Hurricane overhead must have offered considerable comfort, while the use of a single-seat fighter in an ASR role reinforces the fact that a major component in such operations was spotting downed aircrew and guiding surface vessels to them.

• •

SPECIFICATION

HAWKER HURRICANE MK IIC

Powerplant one Rolls-Royce Merlin XX V12 piston engine rated at 1,280hp for take-off

Length 32ft (9.75m)

Height 13ft 3in (4.05m)

Wingspan 40ft (12.20m)

Wing area 257.6sq ft (23.93m²)

Maximum speed at 22,000ft 339mph (546km/h)

Range 460 miles (740km)

Service ceiling 32,400ft (9,880m)

Armament four 20mm Hispano cannon

time to recover a Douglas Havoc pilot. Number 276 Squadron followed on 18 June, plucking a five-man Coastal Command Whitley crew out of the sea three miles from Bude, Cornwall. The Walrus was unable to take off and its pilot instead taxied to Bude harbour; it was the first of several such taxi rescues.

On 23 June, 278 Squadron performed its first Walrus rescue, again demonstrating the aircraft's limitations. A circling Wellington and Hudson guided the aircraft to the survivors of a ditched Wellington, 60 miles off Cromer, Norfolk. The Walrus landed and successfully embarked the five crew but took three attempts to reach sufficient speed to 'unstick' from the water's surface tension and become airborne again.

These early Walrus sorties also revealed to the crews that special techniques would need to be devised for the safe transfer of wet, cold and most likely exhausted survivors from a dinghy or the sea into the aircraft. Before any attempt at recovery was made, however, the pilot needed to approach carefully so as to avoid a bow wave that might upset a dinghy or force a man in the water down.

Ideally, a casualty could catch a rope thrown from the forward hatch and be pulled to the aircraft. He was then allowed to drift aft, under the lower wing to the rear hatch, where a second crewman could pull him in. Where no second crewman was available, the forward man tied the rope to prevent the casualty drifting off, then moved back to the rear hatch himself. Sometimes embarking a survivor was a two-man job, in which case both crewmen worked together. If there was only one, then the pilot allowed the engine to idle while he left the cockpit to lend a hand. It was important not to leave an empty dinghy afloat after a recovery, lest it attract the attention of other would-be rescuers and begin a false new operation.

A task perhaps even more challenging was to find the scene in the first place. The ASR squadrons each covered a large expanse of sea and the slow Walrus was not the best platform for a quick response and search following a Mayday call. Often a fighter was scrambled to fly on ahead and search the Mayday area, calling the Walrus crew to help them fly directly to the site. Any fighter or aircraft in the vicinity would do the trick, but through their regular use in the role, the Hawker Hurricane and Supermarine Spitfire became stalwarts of such operations. So much so, in fact, that both were added to the ASR inventory in specialised variants, equipped to drop supplies on making first contact.

All through the war, the HSL remained the primary source of rescue, especially further out to sea, working alongside the 'spotter' aircraft just as the Walrus crews did. Where there was a strong likelihood of enemy interference, however, the Walrus arguably had the better chance of survival since although slow, it was still faster than an HSL, assuming it was able to take off again.

By late 1941 large gaps in ASR coverage remained, but efforts were continuing to close them. A unit was required to cover the sea to the east, off northern England and Scotland, and 281 Squadron formed for the task on 29 March 1942. The Lysander had been a staple of landplane ASR operations to date but insufficient numbers were available to equip the new unit. Instead, attention turned to the Defiant, a turret-armed fighter that had proven disastrous in combat.

SUPERMARINE SPITFIRE

First flown on 5 March 1936, the Supermarine Spitfire needs little introduction, save dispelling the popular myth that its finest hour came during the Battle of Britain in 1940. That desperate summer's fighting proved without doubt that the Spitfire was a fine fighting machine, but the aircraft in action then represented the beginning of an evolution that continued into the early post-war years.

It is seldom recognised that from the Mk I and II Spitfire flown during the Battle of Britain, a series of increasingly powerful, more heavily armed variants emerged as superlative air-combat fighters, fighter-bombers and long-range photo-reconnaissance platforms, not to mention the carrier-borne Seafire derivatives. Alongside all these, many Spitfires also made it into secondary roles, sometimes modified for their new tasks but commonly on a make-do basis. In 1943, a little over 50 Spitfire Mk II and Mk IIB airframes were modified as the Mk IIC for the ASR role.

The conversion process to Mk IIC included the addition of a rack for marker bombs under the port wing and re-engining with the more powerful 1,240hp Rolls-Royce Merlin XX. Flare chutes were installed in the underside of the Spitfire's centre fuselage as standard and on the ASR.Mk IIs they were equipped to launch Type E sea survival and rescue gear, packed into two small containers and one larger unit. Inside the large container was a dinghy suitable for several men, while one of the smaller units housed water, food, distress flares and a first-aid kit. The second small canister contained 75 yards of buoyant rope that held the dinghy and supply containers together in the water.

Thus equipped, the Spitfire could be on scene relatively quickly and although it was unable to pluck survivors to safety, it could at least provide sustenance and shelter until better equipped help arrived by sea or air. In some cases, the presence of a fighter overhead might also serve to reassure airmen concerned about enemy attack, but the Spitfire's short range soon saw pilots making for home. Modified from weary airframe stocks, the Mk IIC was isolated from the main run of Spitfire evolution and when the 'C' wing was developed for production machines and introduced on the Mk VC, the Mk IIC was redesignated ASR.Mk II to avoid confusion.

Spitfire Mk IIs had been released for Mk IIC conversion as the Mk VB arrived to replace the earlier version on the front line and when the Mk IX began replacing the Mk VB, the latter also found its way on to the ASR squadrons, beginning in 1943 and gathering pace during 1944. Mounting underwing racks as standard, the Mk VB flew its rescue missions unmodified, there being no change required to its flare chutes to accommodate the Type E equipment. There is evidence to suggest that the majority of ASR.Mk VBs had their elliptical wing tips removed in favour of 'clipped' wing tips, improving manoeuvrability at low altitudes.

The even more powerful Spitfire Mk IX also saw ASR service, with 283 Squadron in the Mediterranean theatre. Spitfire ASR.Mk II aircraft flew with 275, 276, 277, 278 and 282 Squadrons, of which 275, 278 and 282 Squadrons apparently had access to a pool of machines rather than having them permanently assigned. The Mk VB served 269, 275, 276, 277 and 278 Squadrons.

SPECIFICATION

SUPERMARINE SPITFIRE MK VB

Powerplant one 1,440hp Rolls-Royce Merlin 45, 46 or 50 V12 piston engine
Length 29ft 11in (9.12m)
Height 11ft 5in (3.5m)
Wingspan 36ft 10in (11.23m)
Wing area 242sq ft (22.48m^2)
Maximum speed at 10,000ft 331mph (533km/h)
Range 395 miles (636km)
Service ceiling 37,000ft (11,280m)
Armament two 20mm Hispano cannon with 60 rounds per gun, and four 0.303in Browning machine guns with 350 rounds per gun

BOULTON PAUL DEFIANT

Hawker's Sydney Camm designed a series of closely related two-seat biplane combat aircraft during the 1920s and 1930s, applying adaptations in equipment and powerplant to optimise them for roles including bombing, training, army cooperation and air-to-air combat. Among them, the Hart bomber proved impossible for contemporary fighters to catch during exercises in 1930 and 1931.

Camm suggested that a Hart Fighter be fielded as a stopgap while more technologically advanced fighters were perfected. The Hart Fighter retained the bomber's rear defensive position and added a pair of forward-firing guns, while its performance matched that of the bomber. Evolving into the Demon, it convinced RAF planners that a two-seater fighter ought to remain in the inventory and thus the Boulton Paul Defiant was commissioned as a modern replacement.

Equipped with a four-gun turret but no forward-firing armament, the Defiant flew for the first time on 11 August 1937. It was envisaged that the Defiant squadrons would attack unescorted bomber formations from abeam, using clever tactics to remain outside the bombers' defensive fields of fire while employing their rear turrets to devastating effect.

The reality in combat was that against enemy fighters the Defiant was woefully vulnerable and by September 1940 it had been withdrawn from daylight operations. Nonetheless, the aircraft's two-man crew was of considerable benefit in the night-fighting role, where darkness considerably reduced its vulnerability. Subsequently equipped with primitive radar sets, the night-fighter Defiants achieved a respectable degree of success before higher-performing Beaufighter and Mosquito fighters entered service in their stead.

Thus, many airframes became available for other roles, including training, target towing and ASR. The Defiant had been designed with provision for hardpoints under its outer wing panels. These had not been used in service, until 70 aircraft were modified for these hardpoints to mount a container holding a Type M dinghy.

Approximately 50 of these ASR-configured machines actually saw service, the first with 281 Squadron, which formed up on the Defiant in March 1942. The type arrived on strength with 275, 276, 277 and 278 Squadrons very soon after, bringing dinghies, four-gun firepower and two sets of eyes to ASR operations, until modified Spitfires and Hurricanes arrived as replacements.

....

SPECIFICATION

BOULTON PAUL DEFIANT MK I

Powerplant one 1,030hp Rolls-Royce Merlin III V12 piston engine
Length 35ft 4in (10.79m)
Height 12ft 2in (3.71m)
Wingspan 39ft 4in (12m)
Wing area 250sq ft (23.23m²)
Maximum speed at 16,500ft 303mph (488km/h)
Range 465 miles (748km)
Service ceiling 30,350ft (9,250m)
Armament four 0.303in Browning machine guns in a dorsal turret

Shown in its day fighter form, this 264 Squadron Defiant was up from Kirton-in-Lindsey, Lincolnshire, in August 1940.

The Lysander's air-droppable ASR kit was modified for the Defiant, although the erstwhile fighter could only carry two containers, compared with four on the Lysander. With its two-man crew, the Defiant worked well as an ASR platform and soon spread among the other ASR squadrons. Later it was largely replaced by the Hurricane and, more importantly, Spitfire.

In the air, the ASRS was increasingly well equipped and better prepared than ever for the influx of US aircraft that was just over the horizon. The story was sadly different on the water. A requirement for 116 HSLs and 80 pinnaces had been identified, but a count on 1 August 1942, revealed just 52 of the former and 22 of the latter. Providing sufficient marine craft was still challenging British resources.

Facing this lack of equipment, the RAF ASRS was pitched into battle on 19 August 1942 in support of Operation Jubilee. An amphibious landing at Dieppe, the operation was effectively a trial for D-Day, helping Allied strategists understand German defensive capability and examine the difficulties of taking and securing a beachhead. Losses among the primarily British and Canadian troops on the ground were devastating, while more than 100 aircraft were lost.

It was planned that the Royal Navy would rescue survivors in the water off the Dieppe

Typical of the new vessels entering service, the 67ft Thorneycroft Whaleback HSL 2586 was undergoing sea trials off the Thames Estuary prior to the type's acceptance to the ASRS in January 1943.

coast, while HSLs out of Dover, Ramsgate and Newhaven would cover the rest of the operation area all the way back home. In total, the ASRS rescued 12 airmen and the Royal Navy two. A fifteenth was saved by a British fishing boat. Between them, the HSLs and Royal Navy craft had responded to 47 calls for assistance, but three HSLs had been sunk.

Rescue operations were to have proceeded under the powerful protection of several squadrons of RAF fighters, but crews often strayed away from their fighter shield in order to effect a rescue. Thus, after two separate attacks by Focke-Wulf Fw 190s, HSL 123 was fired upon from the shore and sank, killing two of its crew. Bombs dropped by Heinkel He 111s reportedly accounted for HSL 122, killing all

but one of its crew, although he later died of his injuries. Finally, aerial attack also accounted for HSL 147. Four crew were killed, two missing and the rest taken prisoner. An Fw 190 attack on HSL 186 wounded two of its crew.

Prior to Operation Jubilee, HSL and rescue launch crews had sailed under instructions to engage enemy vessels and aircraft at every opportunity. This policy changed after Dieppe to one of returning fire only if attacked. Work also began to better arm the HSLs and a variety of guns and turrets was installed to aid their defence.

Still there was a need for more ASR coverage and large parts of the Scottish coast remained without provision. During December 1942 it was decided that the area

between Montrose to the east and Oban on the west coast was dangerously vulnerable. Number 282 Squadron thus came into existence on 1 January 1943, operating a standard mix of Ansons and Walruses. A month or so later, the Air Staff concluded that a major expansion of ASR, dubbed Target H, would be necessary to see the service into 1944.

Before further expansion could be properly considered, existing issues in equipment supply needed to be overcome. The Warwick was taking far longer than expected to reach service and while 280 Squadron took three Wellingtons in an effort to familiarise itself with the related Warwick during February 1943, the larger aircraft was still some way off. Number 279 Squadron was also suffering, with its Hudson complement down eight aircraft to twelve. It too was scheduled to receive Warwicks, but in the event was deselected for the type, which instead went to 281 and 282 Squadrons.

The motto of 275 Squadron, 'They Shall Not Perish', neatly summed up the ASR squadrons' efforts as they gained more proficiency through operational missions. Each of the squadrons became busier, regardless of its area, the crews meeting with success and disappointment in equal measure and taking serious personal risks. On 14 April 1943, for example, a Messerschmitt Bf 109 fighter shot down a 277 Squadron Walrus over the Channel, a second aircraft coming out to rescue the crew. A US Army Air Force (USAAF) Republic P-47 Thunderbolt pilot was recovered in 277 Squadron's 100th rescue, on 12 June 1943.

Long before the Hurricane and Spitfire joined the ASR squadrons, the Anson and Boulton Paul Defiant were providing stalwart service. The twin-engined Avro had been designed for patrol work and although it became outmoded almost immediately at the outbreak of hostilities, it remained an effective tool for ranging out over the sea in search of casualties.

The Officer Commanding 278 Squadron, Squadron Leader PR Smith, was flying with four crewmen searching for a downed Spitfire pilot over the North Sea when they came under attack. A radio call alerted the squadron of the incident, but nothing more was heard.

In June, 278 Squadron performed another magnificent taxi rescue after a crew loaded eight survivors from a USAAF Boeing B-17 Flying Fortress aboard. The pilot taxied to rendezvous with an HSL for a successful transfer.

In May 1943, the ASRS could muster 130 HSLs, 25 pinnaces and seven seaplane tenders, the Royal Navy adding 82 rescue vessels to the total. The airborne lifeboat also saw its first successful use during May, adding a vital new capability. The Walrus could land and take on survivors but was frequently unable to take off again, rendering it little more than a suboptimal, slow boat. Ideally, a rescue aircraft ought to arrive on scene, stop to embark survivors, then fly off without endangering itself on the water. Such a capability was impossible until the helicopter became a practical military tool and the airborne lifeboat remained a useful second best into the immediate post-war period. Droppable radio sets, built into standard dinghies, also arrived, adding an important additional tool to the Very flares and pigeons otherwise employed to alert rescue craft to downed personnel.

Questions were asked during a 1943 review of ASR operations over the efficacy of pigeons. The Director of Aircraft and Aircrew Safety called for the disbandment of the RAF Pigeon Service by November, but the birds retained a degree of utility and remained on strength into the early post-war era. The captain of a North American Mitchell Mk II that ditched on 31 May 1943 after an attack on shipyards at Flushing nonetheless felt it unnecessary to release the aircraft's pigeons, as an abridged extract from *Air/Sea Rescue Note 83* confirms, while also providing a wealth of further insight into the rescue process.

MITCHELL II DITCHED 31.5.43 AT 18.10 HOURS IN A POSITION 51°52'N 01°28'E

Introduction

This aircraft was one of a formation of twelve, which carried out an attack with fighter escort on the shipbuilding yards at Flushing on 31st May from 10,000ft.

The attack was made at 17.31 hours in conditions of good visibility with no low cloud.

Immediately after bombing, a shell burst just beneath the aircraft, splinters hitting both engines, smashing [the] mirror on [the] PA[?] compass and slightly wounding the captain in the left arm.

The aircraft maintained station with the formation, which was losing height from 10,000ft down to 1,500ft for the run home, until 17.40 hours when the starboard engine started to lose power and emit smoke.

This engine was switched off and the propeller feathered to prevent fire. At this time the gyro and the engine instruments became unserviceable even though they were switched over to the port engine.

Two minutes later the air gunner reported that the port engine was also emitting smoke. At the same time, the pilot realised the port engine was losing power, so he gave the crew warning of the possibility of having to ditch the aircraft.

The captain decided not to keep up with the main formation as he considered it essential to endeavour to maintain height when [at] 7,000ft. This proved impossible owing to the failing port engine, but rate of descent was limited to 250ft per minute.

The port engine continued to behave erratically and at 17.50 hours when at 2,000ft the pilot warned the crew to prepare for ditching.

Six Spitfires of the close escort remained with the aircraft until the crew were picked up by HSL 2558.

Preparation for Ditching

The captain jettisoned the escape hatch above the pilot's seat and the wireless operator jettisoned his escape hatch on the starboard side of the fuselage. The navigator passed the W/Op [wireless operator] a DR [dead reckoning] position for transmission but the W/Op reported he was having trouble with his set, and no W/T [wireless transmitter] signal was received from the aircraft.

Although pigeons were carried the captain did not consider it necessary to release one as the six escorting Spitfires were still in company and shipping was seen ahead. The crew took up the following ditching stations.

Pilot strapped in pilot's seat.

Navigator strapped in second pilot's seat.

Air gunner on floor of navigation compartment with back to pilot.

Wireless operator strapped in wireless operator's seat.

Ditching

At 400ft the captain warned the crew that ditching was imminent. He approached the sea in a glide at an indicated speed of 105mph using a flap setting of 15 degrees. The final approach was made on a heading of 290 degrees, the captain deciding that in view of the calm sea and light wind it would be advantageous to ditch as near as possible to the coast, which could be seen ahead.

The aircraft was flown down on to the water in a slightly tail-down attitude.

The aircraft skimmed the water for a second or two and then came two violent shocks. The first of these threw the pilot and navigator forward, breaking the pilot's belt and causing the navigator to hit his head on the co-pilot's control column.

The navigator unfastened his safety belt and then came the second impact shock, which threw the pilot upwards through the escape hatch clear of the aircraft with the navigator close behind him.

The front compartment flooded immediately and the air gunner was floated up to the roof of the navigator's compartment and was then thrown halfway through the astrodome by the second impact shock.

In each case, the Mae Wests were inflated after the exit.

The aircraft came to rest at 18.10 hours with the humped part of its broken back protruding out of the water. The rest of it was half submerged, the wing being awash, the tailplane and the nose underwater.

The pilot and navigator, having been thrown out to the port side of the aircraft, climbed back to the fuselage and helped the air gunner to extricate himself from the shattered astrodome. He was suffering from a severe cut on his head and was slightly dazed.

There was no sign of the wireless operator, so the pilot and navigator climbed further along the fuselage to see what could be done to help him.

The back of the aircraft was broken just aft of the mainplane and through the gap they could see the wireless operator sitting in his seat with his legs trapped by the top turret, which had been forced forward when the back of the aircraft was broken. The wireless operator was quite conscious.

All attempts by the crew to extricate the wireless operator were unsuccessful.

The pilot then released the dinghy by the manual release on the outside of the fuselage and dragged the dinghy out on to the wing. All efforts to inflate the dinghy by the CO_2 bottle were unavailing, although the actual instructions were complied with.

Rescue

Two high-speed launches which had been at rendezvous positions awaiting the return of aircraft from this mission saw the aircraft in trouble and immediately set course for the aircraft's position. Arriving alongside they took the pilot, navigator and air gunner aboard.

Two members of the crew of HSL 2558 jumped into the water and immediately set to work with crowbars passed to them from the launch to reach the trapped wireless operator.

They forced an entry into the plane and found his legs trapped by the turret and had no time to release him as the aircraft sank within 4 minutes of the time they came aboard. The aircraft floated for 15 minutes. The rescued members of the crew were taken to Felixstowe and given treatment. The air gunner was retained in hospital there.

The ASR Walrus crews had come to exhibit a particular expertise, courage and disregard for personal safety, qualities that would endure through the post-war years and right through the helicopter era. They needed every one of those attributes as Allied strategists began planning the invasion of Europe and offensive operations stepped up from the beginning of 1944.

Everything changed in the run-up to D-Day, 6 June 1944. Bomber Command and USAAF Eighth Air Force heavy bombers, flying from bases in England, continued their attacks on German cities and industrial targets by night and day, respectively, but also turned their destructive might against railheads, major transport intersections, military installations, bridges and other infrastructure in occupied France.

Fighter sweeps continued, while there was also an intense effort to photograph the entire 'invasion coast', to a depth of a few miles in, reconnaissance de Havilland Mosquitos, Spitfires and other types gathered imagery even of the areas in which the Allies intended not to invade, thereby denying the enemy any real indication of where to expect the assault. And this crucial effort was repeated at intervals, all of it, ensuring the visual intelligence was as accurate and timely as possible.

Then there were the attacks on coastal defences, employing a variety of RAF and USAAF aircraft, many of them single-seater fighter-bombers. Factor in training accidents, which occurred frequently throughout the war, remember that the 'heavies' fought in formations of several hundred, rather than tens of aeroplanes, and that German air defences were far from beaten, and it becomes clear that the RAF ASRS faced a near impossible challenge.

Late in 1943, 277 Squadron had taken on a new type to supplement the Walrus and, in theory, begin replacing it. The Supermarine Sea Otter was carefully designed to improve take-off capability from the water, at least partially overcoming the major issue Walrus crews faced. The ASR squadrons were also taking on more spotters – primarily Spitfires – many released from combat duties as improved derivatives entered service.

Number 277 Squadron was the busiest of the ASR units, its South Coast location ideal for forays out over the Channel. A good number of the unit's 'customers' were now American, among them Captain George Preddy,

SUPERMARINE SEA OTTER ASR.MK II

Designed to replace the Walrus, Supermarine's Sea Otter never quite took over from the Shagbat during World War II, but survived in RAF service until October 1945 as its last operational biplane. Known initially as the Stingray, the aircraft was the Sea Otter by the time of its first flight on 29 September 1938 and was immediately distinguishable from the Walrus thanks to its tractor propeller arrangement.

In fact, the differences between the two types went far deeper, the Sea Otter's much-improved hull and more powerful Mercury engine enabling it to leave the water far more easily, even with a heavier load. All production Sea Otters came from the Saunders-Roe factory on the Isle of Wight, the first among them, an ABR.Mk I for the Royal Navy, completing its maiden flight in January 1943.

The RAF aircraft were to ASR.Mk II standard, the first reaching 277 Squadron later in 1943. Subsequent production supplied 276 and 281 Squadrons (1944), then 282, 278 and 279 Squadrons (March, May and July 1945, respectively). The Sea Otter also served 292 Squadron in India, between November 1944 and July 1945.

• •

SPECIFICATION

SUPERMARINE SEA OTTER ASR.MK II

Powerplant one 965hp Bristol Mercury XXX radial piston engine
Length 39ft 5in (12.04m)
Height 16ft 2in (4.93m)
Wingspan 46ft (14.02m)
Wing area 610sq ft (55.67m^2)
Maximum speed at 4,500ft 163mph (262km/h)
Range 690 miles (1,110km)
Service ceiling 17,000ft (5,180m)
Armament one 0.303in Vickers K machine gun in the bow, plus two similar weapons in the midships position for self defence

A Royal Navy aircraft, Sea Otter ASR.Mk II RD892 was identical to the Sea Otters employed by the RAF on ASR duties.

38 SQUADRON

Formed at Thetford, Norfolk, on 1 April 1916, 38 Squadron disbanded into 25 Reserve Squadron soon after, only to reappear in its own right on 14 July. It served as a Home Defence unit and then as a ground-attack unit in France, specialising in nocturnal operations. It disbanded at Hawkinge, Kent, on 4 July 1919.

A new 38 Squadron appeared at Mildenhall, Suffolk, on 16 September 1935, as a heavy bomber unit. In November 1940 it moved to the Middle East, before changing roles in January 1942 to become an anti-shipping squadron. Equipped with various marks of Wellington, some equipped to deliver torpedoes, the unit scored notable success over the Aegean in particular, and in late 1944 it moved to Greece.

In 1945 its work focused on supporting the Allied progress through Italy and although it still engaged in offensive operations, its secondary roles of minesweeping and ASR gradually took on more importance. In July 1945 it abandoned bombing entirely, moved to Malta and became a dedicated

ASR squadron, simultaneously swapping its Wellingtons for the Warwick ASR.Mk I.

The Lancaster ASR.Mk III replaced the Warwick in November 1946, with the Lancaster GR.Mk 3 arriving during 1948. The wider role of this 'general reconnaissance' type saw the squadron expanding its duties to once again include a degree of maritime operations beyond ASR, a trend emphasised after December 1952, when the Shackleton MR.Mk 2 ousted the Lancasters.

Although ASR inevitably remained as a secondary task, anti-shipping and anti-submarine sorties now dominated the squadron's schedule, even as it became involved in local crises around Suez, Kuwait and Madagascar. It disbanded at Hal Far, Malta, on 31 March 1967.

The designation reappeared as 38 (Reserve) Squadron, the so-called shadow identity of 236 Operational Conversion Unit (OCU), the Nimrod training unit, at RAF St Mawgan. The Nimrod force was concentrated at RAF Kinloss during 1992, however, and on moving north, the OCU took 42(R) Squadron as its shadow designation. 38 was officially lost as an active unit on 1 October 1992.

221 SQUADRON

With the formation of the RAF on 1 April 1918, D Squadron, Royal Naval Air Service, flying during the Gallipoli campaign, became 221 Squadron, RAF. Post-war it served on policing duties in Russia, where it disbanded on 1 September 1919.

Re-formed on 21 November 1940 as a Wellington unit, 221 Squadron's focus was initially on employing the new ASV equipment in the maritime reconnaissance role. It continued as a Wellington operator throughout the war, flying from stations in England, Northern Ireland, Iceland and the Middle East, achieving considerable success against shipping and, later, land targets.

After a spell in Italy, it returned to the Middle East in October 1944 and set up its final base, at Edku, Egypt, in April 1945. From here it supported detachments at El Adem and Benina, Libya, and Aqir in Palestine, flying rescue missions with the Wellington Mk XIII over the sea and desert.

Its tenure on ASR was brief, however, since it disbanded on 25 August 1945.

Number 284 Squadron personnel with Walrus X9506/C, at Cassibile, Sicily. Aircrew in the front row, from left to right: Sergeant JD Lunn (pilot), Sergeant CS Taylor (wireless operator/air gunner), Warrant Officer N Pickles (WOp/AG), Flying Officer R Eccles (pilot), Flight Sergeant JW Bradley (WOp/AG) and Flight Sergeant EJ Holmes (pilot). Ground crew in the back row, left to right: Aircraftman 1st Class Radford; Flight Sergeant RC Glew; Corporal J Warrington; Leading Aircraftmen S Waight, J Price, JH Crowther and H Walker; and Corporal JE Newall.

283 SQUADRON

Formed at Algiers in February 1943 to provide ASR cover off the North African coast, 283 Squadron initially flew the Walrus Mk II and Hurricane Mk II. As the Allies moved into Italy, so the unit followed, basing its aircraft at Palermo from August 1943. The following April it moved to Hal Far, covering the Mediterranean from the Malta base until disbanding on 31 March 1946.

The Spitfire Mk IX had arrived to bolster 283 Squadron's ranks, and during its stay on Malta it also took the Warwick on strength. Although primarily based in Africa, Italy and Malta, the squadron also operated detachments from Greek facilities.

284 SQUADRON

On 7 May 1943, 284 Squadron was established to provide ASR for the Mediterranean theatre, moving from Gravesend to Hal Far, Malta, in June/July. Operating the Walrus Mk II and later the Hurricane Mk II and Warwick Mk I, 284 Squadron tracked the Allied advance through Italy with detachments at several locations. It disbanded at Pomigliano on 21 September 1945.

Still in the Mediterranean region, 284 Squadron re-formed as a Sycamore and Whirlwind unit at Nicosia, Cyprus, on 15 October 1956. It flew in a variety of roles until 1 August 1959, when it was renumbered as 103 Squadron.

293 SQUADRON

With a history mirroring that of 283 and 284 Squadrons, 293 Squadron was properly established at Blida, Algeria, on 28 November 1943. Equipped with the Vickers Warwick, it soon had detachments in Italy, moving to the country in its entirety during March 1944. In April 1944 it added the Walrus Mk II to its fleet and continued with both types until disbanding at Pomigliano on 5 April 1946.

294 SQUADRON

Established at Berka, Libya, on 24 September 1943, 294 Squadron's area of ASR responsibility covered the Eastern Mediterranean and Persian Gulf, including a detachment at Basra. It flew the Walrus Mk II and the Vickers Wellington in its Mk IC, XI and XIII variants, and later the Warwick Mk I. The unit disbanded at Basra on 8 April 1946.

461 SQUADRON

Another Royal Australian Air Force (RAAF) unit, 461 Squadron formed from a core of 10 Squadron RAAF personnel, at Mount Batten, Devon, on 25 April 1942. From the outset a Sunderland operator, 461 Squadron remained on the type until disbanding on 20 June 1945; it also remained UK-based for the duration.

The unit began operations with an ASR sortie on 12 June, soon extending its duties to include anti-submarine patrols. An Armstrong Whitworth Whitley bomber crew was picked up from the sea in July, and another Whitley crew rescued on 6 August. Considerable success was also achieved against U-boats, but on 28 May 1943, a squadron Sunderland crashed attempting to land alongside a dinghy containing survivors.

The flying boat's captain was killed, and the remaining crew took to their own dinghy. Another 461 Squadron Sunderland arrived the following day to retrieve both crews; it managed to take off despite suffering damage from floating debris, achieving a forced landing close to base. The pattern of ASW and ASR continued as the unit equipped with more capable Sunderland variants, but 461 Squadron was quickly disbanded after the end of the war in Europe.

Corporal W Faulds, Leading Aircraftman G Gregory and Leading Aircraftman L Mansfield (from left to right), 221 Squadron ground crew, load packets of newspapers into Wellington GR.Mk XIII MF263 at Kalamaki/Hassani, Greece. The aircraft was dropping supplies to Macedonian villages cut off by winter snows and destroyed communications. The extensive aerial array of the ASV.Mk II radar is worthy of note.

This USAAF B-17 crew ditched in the English Channel and successfully took to their dinghy after a raid on Germany in July 1943. They were awaiting rescue by RAF HSL.

who abandoned his flak-damaged P-47 on 29 January 1944 after shooting down a Focke-Wulf Fw 190. A fellow P-47 circled to guide the Walrus in and Preddy was taken on board.

Typically, the Walrus was reluctant to 'unstick', but this time the port wing dipped, and its float was torn away. Asymmetric and unbalanced, the Walrus was now incapable of flight but also unable to taxi. Flying Officer FE 'Tug' Wilson therefore walked out to the end of the starboard lower wing to balance the aircraft, remaining there as the pilot taxied home. Preddy had scored his first air-to-air kill on 1 December 1943, against a Bf 109, and destroyed 25 more enemy aircraft plus five on the ground. He downed a pair of Bf 109s on 25 December 1944, before being shot down and killed.

An early 277 Squadron Sea Otter rescue saw the aircraft called to the aid of a Canadian pilot shot down close to France on 16 March 1944.

So close in fact that when the aircraft arrived, the survivor was standing on the mined beach. The Sea Otter crew beckoned him to paddle back out so they might alight without too much risk from enemy fire. He did so, but even then, it was thanks to strafing from the escorting Spitfire and good fortune – the enemy guns found their range just as the Sea Otter took off – that the rescue was accomplished.

The USAAF bomber crews were initially ill prepared for ditching and their aircraft and survival equipment less than adequate in an emergency. The ASRS worked hard to change attitudes and kit, its efforts bearing fruit as more ditched US crews were saved. Then, as a result of a meeting on 8 May 1944, the USAAF established its own rescue squadron.

Alongside a pledge to equip the unit with 25 ASR P-47s equipped with rescue equipment, the US Strategic and Tactical Air Forces headquarters constructed a VHF fixer service based at Saffron Walden as the 6th Control Wing. It was also determined that six Warwicks carrying airborne lifeboats would be available during every large-scale 8th Air Force raid. On 9 May 1944, the 5th Emergency Rescue Squadron (ERS) was formally established, embarking on its first live mission – to retrieve a B-17 crew 240 miles off Great Yarmouth – ten days later. The P-47s ironically lacked the range for the mission and four Mustangs were despatched in their stead.

A complex operation ensued in which an airborne lifeboat was successfully dropped and the B-17 crew embarked. On 21 May, a Danish fishing vessel took the boat and its ten passengers on board. Shots fired from a Warwick failed to stop the vessel, but a flight of four P-47s did the job. A Great Yarmouth HSL then came

Flying Officer G Lockwood, Master of 28 ASRU's HSL 156 out of Newhaven, Sussex, speaks to base from the craft's lookout cockpit on 20 February 1944. The sortie included the rescue of a downed American pilot from his dinghy in the English Channel. With the casualty safely on board, the second coxswain took down his details while Lockwood plotted a course for home and the pilot recouped with a warm drink. Lockwood was awarded the Distinguished Service Cross in 1945, for his skill in rescuing aircrew from the Channel.

20 SQUADRON

Formed at Netheravon, Wiltshire, on 1 September 1915, 20 Squadron was equipped as a scout (fighter) unit flying the Royal Aircraft Factory F.E.2b. After World War I, it served in India as an army-cooperation squadron, fighting in the Third Afghan War.

It continued in the role until 1941, when it added Bristol Blenheim and Westland Lysander aircraft to its Hawker Audax biplanes. Now based as two flights at Bombay and Madras, the squadron temporarily flew coastal patrols but soon began working alongside the Chinese Army, using Lysanders out of Tezpur. Operating a largely unsuitable aircraft in difficult conditions, 20 Squadron moved around the theatre before receiving Hurricanes for tactical reconnaissance in January 1943. Its Lysander Mk IIs were now assigned ASR duties out of Feni, but only until March 1943, when 20 Squadron became a dedicated ground-attack unit.

The squadron remained on offensive duties until 1992, when it relinquished the Panavia Tornado to become the Harrier OCU, a role in which it continued until 2010.

160 SQUADRON

Formed in June 1918, 160 Squadron survived only one month. It re-formed as a maritime reconnaissance and anti-submarine Liberator unit at Thurleigh, Bedfordshire, on 16 January 1942, operating only until early June, when its aircraft moved to Palestine, its ground elements having already set up base in India.

The Palestine element merged with 178 Squadron in January 1943, the remainder of 160 Squadron taking Liberator Mk IIIs in Ceylon for a recommencement of operations in February. A variety of MR, ASW, transport and special missions ensued until June 1946, when the squadron began departing for Leuchars, Fife.

In July its Liberators began giving way to the Lancaster ASR.Mk III, ready for 160 Squadron to fly two missions with the type in September. But those were its only ASR sorties; on 30 September 1946, the unit was renumbered as 120 Squadron.

191 SQUADRON

Similar to 190 Squadron, 191 Squadron served as a home-based night training unit during World War I, forming on 6 November 1917 and disbanding in January 1919. Its next incarnation was at Korangi Creek, Pakistan, on 13 May 1943. Flying Catalinas, convoy escort and MR were its primary roles.

Air-sea rescue was important among its secondary missions, however, and in April 1945 it located and rescued survivors from a downed Liberator. It disbanded again on 15 June 1945.

200 SQUADRON

Mirroring the origins of 190 and 191 Squadrons, 200 Squadron formed on 1 July 1917 as a night training unit; it disbanded late in 1918.

Number 206 Squadron provided a nucleus of personnel for the new 200 Squadron when it re-formed on 25 May 1941. Flying Hudsons, on June 1941, the squadron escorted a force of Hurricanes from Gibraltar to Malta, subsequently flying ASW and convoy patrol work off the African coast. Adding Liberators to its roster, 200 Squadron returned exceptional service until March 1944, when it departed Africa for Ceylon.

Now fully Liberator equipped, the unit continued with its traditional roles but adding ASR as an increasingly important adjunct. It served out its time with an additional variety of reconnaissance and supply-dropping missions, before renumbering as 8 Squadron at Jessore on 1 May 1945.

251 SQUADRON

Established at Hornsea, Yorkshire, in August 1918, 251 Squadron flew Airco DH.6 biplanes on coastal patrols, work that concluded around 30 June 1919, when the unit disbanded.

It reformed at Reykjavik, Iceland, out of 1407 Flight on 1 August 1944, tasked with meteorological reconnaissance using Lockheed Hudsons and Venturas, while a handful of Ansons flew communications duties. It also took on a secondary ASR role, with at least two Hudsons equipped to carry airborne lifeboats. The Fortress Mk II and Mk IIA arrived in March 1945, followed by the Warwick ASR.Mk I in August, replacing the ASR Hudsons. The unit disbanded at Reykjavik on 30 October 1945.

252 SQUADRON

Number 252 Squadron was another of those RAF units formed out of RNAS coastal flights in August 1918, in this instance a unit based at Tynemouth. It continued in operation until 30 June 1919. On 21 November 1940, the squadron stood up again, receiving Beaufighters soon after. Its coastal role continued with convoy escort and it operated various Beaufighter models right through the war, always in maritime roles, from UK and Mediterranean bases.

By April 1945, the squadron was stationed in Greece and, although it was flying Beaufighter Xs, its primary mission was ASR. It disbanded on 1 December 1946.

269 SQUADRON

A strategically important location for monitoring access into the Suez Canal, Port Said, Egypt, boasted an RAF Seaplane Flight equipped with a variety of sea and landplanes. On 6 October 1918, its status was raised to that of a squadron, numbered 269. Thus it continued with routine patrols until 15 November 1919, when it disbanded.

In the midst of the interwar expansion, 269 Squadron re-formed out of 'C' Flight, 206 Squadron at Bircham Newton, Norfolk, before moving north to Abbotsinch, today regenerated as Glasgow International Airport. It flew Avro Ansons until re-equipping with the Lockheed Hudson in April 1940, a type it employed on anti-submarine and anti-shipping patrols along the Norwegian coast.

In 1941 the unit relocated to Kaldadarnes, Iceland, from where its Hudsons covered the mid-Atlantic. The work continued until January 1944, by which time more capable and longer-ranged aircraft had taken over and 269 Squadron returned to Great Britain. Once again equipped with a variety of aircraft, it deployed to Lagens Field on the Azores in March, for anti-submarine, ASR and meteorological (met) reconnaissance duties. To its Hudsons, 269 Squadron added the Walrus, Spitfire Mk VB and Warwick.

Given the regular transatlantic traffic in the immediate post-war period, 269 Squadron remained in place providing ASR cover and met information until disbanding on 10 May 1946. It became active again at Ballykelly, County Londonderry, on 10 March 1952, initially flying the Shackleton MR.Mk 1A and later the Mk 2, on maritime and search and rescue duties. These latter aircraft were particularly important during a 1958 deployment to cover the nuclear tests on the Christmas Islands. The unit disbanded at Ballykelly on 1 December 1958 by renumbering as 210 Squadron.

270 SQUADRON

Numbers 354, 355 and 356 Flights, RNAS at Alexandria, amalgamated as 270 Squadron, RAF in August 1918. The new unit continued in the anti-submarine role and disbanded into 269 Squadron on 15 September 1919.

Re-formed at Jui, Gambia, on the Catalina in November 1942, 270 Squadron was again tasked against submarines but with important secondary roles, including ASR. It disbanded on 30 June 1945, having added the Sunderland to its roster from February 1944.

459 SQUADRON

Established as a Royal Australian Air Force (RAAF) unit at Burg-el-Arab, Egypt, on 10 February 1942, 459 Squadron prepared for operations using Blenheims loaned by 203 Squadron. It entered combat soon after on the Hudson, primarily on anti-shipping duties, but also escorting Hurricanes to Malta and then, in September, detaching aircraft to Aden.

During 1943, a detachment was also established on Cyprus and as the squadron's focus became the Aegean, so attacks on Greek and Cretan targets became more common, as did anti-submarine and ASR patrols. In December the Lockheed Ventura Mk V replaced 459's Hudsons. With this more capable aircraft, the squadron engaged predominantly in bombing missions, until the Martin Maryland took over from July 1944, when the squadron's more familiar mission set, including ASR, was resumed.

The squadron returned to the UK and disbanded on 10 April 1945.

621 SQUADRON

Formed in Kenya for a general reconnaissance role on 12 September 1943, 621 Squadron soon took its Wellington Mk XIIIs into action. Ironically, although it was yet to formally adopt the ASR mission, its first operational sortie led to exactly that, after the aircraft ran out of fuel and force landed. The squadron mounted a search and rescue operation, finding the hapless machine after three days, when a Wellington landed to collect its crew.

Late in 1943 the unit moved to Aden, where an expanded mission set finally included ASR. On 1 May 1944, squadron aircraft located 70 survivors from a sinking ship, adrift in lifeboats and on rafts.

It continued with a variety of combat and rescue work until May 1945, when its primary tasking became transport. In November it moved again, to Egypt, flying a variety of missions, now with Warwick GR.Mk Vs and including searches for aircraft and vehicles lost in the desert. In April 1946 it relocated to Palestine and began operating the Lancaster ASR.Mk III alongside the Warwick. Its tasks continued to include ASR, until the unit was renumbered as 18 Squadron at Ein Shemer, Israel, on 1 September 1946.

The new 18 Squadron continued flying the Lancasters but as GR.Mk IIIs though, even then, survived only two weeks before disbanding. It reappeared the following year as a Mosquito fighter-bomber unit.

Number 269 Squadron Hudson Mk I N7303/UA-B receives attention at Wick, Caithness. The aircraft is rested on trestles for gun testing at the butts. Anson Mk I K6244 is parked beyond.

alongside and embarked the survivors. It was the first operation of many involving the USAAF's own dedicated rescue services.

New surface craft had also arrived in May, four 70ft motor gunboats being made available for ASR. Capable of 45 knots, the vessels were extremely fast and range was added to their speed later in the year, when 19 long-range rescue craft (LRRC) entered service; a further 21 arrived on the front line in 1945.

Further new boat designs entered service as ASR coverage extended around the British Isles. On 31 May 1944, just a week before D-Day, the RAF ASRS included 90 HSLs, six seaplane tenders and 40 rescue motor launches. Royal Navy and US contributions bolstered these numbers significantly. In the hours before the D-Day assault, Allied aircraft were painted with alternating black and white stripes on fuselage and wings as a recognition feature for other aircrew and gunners on the ground. The ASR craft were painted with large stars, similar to the centre of the US marking, on their foredecks.

D-Day was to be a maximum effort, with ASR vessels ready along planned aircraft paths, including those of the diversionary force operating some distance from Normandy where the landings were headed. Three tenders were employed for fighter direction during the assault and each of these was allocated a pair of HSLs for additional cover. Pilots in trouble and flying single-seaters were instructed to leave the aircraft rather than ditch, while large aircraft crews were to ditch north of Allied vessels and signal their friendly status.

Walrus and Spitfire ASR aircraft were already in the air as the invasion fleet began to move from British ports and airfields, their efforts combining with those of the ASR vessels and the massed surface craft of many kinds to ensure that few airmen – or paratroops – were lost at sea. Sources suggest that around 60 men were rescued, some remarkably efficiently. One HSL was positioned ready for a bailing-out Spitfire pilot and retrieved him immediately, while a Dakota ditched so close to a destroyer that its pilot and 18 paratroops took to the water and were quickly picked up, but the co-pilot reportedly walked along the wing to the ship.

After D-Day, the Allies established landing grounds in France within a few days, later operating aircraft from former Luftwaffe airfields as they were liberated. Primarily used by tactical aircraft, these landing grounds and airfields also provided temporary homes for a variety of support aircraft, including those dedicated to ASR. By 26 June, several HSLs were forward based at Mulberry Harbour and other floating installations built to support the invasion forces, but plans were already in hand to base 32 Air-sea Rescue/Marine Craft Units at Cherbourg along with a flight of supporting aircraft.

Three HSLs made the French port home on 7 July, followed by 'A' Flight Lieutenant of 276 Squadron, which arrived with four Walruses and a similar number of Spitfires on 27 July and 1 August. The Allies were in the ascendency, especially in the air, but the enemy remained extremely dangerous and the ASRS responded to non-flying incidents on several occasions. In one, on 14 June, a pair of HSLs out of Weymouth came to the assistance of the frigate HMS *Blackwood* after it hit a mine. The 68ft HSLs evacuated 115 sailors, transferring the least injured to a brace of additional HSLs that came to assist. During the process at least one boat had 86 personnel embarked.

As the inexorable Allied advance took in more occupied territory the ASR units moved to cover greater areas of intensive activity, gradually moving to the north and east. They were poised ready for action, yet stretched to their limits for Operations Market and Garden in September, recovering 181 airmen and soldiers, 92 of them on 19 September alone.

Adding to the urgency of finding new Continental bases to keep pace with demand, the ASRS faced a new challenge. Germany still relied heavily on its beleaguered U-boat force, which was being forced northwards as its bases were overrun. With enemy submarines concentrated in Norwegian waters, Coastal Command massed its air power ready to strike from Scotland and the ASR units repositioned themselves accordingly.

From a Britain-based ASR perspective, the war in Europe had effectively moved north. A reorganisation in units and equipment made sense. The Spitfire became less prevalent in the spotting role and Coastal Command took control of the Warwick and Walrus flights, as well as rescue coordination, while numbers of aircraft fell overall. On 15 February 1945, Coastal Command assumed all responsibility for RAF ASR and 275 and 277 Squadrons disbanded. Standard flying equipment was now the Walrus and/or Sea Otter and Warwick, the latter taking part in perhaps the final maximum effort of the ASRS operating from British bases.

A P-51 Mustang pilot was reported in a dinghy off Schiermonnikoog on one of the Dutch Frisian Islands on 30 March 1945. A 5th ERS Catalina scrambled to his aid with two P-47s as its escort.

Its pilot managed to alight and come alongside the dinghy, at which time a wave caught the aircraft, seriously damaging an engine. The Catalina crew nonetheless attempted to get the Mustang pilot aboard but were unable to reach him before his dinghy drifted off.

Now also at the mercy of the waves, the Catalina crew sent a distress signal. A Warwick launched in response found neither the Catalina crew nor the Mustang pilot. Next morning, a second Warwick, escorted by four Mustangs, spotted the Catalina and dropped an airborne lifeboat nearby. The flying boat captain used the aircraft's remaining engine to taxi towards the craft, but waves caused further damage and the Catalina began sinking.

Another Warwick, again under escort, dropped a second lifeboat. This began to sink as soon as the crew embarked, forcing them back to the semi-submerged Catalina, which then came under fire from a Messerschmitt Me 262 jet. Abandoning their already sinking machine, the Catalina crew took to the aircraft's three dinghies.

After the Me 262 departed, a USAAF B-17 arrived and dropped a US-built airborne lifeboat. The Catalina crew embarked and began making way using the craft's engines. They continued on a roughly north-west heading for 36 hours before the boat's fuel ran dry.

Appalling weather worsened the crew's situation and complicated search efforts. A Beaufighter made it to their general area on 2 April, but crashed into the sea before its crew made any sighting.

Mustangs escorted a pair of Warwicks into the area on 3 April and they received a signal from a transmitter on the dinghy aboard the US airborne lifeboat. The aircraft dropped

VICKERS WARWICK

Owing much to the earlier Wellington, Vickers designed the Warwick as a heavier bomber against a 1935 specification, although changing requirements saw first flight delayed until 13 August 1939. The aircraft's Rolls-Royce Vulture powerplant proved complex and unreliable, so a second prototype was prepared with Bristol Centaurus power. This flew for the first time in April 1940, but not until January 1941 was a production aircraft ordered.

In the event, production then only got underway in June 1942, by which time the Warwick was already obsolete as a bomber and Centaurus supply could not meet demand. Thus the Warwick Mk I was built with a Pratt & Whitney R-2800 Double Wasp powerplant. Although 16 were completed as bombers, in October 1942 it was decided that the type would become a specialist ASR machine, equipped to drop an airborne lifeboat or Lindholme gear.

While the bombers never entered front-line service, the ASR.Mk I entered service with 280 Squadron at Thornaby in October 1943. Subsequent Warwick variants were used for training, meteorological and maritime reconnaissance tasks. The Warwick ASR.Mk I served with 38, 251, 269, 276, 277, 278, 279, 280, 281, 282, 283, 284, 292, 293 and 294 Squadrons.

•••

SPECIFICATION

VICKERS WARWICK ASR.MK I

Powerplant two 1,850hp Pratt & Whitney R-2800 Double Wasp radial piston engines

Length 72ft 3in (22.04m)

Height 18ft 6in (5.67m)

Wingspan 96ft 8½in (29.51m)

Wing area 1,006sq ft (93.46m^2)

Maximum speed 224mph (360km/h)

Range 2,300 miles (3,702km)

Service ceiling 21,500ft (6,550m)

Armament two 0.303in machine guns each in the nose and dorsal turrets, plus four 0.303in machine guns in the tail turret

fuel containers, Lindholme gear and an airborne lifeboat on spotting the survivors. Rowing their powerless boat, the Catalina crew reached the fuel and Lindholme kit and loaded them on board, but the engines would not start, even after refuelling. More fuel and Lindholme equipment were dropped as the day progressed, followed by another lifeboat that evening.

It made little odds, since the crew had no reserves of strength left with which to reach it. More importantly, the last search aircraft of the day surrounded them with sea markers in the hope of guiding in the HSLs that had already been launched. The plan failed.

The following morning, as Warwicks and Mustangs scoured the area, an HSL found the lifeboat off Heligoland and boarded the Catalina crew, carrying them safely to Great Yarmouth, where they arrived next morning.

A variety of units found the capacity for ASR following the initial D-Day effort, among them 190 and 196 Squadrons, both using the Short Stirling primarily on transport, glider towing and special duties work. Number 220 Squadron had dabbled in ASR as early as 1942, but expanded the mission after March 1945. For 248 Squadron, the ASR association began in 1941 and it essentially became the unit's sole task after VE Day. Similarly, 254 Squadron flew its first ASR mission in 1942 and concluded its wartime service with an ASR sortie on 11 May 1945. Finally, 461 Squadron, a Royal Australian Air Force (RAAF) unit, performed ASR as a secondary task to its primary anti-submarine work throughout its existence.

The ASR squadrons launched on so many rescues that to detail them all might take several volumes. Of course, the HSLs were active too and often worked in harmony with the ASR squadrons, but by war's end 277 Squadron alone had recorded 598 rescues.

The airborne lifeboat

Famously remembered for his controversial leadership of Bomber Command, in 1940 Air Vice-Marshal (AVM) Arthur Harris had suggested that a glider boat might be towed to downed crew by a suitable aircraft. The idea was not without merit. In September 1941, Group Captain Waring, latterly of RAF Lindholme, transferred to the Air Ministry, where he worked with Royal Navy Volunteer Reservist Lieutenant Robb, to plan a wooden lifeboat that might be dropped from a suitably modified aircraft.

Creating such a vessel posed serious challenges. It could be slowed by parachute on its descent but would still need to be sufficiently robust to survive contact with a rough sea, yet light enough for a Hudson – then the only suitable carrier – to lift. Anti-capsize equipment, a sea anchor, shelter, sail and powerplant, operating instructions and essential supplies and rations also had to be provided so that a crew might at least stay reasonably safe and at best sail towards rescue.

The conundrum was such that Robb approached yacht designer Uffa Fox for advice on one or two of the lifeboat's requirements. Intrigued, Fox threw all his experience into the project and between them, he, Robb and Waring created and saw tested a boat that may have been ready for service by winter 1942/43. Trials flown in July and August 1942, proved the concept and the effort to build Mk I boats was approved on 19 September.

Fox had been commissioned to construct them, but even his genius was stretched by a combination of technical and regulatory challenges that elongated the development time frame to the extent that the larger, more

These Warwick ASR.Mk Is were with the Warwick Training Unit (later the ASR Training Unit) at Bircham Newton, Norfolk, on 4 September 1943. The aircraft in the foreground, BV277/T, later served in the MTO with 284 and 293 Squadrons.

27 SQUADRON

Formed, as were many RAF squadrons, as a Royal Flying Corps unit on 5 November 1915, 27 Squadron was associated primarily with attack and transport roles, yet had a brief and unusual flirtation with search and rescue.

After debuting the Beaufighter spectacularly into combat in the Far East, during 1945 27 Squadron found itself employing the Beaufighter X on supply-dropping and rescue missions over the jungles of the Dutch East Indies. Disbanded in February 1946, the squadron re-formed as a transport outfit in 1947, but lasted only until 1950. Re-formed again in 1953, it became an English Electric Canberra-equipped bomber squadron, subsequently flying the Avro Vulcan and Panavia Tornado.

In 1993 the 27 Squadron number plate passed to 240 OCU, the combined Chinook and Puma training unit, as 27 (Reserve) Squadron. The Reserve status was lost in January 1998, however, with the unit joining the front line as a Chinook operator. It retained the Chinook into 2020; less than ideal as a SAR platform, the Chinook nonetheless performs an essential humanitarian mission at home and overseas.

179 SQUADRON

From its formation at Wick, Caithness, on 1 September 1942 to 1946, 179 Squadron was a dedicated anti-submarine unit, operating from the UK and Gibraltar, equipped first with Wellingtons and later Warwick Mk Vs.

In 1946, the unit reconfigured as 8 and 179Y Squadrons, which continued on the Warwick. In June, 179Y Squadron renumbered as 210 Squadron, with 179X joining it on 30 September.

212 SQUADRON

Some uncertainty surrounds the origins of 212 Squadron, which may reside with the redesignation of a scout flight at Great Yarmouth in August 1918. The unit disbanded on 1 February 1920, but may not have taken the 212 Squadron moniker.

A 212 Squadron was definitely formed at Heston on 10 February 1940, before combining with the

Photographic Reconnaissance Unit in June. It re-formed as an MR squadron on 22 October 1942. Equipped with Catalinas, the unit began convoy escort missions in December. Operating multiple detachments, it performed doggedly, adding ASR in support of the US Army Air Force's 20th Bomb Group (raiding Singapore) and supply flights to its regular tasking in 1945. It renumbered as 240 Squadron on 1 July 1945.

224 SQUADRON

On 1 April 1918, the bombing flights of 6 Wing, RNAS at Otranto, Italy, were formed into 224 Squadron, RAF. Serving on with a mix of Airco DH.4 and DH.9 aircraft, the unit disbanded in May 1919.

It re-formed as one of several Anson GR units, at Manston, on 1 February 1937 from a nucleus of 48 Squadron. In May 1939, it introduced the Hudson into RAF service, operating the type until September 1942, although with the addition of a Tiger Moth detachment in December 1939.

Maritime reconnaissance and anti-submarine warfare (ASW) were also the primary tasks with the Liberator and by war's end the squadron had achieved 11 U-boat kills and three shared. In October 1946 the Lancaster ASR3 replaced the Liberator and ASR became a new mission, but only until 10 November 1947, when 224 Squadron disbanded.

It re-formed on 1 May 1948 as a Halifax GR6 meteorological recce unit at Aldergrove, with a detachment on Gibraltar. The latter also took on a maritime patrol mission and for this it took the Shackleton MR1A in August 1951. The MR2 followed from May 1953 and, along with various overseas deployments and tours, 224 Squadron continued until disbanding on 31 October 1966.

233 SQUADRON

In August 1918, RNAS units at Dover and Walmer were merged to form 233 Squadron, RAF. The new organisation flew patrols over the Channel, beginning a long association with maritime flying. It disbanded on 15 May 1919.

The resurrected 233 Squadron was part of the pre-war expansion of Coastal Command, re-forming at Tangmere on 18 May 1937. Equipped with Ansons, it moved through a succession of bases and began re-equipping with the Hudson even as it began its wartime patrol and anti-submarine mission. This set the theme for its combat service and,

by December 1942, the squadron was stationed at Gibraltar.

From there its primary duties were to protect convoys sailing along the Portuguese coast and patrols over the Western Mediterranean, before the focus turned to the invasion of North Africa, a very hectic time for the squadron. As Allied forces moved eastwards, 233 Squadron detached to Agadir, from where its anti-submarine role took precedence, but ASR and met recces were also flown. The primary maritime work kept 233 Squadron busy over the Mediterranean, and North and South Atlantic until February 1944.

In April, the unit returned to operations as a transport squadron, including casualty evacuation (casevac) from Continental Europe, continuing as such after an August 1945 move to Burma. In the Far East, the focus was on supply dropping, delivering food and other vital supplies, before 233 Squadron merged with 215 Squadron on 15 December 1945 and ceased to exist.

It returned as a restructuring of 84 Squadron's (Vickers) Valetta Flight on 1 September 1960, ranging widely on transport, supply dropping and humanitarian missions from Khormaksar, Yemen, before disbanding in Aden on 31 January 1964.

240 SQUADRON

Three RNAS seaplane flights, 345, 346 and 410 at Calshot, were amalgamated into 240 Squadron, RAF in August 1918. The primary task was anti-submarine patrolling and the unit continued until 15 May 1919. It re-formed on 30 March 1937, similarly equipped with seaplanes, as an enlargement of 'C' Flight, Seaplane training Squadron, still at Calshot.

Equipped successively with Supermarine Scapa, Short Singapore III and Saro London aircraft, 240 Squadron flitted between training and operational roles, before beginning anti-submarine and patrol work in earnest as war broke out. It re-equipped with Stranraers in May 1940, returning to operations only to re-equip again, with the Catalina, in March 1941.

In February 1942, the squadron began a long transition to the Middle and Far East, via operations over the Mediterranean. Once established in its new theatre, 240 Squadron added special duties flying to its regular operations, subsequently adding ASR and other missions from February 1945. It disbanded on 1 July 1945, with Sunderland-equipped 212 Squadron simultaneously renumbering into a new 240 Squadron, which itself disbanded on 13 March 1946.

On 1 May 1952, 240 Squadron was established for the final time, on the Shackleton MR1 at St Eval. Subsequently flying from Ballykelly, it fulfilled the usual gamut of Shackleton duties before renumbering as 203 Squadron on 1 November 1958.

265 SQUADRON

A combination of 265, 266 and 364 Flights, RNAS at Gibraltar created 265 Squadron, RAF during August 1918. It flew anti-submarine patrols and disbanded the following year. When it re-formed at Mombasa on 11 March 1943, 265 Squadron was still in the maritime business. Flying Catalinas, it began its second career with an ASR mission on 6 May.

The remainder of its service was primarily on patrol and ASW, with photographic survey and transport becoming more important as it neared disbandment on 30 April 1945. Ironically, on a survey mission to the Bassas da India reef in October 1943, a 265 Squadron aircraft had discovered survivors from a torpedoed ship, marooned there four months previously.

292 SQUADRON

Formed at Jessore, India, on 1 February 1944, and disbanded at Agartala, India, on 14 June 1945, 292 Squadron provided ASR cover in the Far East. It flew the Walrus Mk II, Warwick and Sea Otter Mk II, replacing its Warwicks with the long-range Liberator GR Mk VI when the Warwick proved less than ideal for operations in the region's heat and humidity. The squadron relocated from Jessore to Agartala in February 1945 and disbanded there on 14 June, its operational duties continuing with three smaller, independent units, 1347, 1348 and 1349 Flights. The latter survived until 1946, when it disbanded at Mauripur.

413 SQUADRON

During World War II, several RAF units were established with a core of overseas personnel. Postings and losses generally diluted national content over time, but many of these squadrons retained the traditions and ethos of their home air arms and 'returned' to them post-war.

Among the Royal Canadian Air Force (RCAF) units serving under RAF command, 413 Squadron was established on the Catalina Mk I at Stranraer on 1 July 1941. It flew patrol missions until March 1942, when it began moving to Ceylon. Returning to Catalina operations from its new base at Koggala it focused on seeking out Japanese forces that might be threatening invasion.

The work carried on in a similar manner into 1943, when anti-submarine and other missions were added, including ASR. Thus the squadron continued while maintaining detachments at other stations in the theatre. It returned to the UK and disbanded on 23 February 1943.

On 1 April 1947, the RCAF renumbered 13 (Photographic) Squadron as 413 (Photographic) Squadron, the new unit subsequently flying in the survey, transport and fighter roles, before disbanding on 30 December 1961. Number 413 Squadron then renewed its acquaintance with the rescue mission, when 103 Rescue Unit was redesignated as 413 Rescue Squadron on 18 July 1968.

In 2020, 413 Transport and Rescue Squadron had responsibility for providing SAR across the whole of eastern Canada, operating a mix of CC-130 Hercules and CH-149 Cormorant helicopters.

1347, 1348 AND 1349 (ASR) FLIGHTS

On 15 June 1945, 292 Squadron disbanded into 1347, 1348 and 1349 (ASR) Flights at Agartala, India.

Number 1348 Flight was initially involved in converting Warwick crews to Liberators, but moved to Pegu, Burma, in January 1946 and received Lancaster ASR IIIs the following month. It disbanded on 15 May 1946.

Number 1349 Flight moved with its Liberators to Mauripur in October 1945, disbanding there in 1946.

1350 (ASR), 1351 AND 1352 FLIGHTS

Number 1350 Flight was based in India, while no information has emerged concerning 1351 Flight.

Established in India, 1352 Flight moved to Mingaladon, Burma, then to St Thomas Mount in August 1945.

A 224 Squadron Hudson crew prepares for a sortie from Leuchars, Fife. The wireless operator/air gunner (far right) is carrying his logbook, rations and a wicker carrier containing a homing pigeon. The latter proved to have some utility as standard equipment for emergency communications.

An airborne lifeboat parachutes down to a B-17 crew after release by 279 Squadron Hudson flying from Bircham Newton. The Flying Fortress crew had difficulty getting into their dinghy after a forced landing in the North Sea on 25 July 1943.

capable Vickers Warwick was expected to have supplanted the Hudson in the long-range ASR role before the first lifeboat was delivered. The Mk I lifeboat had been designed for the Hudson and would need modification, as the Mk IA and Mk II, to suit the Warwick.

It was decided that since compatibility with the Hudson had been tried and tested, 279 Squadron should proceed to equip with modified aircraft and lifeboats. In the meantime, an RAF team was touring flying stations, including US Army Air Force facilities from summer 1942, demonstrating the lifeboat and its content. From many aircrew it received amazed appreciation that so much was being

done to rescue them should the need arise, but many others, especially the Americans, were less enthusiastic, preferring to believe it was a device they would never require.

History records the Warwick as a troublesome design that only entered service in its primary ASR role in October 1943, by which time the Hudson had demonstrated the Mk I lifeboat's worth in action. The first such demonstration came on 5 May 1943, when a 102 Squadron Halifax crew ditched shortly after 03.00 off the Dutch coast. A 279 Squadron Hudson found them in their dinghy at 06.25, circling until 08.20 when two more squadron Hudsons arrived, one equipped with a Mk I lifeboat.

Much of the craft's equipment failed to activate or activated incompletely, but it landed safely, just 75ft from the dinghy. The Bomber Command crew climbed into the dinghy and although the equipment failures caused them difficulty, they had the engines running and began making way. Fog descended, adding to their woes and causing the Hudsons to lose contact at 11.15. Soon after, the starboard engine stopped. Struggling to erect the mast and rigging, the crew relied on the port engine, until this also failed.

Search aircraft spotted the lifeboat again at 13.00, vectoring HSL 2579 and two Royal Navy rescue launches towards it. The RAF vessel arrived first, recovering the Halifax crew in the midst of a minefield and taking the Mk I in tow. The lifeboat hampered their progress, however, and they moored it to a buoy, leaving the Royal Navy to recover it the next day, while they made all haste for their home base at Grimsby.

Many more airborne lifeboat missions followed, with varying degrees of success.

Above: Number 269 Squadron Warwick ASRI BV508/HK-B was being loaded with a Mark II lifeboat at Lagens, in the Azores, during April 1945.

Below right: Another 269 Squadron Warwick, BV356/HK-E was up from Lagens, flying over Terceira in April 1945. Carrying a Mark II lifeboat, it also demonstrates the type's comprehensive ASV antenna fit.

Below left: This September 1944 image shows how the lifeboat is fitted beneath the Warwick's bomb bay.

ASR Flight Wellington IC Z9027/Z takes off from Bir El Beheira, Libya, in July 1942.

Air Vice-Marshal Sir Keith Park (second from right), Air Officer Commanding Air Headquarters Malta, employed an HSL during an inspection of RAF bases on the island in August 1942.

Among the more notable releases, that of 15 July 1943 saw a 279 Squadron Hudson drop a Mk I to a ditched Vickers Wellington crew. Another accurate release saw the boat land 90ft from the casualties, after which the Hudson departed with four Hawker Typhoons of 12 that had escorted it to the scene. The remaining Typhoons then fought a pitched battle that kept 16 Focke-Wulf Fw 190s away from the rescue scene, downing two of the fighters before Supermarine Spitfires arrived and drove off the survivors. The Wellington crew spent three and a half hours in the Mk I before HSLs 177 and 190 picked them up.

On 24 November 1943, a 280 Squadron Warwick dropped a Mk IA lifeboat to a Wellington crew ditched 65 miles off Land's End. The vessel was apparently damaged, for it began taking on water. The downed flyers were left stranded in a sinking lifeboat around 11.35 after their dinghy drifted away. Seeing the lifeboat in trouble, the Warwick crew dropped Lindholme gear, but this also failed.

Lindholme gear was again dropped at 13.10, this time working properly. But the crew was unable to board the dinghy. Visual contact with the lifeboat was then lost and despite a desperate search by another Warwick, a Hudson and a Wellington, no trace of the crew was seen. The search continued until 2 January 1944, but without result.

The final confirmed RAF airborne lifeboat drops of World War II were all performed by 280 Squadron Warwicks on 18 April 1945. Two Warwicks launched from Beccles at 09.24 to search around the Frisian Islands. A column of smoke drew them to a spot where they found seven survivors in the water, wearing Mae West lifejackets and arranged in two groups

SHORT SUNDERLAND

The Sunderland was the most heavily armed of the RAF's wartime flying boats, literally bristling with machine guns in a fearsome configuration that led German pilots to bestow the nickname 'Flying Porcupine'. A superlative warplane, the Sunderland had its origins in the luxurious pre-war 'C'-Class Empire airliner, the prototype flying for the first time on 16 October 1937.

Numbers 230 and 210 Squadrons, in Singapore and at Pembroke Dock respectively, were first into service with the Sunderland Mk I in June 1938. Three Coastal Command squadrons were equipped by September 1939, 204 and 228 Squadrons demonstrating the type's ASR ability almost as soon as war broke out.

The freighter *Kensington Court* was torpedoed on 18 September 1939 in the Atlantic Ocean, 70 miles off the Scilly Isles. One Sunderland from each squadron joined the rescue, the first alighting on a rough sea to collect 20 survivors only 10 minutes after the ship sank. The second aircraft recovered the remaining 14 sailors and all were safe and back on dry land less than 60 minutes after the sinking.

Heroic combats with submarines and enemy aircraft soon followed as Sunderlands ranged wide through every theatre of war. The aircraft was on hand for many rescues and even passenger evacuations, a 228 Squadron lifting 82 passengers during the evacuation of Crete in April 1941.

The Sunderland appeared in steadily improved Mk II, III and V variants, the latter with Pratt & Whitney Twin Wasp engines. It is worth noting that the Sunderland Mk IV development became so different to the original aircraft that it matured as the post-war Seaford Mk I. The Sunderland served on after the war, as a general reconnaissance type and makeshift transport, especially during the Berlin Airlift in 1948 and along the Korean coast during the three years of conflict in the peninsula. The type remained active until 15 May 1959.

··

SPECIFICATION
SHORT SUNDERLAND MK III
Powerplant four 1,066hp Bristol Pegasus XVIII radial piston engines
Length 85ft 4in (26.03m)
Height (on beaching gear) 32ft 2in (9.81m)
Wingspan 112ft 10in (34.39m)
Wing area 1,487sq ft (138.14m²)
Maximum speed 212mph (341km/h)
Range (at 145mph/233km/h) 3,000 miles (4,828km)
Service ceiling 15,000ft (4,750m)
Armament one (or two) 0.303in Vickers machine gun in the nose turrets, plus two 0.303in Browning machine guns in the mid-upper turret, four similar weapons in tail turret, four fixed to fire forwards and one 0.5in Browning firing from each waist hatch; up to 4,960lb of stores

A pair of Sunderland Is, moored in Messinia Bay, Kalamata, on 29 April 1941 during the evacuation of RAF personnel from Greece.

of two and five. One Warwick dropped its lifeboat to the two-man group, the second aircraft following up with a drop to the other five. The men were too exhausted to reach, let alone climb into the lifeboat, and dinghies plus additional Mae Wests were dropped.

Assistance was called for from a Walrus or Catalina, either of which may have been able to alight and offer immediate assistance, and it was stressed that a powerful escort ought to be sent to protect the seaplane as it was so close to enemy territory. A third Warwick arrived to relieve the initial pair, remaining on station until 17.08, when it became evident that all seven men had perished.

Back at Beccles, another Warwick had departed at 14.01 on a search close to the site of the two-aircraft sortie. Its crew dropped their lifeboat to an individual in the water at 15.29. He made no attempt to reach it, however, so two sets of Lindholme gear were deployed, but again with no reaction. Remaining on station, the Warwick oversaw the arrival of a Catalina, which set down to recover three bodies, but no survivors.

By its nature, air sea rescue delivered more than its fair share of tragedy, offset by the occasional spectacular success. It ought to be noted that the important contribution of the airborne lifeboat operators continued alongside the inestimable efforts of the marine craft and the Walrus and, later, Sea Otter crews with the other dedicated ASR squadrons. To their efforts must be added the work performed by the Consolidated Catalina, Short Sunderland and other squadrons that regularly performed ASR as a secondary tasking to their primary anti-submarine, anti-shipping and maritime patrol missions.

OVERSEAS ASR

The Mediterranean and Africa

Beginning in late 1940, the RAF switched from a defensive to an offensive position. The ultimate aim was to invade and liberate continental Europe and more than four years of intensive combat ensued. Elsewhere, British forces were simultaneously fighting overseas, around the Mediterranean, in North Africa and the Middle East, and in the so-called China, Burma, India (CBI) theatre of operations. In every case, air power was exercised and wherever aircraft risked coming down on water, ASR coverage was required.

Yet, until 1943, there was no formal ASR organisation in the Mediterranean. There was ASR coverage, typically provided by various vessels and RAF Blenheim and Wellington bombers. On the other hand, the Middle East ASR Flight, initially comprising only RAF personnel, was established during summer 1941. At first operating Wellingtons out of Kabrit, Egypt, it later added a Fleet Air Arm (FAA) manned flight operating the Walrus, and based near Benghazi, Libya. It also had access to individual Grumman and Fairchild 91 amphibious seaplanes, the latter among just four of the type built, originally as an eight-seater airliner. Even so, primary ASR cover came from a single Malta-based HSL, augmented by a variety of civilian craft. Two more HSLs arrived in October and another pair in November.

Elsewhere, 230 Squadron had arrived with its Sunderlands from Ceylon, setting up a new base in Egypt. From there, the unit began experiments with equipment similar to the Thornaby bag, hinting at the big flying boat's ASR potential. Indeed, the Sunderland

This ASR Flight Wellington IC was based at Landing Ground 'X'/Abu Sueir North, in Egypt. It performed a joint Mediterranean search operation with HSL 2518 on 25 October 1942.

Flight Lieutenant DD Browning, Master of 251 ASRU's HSL 139 guides the craft at speed along the Algerian coast.

Walrus I X9498/B with 284 Squadron undergoes maintenance at Cassibile, Sicily. Hurricane Mk IIC KW980, parked alongside, belonged to the Mediterranean Air Command Communications Unit, based at Maison Blanche, Algeria. Beyond is the medieval building that served as the airfield control tower.

contributed to many rescues in all theatres, but its contribution is easily overlooked since it never formed the sole equipment of any dedicated wartime ASR unit.

As more HSLs came into the theatre, so the airborne ASR provision also expanded, although it fell far short of the aircraft numbers required. The Air Ministry believed 60 aircraft, comprising Catalinas and Hudsons, would be adequate but was only able to offer 20 Warwicks and half that number of Walruses, and none until August 1943. Airborne lifeboat-capable Warwicks were not expected in the theatre until even later in the year.

In the meantime, 283 Squadron was established on the Walrus at Hussein Dey, Algiers, in February 1943, operating detachments to cover more of the area than would be possible from a single base. Its first live mission, on 5 February, recovered a dead German pilot. Three more rescues

in succession then retrieved three German soldiers, a flyer and, on 24 February, a Junkers Ju 88 crew. Subsequently, much of its 'trade' came from downed US airmen.

Tragedy struck on 27 May after a Walrus suffered damage when it alighted to assist a US Lockheed P-38 Lightning pilot. The crew called to report their aircraft was sinking and their dinghy faulty, and all were lost. Two dinghies became standard for the Walrus thereafter. In August, 283 Squadron moved to Palermo, Sicily, keeping up with the Allied advance.

A second ASR unit, 284 Squadron, arrived on Malta in July 1943, with a detachment at Algiers. It had moved in its entirety to Cassibile, Sicily, by the end of the month. Its first rescue, on 27 July, recovered a US pilot who had spent 13 hours paddling his dinghy away from enemy-held territory.

Both squadrons included experienced crew from the home-based ASR units, in particular 277 Squadron, and there was also an interchange of personnel between them.

In July 1943 the Allies had invaded Sicily, with the generally inadequate ASR bolstered by 230 Squadron's Sunderlands. Then, in September, mainland Italy was invaded. With air power on the ascendancy, the ASR task became more important than ever and 614 Squadron lent a hand, flying ASR patrols with its Blenheim Mk Vs out of Borizzo. Given Italy's extensive coastline and elongated shape, several HSLs were called into action and it made sense for 283 Squadron to do most of its work along the west coast, with 284 Squadron

to the east. Many of the squadrons' 'customers' were American, including a B-17 crew saved by 284 Squadron on 1 May 1944, although the arrival of a sixth casualty, a South African, came as a surprise.

The bomber had gone down on 30 April, but its crew was only located by a Spitfire pilot the next day. Under escort from more Spitfires, the 284 Squadron Walrus alighted alongside the crew, only to be struck by a rogue wave that damaged its forward fuselage and cockpit. Cracking on, as was their way, the two-man ASR crew embarked the B-17 survivors in preparation for a long taxi to Ortona, at which

Number 284 Squadron aircrew rest at Cassibile between sorties.

VICKERS WELLINGTON

First flown in prototype form on 15 June 1936, the Vickers Wellington equipped 21 Bomber Command squadrons by the winter of 1941/42 as the cornerstone of the RAF's long-range bombing capability. It remained so until the four-engined heavy bombers came on line, but by then the Wellington was already demonstrating its abilities in the maritime strike and reconnaissance roles.

A few 'bomber' Wellingtons found themselves on rescue duties, but the majority of ASR-tasked airframes were maritime marks. The latter were radar equipped and included the Hercules VI- or XVI-powered Wellington Mk XI with anti-surface vessel (ASV) Mk III radar featuring an undernose antenna housed in a streamlined radome, the Hercules XVII-engined Mk XIII with ASV.Mk II and associated mast aerials, and Mk XIV, incorporating Hercules XVII engines, ASV.Mk II and a retractable Leigh Light.

Squadrons engaging in regular Wellington ASR operations were 38 (Mk XIV), 221 (Mk XIII), 281 (Mk XIV), 294 (Mks IC, XI and XIII) and 621 (Mks XIII and XIV). Some 11,460 Wellingtons were built and the type remained in RAF service, latterly as a trainer, until 1953.

••

SPECIFICATION

VICKERS WELLINGTON MK IC

Powerplant two 1,000hp Bristol Pegasus XVIII radial piston engines

Length 64ft 7in (19.72m)

Height 17ft 5in (5.33m)

Wingspan 86ft 2in (26.27m)

Wing area 840sq ft (78.04m²)

Maximum speed at 15,500ft 255mph (410km/h)

Range (with 4,500lb bomb load) 1,200 miles (1,931km)

Service ceiling 18,000ft (5,490m)

Armament two 0.303in machine guns in each of the nose and tail turrets, plus two similar weapons in beam positions; up to 4,500lbs of bombs or other stores

point a parachute came into view, under which hung a South African Air Force (SAAF) Spitfire pilot from the escort detail. With his engine failing, he had bailed out close to certain rescue.

With six survivors aboard, the Walrus began its journey, with a boat heading out from Ortona hopefully to make a rendezvous. But they were still close to shore, from which the enemy began firing. The Walrus was hit, leaving the pilot with no choice but to beach it. All eight on board survived the encounter.

Meanwhile, back in Britain, personnel from 283 and 284 Squadrons had combined to form a new unit on 20 October 1943. It was numbered 293 Squadron on 28 November and began operations out of Algeria with Warwicks. Later absorbing some Walrus detachments from 283 Squadron, it joined the latter serving Italy's west coast.

In January 1944, ASR strength in the Mediterranean included 45 HSLs, with another 21 assigned to the Middle East and new variants arriving. In the air, all the local ASR squadrons soon had Warwicks on strength, 283 Squadron completing its first, inauspicious, live airborne lifeboat drop on 22 July. Engine trouble had forced a Spitfire pilot out of combat with a Junkers Ju 88 and a Warwick flew to his position. It released Lindholme gear and the pilot climbed into the

Top right: A Mediterranean HSL pick-up, probably in 1943.

Right: The Malta ASRU came to the aid of Sergeant D Goodwin on 28 January 1943, after he ditched his 229 Squadron Spitfire 30 miles west of the island.

Far right: A Spitfire overflies a seaplane tender as it returns to harbour in Malta. Such craft often supported rescue operations.

Lindholme dinghy. A second Warwick arrived to deliver the airborne lifeboat, which was destroyed on impact with the water after its parachute detached during the drop. An HSL then arrived to collect the Spitfire pilot.

It fell to 293 Squadron to perform one of the most spectacular series of rescues of the war, not for their derring-do, but for the fact that they involved the same SAAF North American

Mustang pilot. On 2 April 1945, Lieutenant Ray Veitch's 260 Squadron Mustang was hit by ground fire, obliging him to leave it over the sea. He drifted down into a minefield, on to which a 293 Squadron Walrus crew thought it best not to land. Instead, the same squadron sent a Warwick, which dropped an airborne lifeboat. Veitch boarded the craft, got it running and sailed out of the minefield to a US Catalina.

Above left: A 520 Squadron Hudson Mk III overflies 71 ASRU's HSL 181 as it returns to Gibraltar.

Above right: Thorneycroft built the 67ft Whalebacks. Photographed in 1944, HSL 2734 was the fourth from last built.

Top: HSL 2546 was the first vessel of the last batch of 63ft HSLs. It was photographed during its MTO service.

Engaging rail traffic on 5 April, Veitch found himself again hit by ground fire and forced to his parachute. Again landing in a minefield, he became the subject of a race between enemy craft dashing to his position and a 293 Squadron Warwick, which again released an airborne lifeboat. Friendly fighters kept the enemy at bay while Veitch, now quite practised with the lifeboat, again got underway towards a Catalina.

When ground fire brought another of his Mustangs down on 30 April, Veitch took to his dinghy, not far from shore. No minefields were involved, yet the 293 Squadron Walrus suffered engine problems and returned to base, leaving a Catalina to complete the rescue.

A further dedicated ASR squadron operated over the Mediterranean from 1943, employing various Wellington variants, among them the radar-equipped Mks XI and XIII, Walrus and Warwick.

Squadrons dabbled with ASR in every theatre of war as circumstance and orders demanded, many seeing aircraft freed up for the work as combat eased off. With the enemy in retreat, units often found themselves with free capacity for ASR, often employing aircraft equipped with the latest anti-surface vessel (ASV) radar for their primary task, which could be usefully employed looking for downed aircraft and dinghies. The Wellington was typical of such aircraft and 38 Squadron used it to good effect as an ASR platform, before moving to Malta and the Warwick in July 1945. Similarly equipped, 221 Squadron also flew ASR briefly during 1945, as well as desert rescue. Faced with a lack of targets, Greece-based 252 Squadron latterly turned its Beaufighters to ASR, while 459 Squadron, also stationed in Greece, flew ASR with its

Marylands. Finally, 621 Squadron flew ASR as a secondary tasking from bases in Kenya, Aden and Egypt.

With U-boats threatening Allied shipping and Great Britain dependent on supplies from the US and Canada, maritime reconnaissance and anti-submarine operations ranged far out into the Atlantic from British bases and stations in West Africa. As ever, where warplanes were going into action, ASR cover was required, locally based aircraft also covering some of the routes used by aircraft ferrying to Europe from the US. Other ferry routes, to the north, necessitated ASR coverage out of Iceland.

An ASR officer was posted to Air Headquarters West Africa in October 1942, where he found a single Sunderland, based at Jui, Gambia, providing the entirety of ASR coverage and using a Thornaby bag-like device of local design. That month, the Sunderland located six lifeboats from the torpedoed SS *Oronsay*, dropping a radio and other equipment that enabled the Royal Navy to effect a rescue. The next day, the Sunderland found another nine lifeboats, followed by three more on the third day.

In November 1942, 270 Squadron arrived with Catalinas and a secondary ASR mission and in December, 200 Squadron at Jeswang, Gambia, received Lindholme gear for its Hudsons. The Royal Navy had provided launches, but from July 1943 HSLs began arriving, joining forces with USAAF and Free French vessels to cover the vastness of the seas off West Africa.

Airborne rescue assistance also came out of the Azores, an important staging post for aircraft ferrying to the Middle East.

CONSOLIDATED CATALINA

The Catalina had been in US Navy service five years by the time the first Catalina Mk I reached the RAF. The Marine Aircraft Experimental Establishment had trialled a single machine at Felixstowe, Suffolk, in 1939, resulting in orders for 90 aircraft equivalent to the US Navy PBY-5.

Such was the urgency for modern, rugged flying boats for patrol, anti-submarine and other maritime tasks, including ASR, that the Catalina Mk I entered service with 240 Squadron in March 1941; by May the type was intimately involved in the campaign against the German battleship *Bismarck*.

Although its load was smaller, the Catalina could operate from considerably heavier seas than the Sunderland, suiting it to the task of alighting to embark survivors, even in a 6ft swell. It was also an exceptional combat aircraft and Britain acquired a total of 640 Catalinas, in Mk I, IB, II, III, IVA, IVB and VI versions, the Mk III standing out among them as an amphibian, thanks to its retractable tricycle undercarriage.

Another of the type's advantages over the Sunderland was its superior performance in hot, humid conditions, suiting it especially to service in the Far East. The final RAF Catalinas were retired by 240 Squadron, at Red Hills Lake, India, in October 1945.

SPECIFICATION

CONSOLIDATED CATALINA MK IB

Powerplant two 1,200hp Pratt & Whitney R-1830 radial piston engines
Length 65ft 2in (19.87m)
Height 17ft 11in (5.47m)
Wingspan 104ft (31.70m)
Wing area 1,400sq ft (130.06m²)
Maximum speed at 10,500ft 190mph (306km/h)
Range 4,000 miles (6,437km)
Service ceiling 24,000ft (7,320m)
Armament one 0.303in machine gun in bow, plus a similar weapon in each side blister and a ventral position; up to 2,000lb of stores

Catalina I Z2147/AX-L flew with 202 Squadron from Gibraltar. Seen here over Europa Point, it was returning from an anti-submarine patrol on 28 March 1942. It completed nine successful attacks against submarines, although the Catalina also took part in many ASR operations.

Number 269 Squadron was stationed there from early 1944, having transferred from the far less favourable climate of Iceland. Operating from outposts somewhat removed from the main effort of war, 269 Squadron only replaced its Hudsons in August 1944, when six Warwicks arrived. Number 251 Squadron had taken 269's place in Iceland, using a mix of aircraft that included perhaps the last lifeboat-carrying Hudsons in service. It replaced the aircraft with Warwicks only in 1945.

The Far East

Air Sea rescue in the CBI Theatre of Operations, and even further east, posed particular problems through the expanse of the areas to be covered and problems of supplying aircraft when they were so badly needed in the European Theatre of Operations. An ASR officer was assigned to Air Headquarters Far East in October 1941, with responsibility for Malaya and Singapore. At his disposal he had two RAF vessels, neither of them HSLs, and in the air he relied on lightplanes flown by the Malay Volunteer Air Force and capable only of dropping smoke floats and lifejackets. A few rescues were accomplished before Singapore fell to the Japanese.

In India, the FAA and Royal Navy provided ASR coverage using surface vessels and Walruses, on the proviso that the precious amphibians were not required for other duties. Meanwhile, Air Headquarters India was informed that it would receive aircraft and vessels as early as possible in 1943. Aside from the problems of supply, there was the rapid Japanese advance to consider, with the number of boats and aircraft required reducing as more

Although not an ASR mission, this historic image does portray Sunderland GR.Mk V ML778/NS-Z, flown by Wing Commander J Barrett, Officer Commanding 201 Squadron, based at Castle Archdale, County Fermanagh, undertaking Coastal Command's last operational wartime patrol, escorting an Atlantic convoy south-west of Ireland.

territory was denied them, and yet the force would need to expand once the Allies turned on to the offensive.

Some relief came in summer 1942, when the US pledged to cover ASR in its areas of operation. Taking this into account, it was believed the RAF needed 30 HSLs in India, ten for East Africa and 30 in work for the future. The promise of deliveries 'as early as possible in 1943' foundered when operations in the Mediterranean and Africa placed greater demands on ASR resources. By the end of July, only nine HSLs has reached India and no more arrived until January 1944.

A force of 20 long-range ASR aircraft was also planned, and an ASR officer assigned to India in March 1943, but no Warwicks were

expected to become available until June 1944 at the earliest. Mercifully, air warfare in the region was less intense and ASR requirements were met in part by the few HSLs in theatre, while local general reconnaissance squadrons also performed admirable work.

Among them, 20 Squadron employed the veteran Lysander only briefly on ASR operations in spring 1943, while a variety of units, including 160, 191, 200, 212, 240 and 413 Squadrons, variously served across the region adding ASR to their duties primarily on the Consolidated Catalina and Liberator. A number of ASR Flights also formed, some quite transient and engaged primarily in training. In November 1943, Lindholme gear and Bircham barrels arrived in India, the former going into

A Hurricane of 222 Group leads 203 ASRU HSL 164 out of Colombo, Ceylon, into the Indian Ocean, for a search around February 1943.

action during the month when it was dropped to a USAAF bomber crew.

Most significantly, a dedicated ASR squadron was planned. Number 292 Squadron was expected to begin operations in February 1944 with the first of an expected complement of 20 Warwicks. The Royal Navy was scheduled to release five Walruses to 292 Squadron in September. No Warwicks arrived until April, by which time the Navy had begun the early release of Walruses, and Sea Otters were on their way by ship. The unit therefore began its formation proper, ultimately sending a Warwick detachment to Bombay, Warwicks and Walruses to Ceylon, and Sea Otters to Chittagong.

With such a vast area to cover, even this improved provision was stretched and aircraft from other RAF squadrons, particularly Wellingtons, made an important contribution. More HSLs also arrived to ease the burden and by June 1944 a total of 45 ranged from Karachi all the way to Chittagong. Coordination remained a difficult issue given the distances and often inhospitable terrain, but a more profound problem was about to arise.

The long-awaited Warwick, developed from the pre-war Wellington, employed fabric over metal construction. More than adequate for operations over Europe, it was less than ideal in the tropical conditions of the Far East. Ground crew found it in need of regular attention, while the aircraft's Hercules engines also became troublesome. The Lancaster was an obvious replacement, but Bomber Command's campaign against Nazi Germany took the bulk of Lancaster production. Instead, it fell to the region's Catalina and general reconnaissance Liberator squadrons to fill the void.

Number 212 Squadron was thus re-roled for dedicated ASR over the Indian Ocean and stationed at Karachi. Its Catalinas worked hard, with relief only coming in January 1945, when the USAAF's 7th ERS formed, also on Catalinas.

An effort was made to cover Africa's east coast, aircraft stationed there also ranging out over the Indian Ocean to augment 212 Squadron's work from Karachi. In place at Mombasa, Kenya, from 11 March 1943, 265 Squadron also flew Catalinas and flew ASR sorties from May that year through until its disbandment in April 1945.

The RAF was also struggling to furnish a suitable long-range, high-speed craft for surface rescue in a region where wooden hulls were prone to parasitic attack; metal protection could be applied, but at great cost in outright speed. As a temporary expedient, the Air Ministry struggled to have the Admiralty release a number of its D-type Fairmile launches, but internal dispute continued until the Japanese surrender on 15 August 1945 and none were delivered. On the other hand, changing fortunes in the Middle East and Mediterranean allowed more HSLs to be launched for service in the Far East.

Changes to the airborne coverage had seen 292 Squadron disbanded into three dispersed flights equipped with Warwicks treated with aluminium dope to help stave off the worst ravages of the local climate. Re-equipment was

AVRO LANCASTER ASR.MK III

Avro designed the twin-engined Manchester heavy bomber against a 1936 Air Staff requirement, choosing the complex but powerful Rolls-Royce Vulture as its powerplant. Rolls-Royce was busy perfecting its new Merlin engine, primarily for the Hurricane and Spitfire, so when the Manchester first flew on 25 July 1939, it relied on an engine that was far from mature.

Introduced into combat by 207 Squadron on 24/25 February 1941, the Manchester was plagued by engine failure but had the makings of a fine bomber. It featured a bomb bay capable of accommodating 14,000lb of bombs, although the 1,760hp Vulture's inefficiencies denied it this weight-lifting capability.

The Manchester's shortcomings were realised early on and this led Avro to modify it with a longer-span wing providing space for four less powerful Merlins. The resulting Mk III was otherwise little modified but proved immediately successful, transforming the troublesome twin into the exceptional Lancaster.

The new bomber flew its first operational mission on 3 March 1942. It will always be associated with the Dambusters' raid of 16/17 May 1943, but its greatest contribution was as the stalwart of Bomber Command's efforts against Nazi Germany, initially as a strategic bomber and later tasked against tactical targets in the build-up to D-Day and beyond.

Just three variants accounted for the majority of wartime Lancaster production, the Rolls-Royce Merlin-powered Mk I, Bristol Hercules-engined Mk II and Packard Merlin Mk III. The latter employed Merlins built in the US by Packard but was otherwise similar to the Mk I. Indeed, after a period in service during which engines might be swapped between airframes and new engines installed to replace damaged equipment, it became common for Mk I and III airframes to feature a mix of Rolls-Royce and Packard engines, some even accumulating four engines of the opposite type, which ought to have changed their mark number.

The end of hostilities saw the RAF with huge stocks of surplus Lancasters, but also an urgent need for MR and ASR machines as US-supplied Liberators and Catalinas were returned off Lend-Lease. Thus the Lancaster began a new career, initially modified as the ASR.Mk III or, after UK military aircraft designations changed in their entirety from using Roman to Arabic numerals, ASR.Mk 3.

The Lancaster had proven its ability to withstand the rigours of long-endurance, low-level maritime flying during wartime patrol missions and, given the surfeit of airframes and the type's lifting capability, it was the ideal candidate for ASR conversion. Cunliffe-Owen was tasked with modifying a number of late-production B.Mk III aircraft, including deletion of the mid-upper gun turret and provision for an air-droppable lifeboat to be carried below the bomb bay.

Other work included fitting observation windows ahead of the tailplane, while all the conversions featured H2S ground mapping radar. The ASR.Mk 3 was re-roled in 1950 as the General Reconnaissance (GR), soon Maritime Reconnaissance (MR) Mk 3. The ability to carry a lifeboat remained, but reconnaissance was now the primary mission, so that all MR aircraft were capable of ASR and some maritime. Squadrons flew the MR, themselves on occasion flying the type of rescue sortie that has remained common for all MR aircraft.

The final operational RAF Lancaster, an MR.Mk 3, was retired on 15 October 1956.

• •

SPECIFICATION
AVRO LANCASTER B.MK III

Powerplant four Packard Merlin 28, 38 or 224 inline piston engines each rated at 1,390hp for take-off

Length 68ft 11in (20.70m)

Height 19ft 6in (5.97m)

Wingspan 102ft (31.09m)

Wing area 1,297sq ft (120.49m^2)

Maximum speed at 19,000ft 270mph (435km/h)

Range (with 14,000lb bomb load) 1,160 miles (1,867km)

Armament two 0.303in machine guns in each of the nose and dorsal turrets, plus four similar weapons in tail turret; normal load up to 14,000lb expected, with Lancasters, later in 1945, while Lancasters and Catalinas were expected as the equipment of a new long-range ASR unit. Catalina operator 212 Squadron was to retire the type in favour of the Sunderland Mk V, but all these plans were abandoned at VE-Day.

There remained an ASR need, however, since aircraft were an important means of supplying the many prisoner of war camps dotted throughout the region and rescue coverage was required for the disparate types serving them. Typical of these units and demonstrating their disparity, 27 Squadron flew both rescue and supply missions using Beaufighters, while 233 Squadron arrived in India after VE-Day and immediately set its Dakotas to work on food and supply drops. Ironically, ASR had featured in the squadron's duties two years earlier.

The British Power Boat Company built the 68ft 'Hants and Dorset'-class HSL, of which HSL 2714 was based in Ceylon and photographed in the Indian Ocean during July 1945.

Post-war ASR

Even before VE-Day, the RAF had begun drawing down units or preparing them for continued service in the Far East. When the atomic bombs dropped on Hiroshima and Nagasaki brought Japan to its knees, the war against that country came to an abrupt end, speeding the RAF's contraction. Every area of operations was affected, not least ASR, which concluded the war with a stronger airborne component than ever before and as many as 300 HSLs, plus many more supporting craft.

Massive operations to supply, extract and then repatriate prisoners of war were under way, directly and indirectly involving the ASRS, while the occupation forces also placed considerable demands upon air power. Peace had returned, but the politicians and strategists alike realised it was unlikely to last, and important capabilities, including ASR, needed to be retained and practised.

The post-war Marine Craft Section (MCS) was reduced through retirement of many of its supporting craft, but the RAF still relied on the Sunderland for its great utility in combat and transport and while the Service operated flying boats it would require an MCS. In fact, the MCS was elevated in importance, becoming the RAF Marine Branch on 11 December 1947. Then, from 25 June 1948, Marine Branch vessels were granted the honour of becoming known as His Majesty's Air Force Vessel and permitted to fly the Union Flag between dawn and dusk, as were Royal Navy craft.

High-speed launch numbers naturally reduced and there was a wholesale disbanding of ASR flying squadrons. As the Sunderland faded from service, there was limited need for

HMAFV 2758, an RTTL Mk II built by Vosper, Portsmouth, in 1957. It was later converted to a Fast Motor Yacht and subsequently to a luxury vessel based in Malta.

surface craft. Less auspicious duties, including range patrol and other support functions, became increasingly important through the 1950s and into the early 1960s, such that new Rescue and Target Towing Launches (RTTLs) entered service from the late 1950s.

By then, the optimal solution of flying out to an incident, stopping to retrieve casualties and flying back without touching the water had been achieved thanks to the helicopter and air sea rescue had merged into search and rescue. But helicopters struggled with poor visibility, lacked range and generally were unable to fly at night, so that the RTTLs remained an important back-up at home and overseas, completing a number of important and audacious rescues. New designs were also introduced, but overall the Marine Branch remained in decline.

As late as 1971 the Service debuted a new marine tender for its RTTLs, but by then the Marine Branch was but a shadow of the post-war MCS. The drawdown continued into the 1980s and the final Marine Branch support tasks passed to a contractor in 1984. Eleven seagoing vessels and one harbour boat remained, and these were disposed of to civilian operators. On 31 March 1986, the RAF Marine Branch disbanded.

In the air, the recalcitrant Warwick had rapidly given way to the Lancaster ASR.Mk III. Converted from surplus B.Mk III bombers, these aircraft were equipped with the Mk II airborne lifeboat – the helicopter was on

Photographed in December 1946 carrying an airborne lifeboat, Lancaster ASR.Mk III RF310/RL-A was with 38 Squadron.

the horizon but yet to become a truly practical military machine.

Even so, the Lancaster remained a dedicated ASR platform for little more than four years, adopting a maritime patrol mission, with ASR secondary, from 1950. It was a switch that shaped the future of fixed-wing RAF search and rescue, in which landplanes became an essential adjunct to the helicopter rescue mission. They provided a means of reaching distant survivors quickly and dropping emergency supplies and equipment to them, and carried all the communications equipment to guide rescue vessels or helicopters to them. For long-range work they acted as radio relays

and provided reassurance to helicopter crews that should they ditch, cover was on hand.

The Shackleton naturally replaced the Lancaster, and while a Mk III airborne lifeboat was designed for it, the time of the helicopter had more or less arrived and the vessel did not enter squadron service.

Among several ASR/GR/MR Lancaster operators, 179 and 224 Squadrons operated it only briefly. Numbers 279 and 621 Squadrons also flew the ASR.Mk III, while 18, 38, 120, 160, 203 and 210 Squadrons all operated the GR/MR.Mk III.

CHAPTER 3

ROTARY REVOLUTION

STOPPING FIRST...

Helicopter search and rescue (SAR) emerged as a useful military capability in the Far East theatre of operations towards the end of World War II. The United States Army Air Force had an experimental flight of three Sikorsky R-4 helicopters in the region and these were called into action after three members of General Orde Wingate's Chindits were stranded in Japanese-held territory.

The Stinson L-1 Vigilant light aircraft sent to evacuate them suffered engine failure; the pilot force landed in a paddy field. The 1st Airborne Commando's Lieutenant Carter Harman, USAAF, was despatched from the rear base at Lala Ghat to rescue them. He and his diminutive, experimental craft faced a 600-mile flight, over mountains rising to 5,000ft, just to the battle zone. Several stops later, he successfully lifted all four personnel out of the Japanese-held territory, two at a time.

It was the first of many 1st Airborne Commando operations that proved the helicopter's value as an air sea rescue vehicle. As helicopter capability subsequently grew through the late 1940s and into the 1950s, the air sea rescue role became that of search and rescue, better reflecting the ability of longer-ranged, more powerful multi-crew helicopters to search as well as rescue.

Post-war and even into the early 1950s, the RAF gave little thought to helicopters. As the Cold War developed, the Service's focus was on the new generation of jet aircraft, the Gloster Meteor, de Havilland Vampire, Hawker Hunter and English Electric Canberra. They brought with them a quantum leap in performance and increasingly complex technology, posing a considerable challenge to an air force facing the simultaneous requirements of drawing down after conflict and wholesale re-equipment.

As there had been in wartime, there were always aircraft and crew losses to non-operational causes, a situation exacerbated by the nascent technologies embodied in the latest warplanes and the tactics employed to exploit them. The British mainland was reasonably well equipped to rescue or recover downed aircrew, but the peacetime RAF tended not to focus its activity over the English Channel, while its new aeroplanes flew faster, climbed higher and, in some cases, ranged wider, requiring an extended air sea rescue service in support.

It soon became clear that a UK-wide search and rescue (SAR) service was needed. Moreover, agreement had been reached in 1947 for the Air Ministry to assume responsibility for the operation and administration of all SAR arrangements in support of military and civil aviation.

Meanwhile, the Royal Navy had been evaluating the helicopter as a possible successor to the Sea Otter and as a much more economical replacement for its escort destroyers. These vessels always followed an aircraft carrier during flying operations, ready to retrieve aircrew should there be an accident.

In 1947, Westland Aircraft took a licence from Sikorsky to build its S-51 in the UK. It began the Somerset company's long association not only with helicopters, but also with Sikorsky, which it maintained through the subsequent Whirlwind and Wessex to the Sea King. Certain the helicopter would find a regular place in service, the Royal Navy ordered an eventual total of 72 Westland Dragonfly helicopters.

The first Dragonfly completed its maiden flight on 22 June 1949 and the Dragonfly HR.Mk 1 was delivered to 705 Squadron, HMS Siskin, Naval Air Base, Gosport, Hampshire, the following January. Built to Mk 1, 3 and 5 standards for the Royal Navy, the Dragonfly did much to pioneer helicopter SAR

from ship and shore, proving itself in particular on the night of 31 January/1 February 1953.

Extraordinary weather conditions over north-west Europe caused devastating floods in the Netherlands and along the east coast of England. The full operational strength of 705 Squadron deployed to the Netherlands and the English coast to assist in rescuing people stranded on rooftops, in flooded fields, and from boats and dykes, and to ferry medical personnel, supplies and food to remote areas; around 800 people were lifted to safety.

While the operation proved, without doubt, the helicopter's utility as a SAR platform, it was also the backdrop for a rather more prosaic development. The standard method of lifting stranded aircrew had been to attach a hook on the winch line to the survivor's Mae West lifejacket. It was a not entirely satisfactory method and generally unavailable when rescuing civilians. Instead, a Royal Netherlands Navy officer developed a rescue strop, essentially a wide strap connected to the winch cable and passed under the arms of the casualty, leaving their body weight to help secure them on the ascent to the aircraft. Further developed at Royal Navy Gosport, it became the standard NATO Rescue Strop.

Slowly waking to the possibilities of rotary-wing flight in the maritime environment, the RAF belatedly placed Hoverfly Mk 1 and 2 helicopters with the Air/Sea Warfare Development Unit. The Mk 1, based on the Sikorsky VS-316, known in USAAF service as the R-4 and modified for British use, had entered Royal Navy service in February 1945 and joined the RAF's Helicopter Training Flight, at Andover, in May. The Hoverfly

Some 45 Hoverfly Mk I helicopters, equivalent to the US military R-4B, were procured. This aircraft, KL104, was employed on search and rescue trials early in 1946. Arabic numerals replaced Roman numerals in aircraft designations during 1948, the Hoverfly Mk I therefore becoming Hoverfly Mk 1.

Mk 2 (R-6A) arrived in 1946, again with both Services, the RAF flying it with 657 (Air Observation Post) Squadron on army cooperation duties.

Both marks were diminutive craft of only marginal utility, and while the Royal Navy moved over to the Dragonfly, the Air/Sea Warfare Development Unit abandoned the helicopter idea when it became apparent the Hoverfly had no useful function in maritime rescue or anti-submarine operations. This damning, but entirely justified conclusion was probably not helped by standardisation of the Royal Navy Hoverfly fleet on the Mk 1, while the RAF and British Army consolidated the Mk 2 fleet. The latter was especially prone to oil leaks and resulting reliability issues.

Meanwhile, the RAF had also wrestled a few Dragonflys from the initial Royal Navy order, the latter providing pilot training at Gosport. There was an accident just as the initial batch of RAF students were arriving at the Hampshire station, however; the first Dragonfly ending up

on its side after a mishap. The Hoverfly Mk 1 was pressed into service while a replacement Dragonfly was awaited, hover training resuming at a maximum altitude of just 6ft.

But a new helicopter did eventually arrive, and aircraft and crews set out for Singapore in April 1950 to commence operations in June. Between then and 275 Squadron's resurgence in April 1953, the RAF's operational helicopter force comprised the Far East Casualty Evacuation Flight. Formed at Seletar, it provided casualty evacuation for troops engaged in the remote jungle areas of Malaya during Operation Firedog, the Malayan Emergency. Initially equipped with the Dragonfly, the unit later competed, along with other newly forming helicopter units in the Middle East, with 275 Squadron for Sycamore allocations. The Casualty Evacuation Unit met with resounding success from the outset, operating across Malaya for 20 months before losing its first aircraft to the far from neutral jungle. On 1 February 1953,

BRISTOL SYCAMORE

The Sycamore pioneered the modern era of RAF helicopter search and rescue, as well as taking a leading role in developing other aspects of the Service's tactical rotary-wing employment. Built against a 1945 specification, the Bristol Type 171 Mk I prototype flew for the first time on 24 July 1947. The subsequent Type 171 Mk 3 initial production variant was developed into the Sycamore HR.Mk 12 for SAR and anti-submarine work.

Coastal Command began trials with the HR.Mk 12 in February 1952 and two examples of the improved HR.Mk 13 entered service with Fighter Command's 275 Squadron at Linton-on-Ouse on 13 April 1953. Eighty of the definitive Sycamore HR.Mk 14 followed, serving 275 Squadron and several other units, but the initial operator remained the only SAR-dedicated Sycamore squadron.

••

SPECIFICATION

BRISTOL SYCAMORE HR.MK 14

Powerplant one 550hp Alvis Leonides 73 radial piston engine

Length (rotors folded) 46ft 2in (14.08m)

Height 12ft 2in (3.72m)

Main rotor diameter 48ft 7in (14.84m)

Maximum speed at sea level 127mph (204km/h)

Endurance 3 hours

A Sycamore HR.Mk 14.

the expanded unit was redesignated as 194 Squadron.

Back in the UK, the Air/Sea Warfare Development Unit had moved to RAF St Mawgan, Cornwall, in December 1951, where it took delivery of the new Bristol Sycamore in February 1952. Rather more capable than the Hoverfly, the Sycamore enabled the development of maritime helicopter operations and provided the impetus that led to the formation of the RAF's helicopter SAR force.

The RAF trailed the Royal Navy in terms of SAR equipment, however; at the end of 1952, the Sycamore's standard rescue fit comprised a rope ladder and safety lines. That October, Exercise Ardent tested UK air defences and a Sycamore was deployed to RAF Linton-on-Ouse to provide daily SAR cover out of Patrington. During the manoeuvres it became evident that a winch was essential for sea rescues and the first example was delivered in 1953. It was allocated to the re-forming 275 Squadron at Linton.

TOWARDS A SAR FORCE

In October 1952, the global strategy envisaged the formation of two 16-helicopter SAR squadrons, a Fighter Command unit equipped with Dragonflys and a Coastal Command squadron flying Whirlwinds. Almost immediately, a 12 per cent cut in expenditure caused the figures to be halved, although the Sycamore was to be substituted for Fighter Command's Dragonflys. The Sycamore was deemed sufficiently powerful for the rescue of fighter aircrew, but the more powerful

Taking part in a survival course during October 1969, these Central Flying School (Helicopter) Whirlwind HAR.Mk 10s serve to illustrate the revised contours of the turbine-engined variant. Like the accompanying 22 Squadron photograph, this image is also part of a series, in this case possibly taken at 2 Air Navigation School, RAF Gaydon, Warwickshire.

Whirlwind was needed for the crews of heavier aircraft (five men at 100nm range).

Also establishing an enduring system of detached SAR flights, between them 22 and 228 Squadrons maintained pairs of Whirlwinds at bases close to the coast all around the British mainland. Each flight was held at a level of readiness, primarily to respond to military incidents – most likely an aircraft down over the sea or land, or to recover an ejectee – but mostly in response to civilian emergencies.

From 1962 the piston-Whirlwinds were withdrawn from SAR duties in favour of the HAR.Mk 10, powered by a 1,050shp Bristol Siddeley Gnome H1000 turboshaft. Accommodating the new engine in a longer nose section, the new model took is first flight on 28 February 1959. The type served

WESTLAND WHIRLWIND

Developed by Westland from Sikorsky's S-55, the Whirlwind continued the evolution of helicopter SAR begun with the Sycamore. Marginally more powerful than the Bristol design, the Whirlwind was a larger machine of greater versatility, its maintenance aided by mounting its Pratt & Whitney engine in the nose, behind a pair of clamshell access doors.

The Sycamore HR.Mk 13 was already in service with 275 Squadron when the Whirlwind HAR.Mk 1 took its maiden flight on 15 August 1953. The model served only with the Royal Navy, the HAR.Mk 2 preceding the improved HAR.Mk 4 into RAF service. The latter model's revised powerplant was optimised for operations in tropical conditions and, as such, 155 Squadron flew the Mk 4 on rescue and transport duties in the Malayan jungle.

Nonetheless, it was the Mk 2 that entered widespread SAR service with Coastal Command, 22 Squadron taking its first examples at Thorney Island from June 1955. The aircraft adopted the yellow rescue colour scheme pioneered on the Sycamore as standard, establishing an instantly recognisable RAF SAR 'brand' that remained until the Sea King stood down in 2015.

From 1962 the piston-engined Whirlwinds were withdrawn from SAR duties in favour of the HAR.Mk 10, powered by a 1,050shp Bristol Siddeley Gnome H1000 turboshaft. Accommodating the new engine in a longer nose section, the new model took its first flight on 28 February 1959. The type served as transport and assault transport with several units, but its primary SAR tenure was with 22 and 202 Squadrons, the former taking its first aircraft in August 1962.

The HAR.Mk 10 served on with 22 Squadron, alongside the Wessex, until 30 November 1981, while 202 Squadron employed the type from August 1964 until July 1978, transitioning directly onto the Sea King HAR.Mk 3. In Cyprus, the Whirlwind Mk 10 joined 84 Squadron in January 1972 for all manner of operations in support of the local UK military presence, including SAR. It remained on strength until the Wessex arrived to replace it in March 1982.

SPECIFICATION

WESTLAND WHIRLWIND HAR.MK 2

Powerplant one 600hp Pratt & Whitney R-1340-40 radial piston engine
Length (overall) 62ft 1½in (18.94m)
Height 13ft 2in (4.02m)
Main rotor diameter 53ft (16.15m)
Maximum speed at sea level 99mph (159km/h)
Service ceiling 8,600ft (2,620m)
Range 335 miles (539km)

This 22 Squadron Whirlwind HAR.Mk 2, apparently embarking RAF Valley's Medical Officer, was involved in a mountain rescue training exercise on 11 July 1956.

194 SQUADRON

Flying Lockheed Hudsons and then Dakotas on transport and resupply duties, 194 Squadron formed at Lahore on 13 October 1942. It flew its missions through India, Burma and Thailand, adding a flight of Stinson Sentinel light transports in January 1945. These aircraft were suitable for a variety of tasks, including casualty evacuation from short jungle airstrips. The squadron disbanded on 15 February 1946.

The Far East Casualty Evacuation Flight was subsequently established, operating much as 194 Squadron's Sentinels had, but with Westland Dragonfly helicopters. On 1 February, 1953, the Flight was expanded and redesignated as 194 Squadron, flying a variety of new missions, including jungle rescue, as well as casevac, during the Malayan Emergency.

From 1955 the Sycamore began replacing the Dragonfly, and although the squadron maintained a frenetic pace, it began suffering from serviceability and spares availability issues. These had become acute by October 1958, and so, after three Sycamore crashes in early 1959, 194 Squadron was grounded. On 3 June its personnel amalgamated with those of Whirlwind-operating 155 Squadron to create a new 110 Squadron.

A 194 Squadron Sycamore HR.Mk 14 prepares to evacuate a casualty in Malaya. A pair of stretchers could be mounted across the helicopter's cabin, one above the other, although the upper position was seldom used. The Mk 14 Sycamore was equipped with larger doors to ease stretcher loading, although stretchers were sometimes not available and on-the-spot improvisation was necessary.

110 SQUADRON

From its establishment on 1 November 1917, 110 Squadron served as a bomber unit, disbanding on 27 August 1919. It reprised the role from 18 May 1937, initially operating the Blenheim before moving to the Far East in 1942. It flew the Vengeance from October 1942 to January 1945, having begun a transition to the Mosquito in November 1944. On 20 August 1945, it flew the RAF's final attack on Japanese positions.

After combat in Indonesia, 110 Squadron disbanded in April 1946, only to reform on the Dakota by a renumbering of 96 Squadron in June. Alongside ad hoc and route transport tasks, it dropped supplies and stood by to evacuate personnel affected by the region's typhoons. It disbanded again in July 1945, but re-formed at Changi in September.

Still on the Dakota, it flew support for the Malayan Emergency as well as regular transport, before creating ASR detachments at Negombo, Ceylon, and Kai Tak, Hong Kong. From the former, Dakota crews were expected to locate survivors or ships in distress, before leading rescue vessels to them. Re-equipment with the Valetta began in 1951, and the squadron was operating only the Vickers twin when it disbanded again on 31 December 1957.

On 3 June 1959, 155 Squadron's personnel and Whirlwind HAR.Mk 4s were combined with personnel from the recently grounded 194 Squadron to create a new 110 Squadron at Kuala Lumpur. Flying the Sycamore HR.Mk 14 alongside its Whirlwinds, the unit continued the jungle resupply and casualty/medical evacuation (casevac/medevac) duties of its predecessors.

By then equipped with the Whirlwind HAR.Mk 10, in 1963 the squadron moved to Borneo, while its headquarters moved to Seletar, where its 'B' Flight became 103 Squadron. Number 110 Squadron continued in Borneo until October 1967, after which it kept a detachment in Hong Kong, before disbanding for the final time on 15 February 1971.

103 SQUADRON

Formed at Beaulieu on 1 September 1917, 103 Squadron served until 1919 as a bomber unit. It re-formed in August 1936 to continue the role, operating the Hawker Hind, Fairey Battle, Vickers Wellington, Handley Page Halifax and, finally, Avro Lancaster. In November 1945 it was renumbered as 57 Squadron, but reappeared as a Canberra operator in 1954, only to disband in August 1956.

Three years later, 284 Squadron was renumbered as 103, which therefore began a new era as an SAR unit equipped with the Sycamore HR.Mk 14 on Cyprus. In 1960 it also managed a flight at El Adem, while the Cyprus portion of the squadron added army support to its mission.

Nonetheless, SAR remained a primary role and on 7 December 1960 the unit effected an exceptional rescue, lifting 13 sailors from the stricken freighter *Snjeznik*, as well as the crew of a Sycamore that crashed during the operation.

On 31 July 1963, 103 Squadron's presence on Cyprus was redesignated 1563 Flight, while its El Adem detachment became 1564 Flight and the squadron ceased to exist.

It returned in August as 'B' Flight, 110 Squadron expanded into a squadron at Seletar. Flying the Whirlwind HAR10, the new 103 Squadron

Sycamore HR.Mk 14 XE311/B was with 110 Squadron at Butterworth, Malaya, in 1962, supporting British forces based in the north of the country after the end of Operation Firedog.

worked with army units in combat in Borneo and Singapore, as well as providing SAR coverage for the latter. In 1972, the Wessex HC2 took over from the Whirlwind and remained on strength until 103 Squadron disbanded at Tengah on 31 July 1975.

1563 FLIGHT

Number 1563 Flight has existed in meteorological (1942–1946), SAR (1963–1972) and tactical support (1975–1991 and 2004–2009) roles.

As a SAR unit, 1563 Flight formed from 103 Squadron on 31 July 1964, operating Sycamore and, later, Whirlwind HAR.Mk 10 helicopters on Cyprus. In January 1972, it combined with sections of 230 Squadron and disbanded into 84 Squadron, which continues to provide the island's military SAR coverage.

Meanwhile, a detachment of four 230 Squadron Westland Puma HC1 helicopters, sent to Belize in November 1975, was designated as 1563 Flight. Its primary support role to locally based British Army units was supplemented by SAR for military and civilian emergencies. It disbanded in 1991 and a subsequent incarnation, in Iraq from 2004 to 2009, did not involve SAR.

22 SQUADRON

Established as a scout unit at Gosport on 1 September 1915, 22 Squadron deployed to France, returning to disband on 31 December 1919. It re-formed for experimental duties in 1923, changing roles on 1 May 1934 in a simultaneous disbandment/re-formation.

Now its long association with maritime operations began, initially with the Vickers Wildebeest torpedo bomber. It took the outdated biplane to war, but only briefly, since the Bristol Beaufort replaced it in November 1939. With its Beauforts, the squadron wreaked havoc on enemy shipping, including a daring solo attack on *Gneisenau* that earned Flying Officer Kenneth Campbell a Victoria Cross.

In January 1942 the squadron moved to Ceylon but, finding a dearth of coastal targets, turned its attention to patrols, convoy escort and ASR, thus embarking on the role for which 22 Squadron is perhaps now best remembered. Nonetheless, this first dalliance with rescue was relatively short-lived, offensive operations ramping up again with Beaufighter deliveries from May 1944. The unit continued in the Far East with Beaufighters and Mosquitos until disbanding on 30 September 1945.

It re-formed at Thorney Island almost a decade later, on 15 February 1955, as a dedicated SAR unit flying the Sycamore HR.Mk 14 and Whirlwind HAR.Mk 2. Thus equipped, the squadron divided into flights at airfields on the east and south coasts, although the Sycamore's tenure was brief.

The Whirlwind, latterly as the HAR.Mk 10, which arrived in 1962 and replaced the HAR.Mk 2 from 1963, was instrumental in a number of heroic rescues, including a 1956 mission in which Aircraftman 2nd class (AC2) Martin was awarded the George Medal for winching two unconscious crew from a sinking yacht. The following spring, Flight Sergeant Prim lifted 11 crew off a stricken trawler, a remarkable feat for the underpowered Whirlwind HAR.Mk 2.

In July 1959 the unit established an additional flight at St Mawgan, dedicated to training, later adding the Wessex HAR.Mk 2 to its roster. The two helicopter types served 22 Squadron side-by-side from May 1976, until the Whirlwind HAR.Mk 10 was withdrawn on 30 November 1981.

The squadron's first Sea King HAR.Mk 3s entered service in August 1978, the Mk 3A following in May 1997 and enabling withdrawal of the Wessex in June. 22 Squadron remained operational on the Sea King until October 2015, when 'A' Flight at RMB Chivenor stood down prior to the squadron disbanding.

Once again operating from Valley, a 22 Squadron Wessex HC.Mk 2 demonstrates winching with far more advanced equipment than that available in 1956. This image is from another mountain rescue exercise, but in February 1989.

as a utility and assault transport with several units, but its primary SAR tenure was with 22 and 202 Squadrons, the former taking its first aircraft in August 1962.

The HAR.Mk 10 served on with 22 Squadron, alongside the Wessex, until 30 November 1981, while 202 Squadron employed the type from August 1964, until July 1978, transitioning directly onto the Sea King HAR.Mk 3. On Cyprus, the Whirlwind HAR.Mk 10 joined 84 Squadron in January 1972, for all manner of operations in support of the local UK military presence, including SAR; it remained on strength until the Wessex arrived to replace it in March 1982.

It took the years 1953–1956 to build the force up to the point where the nine planned deployed flights could offer standby cover over the whole of the east and south coasts, Wales and part of the Irish Sea. The Whirlwind 2s and Sycamores had an effective maximum radius of action of 50nm and during its first two years the embryonic 275 Squadron, with only a few Sycamores on strength, spent much of its time moving from one detached location to another in an attempt to provide SAR cover wherever fighter exercises were taking place. The pattern of permanently detached flights established at the end of 1956 remained in place until 2015, albeit with changes in aircraft numbers, location and type.

Number 275 Squadron was re-formed as part of 13 Group, Fighter Command, at RAF Linton-on-Ouse on 13 April 1953. Its initial cadre included three Sycamore pilots, among them the unit's Officer Commanding, Flight Lieutenant DC Kearns, and three crewmen/navigators. Its initial equipment comprised the second Sycamore, which arrived on 16 April 1953. Remarkably, the squadron's SAR standby commenced on 20 April, at ten-minute readiness during normal working hours and one hour otherwise, restricted to daylight operations only. Its first operational sortie had been flown on 18 April 1953, an abortive search for a reported ditching.

With two Sycamore Mk 13s, the unit responded to demands for operational SAR standby at various places along the east coast. Maintained for a few hours or days at a time, these mirrored the later pattern of fixed detachments, aircraft visiting, for example, Bridlington Bay, Patrington, Sutton-on-Hull and Thornaby, Yorkshire; Strubby, Lincolnshire; North Weald, Essex; Coltishall, Horsham St Faith and Marham, Norfolk; Acklington and Boulmer, Northumberland; Manston, Kent; and Bampton, Oxfordshire.

Compared with wartime, the early and mid-1950s saw more frequent aircraft crashes on land than on water. Large numbers of Meteors, Vampires and Venoms were in service, and with jet flying on such a scale still in its infancy, crashes and bail-outs were not uncommon. 275 Squadron's first rescue, in August 1953, recovered a Venom pilot from Boulmer (then under care and maintenance) to Acklington, Northumberland.

In 1954, the squadron acquired an Auster Mk V, two Hiller HT.Mk 1 helicopters borrowed from the Royal Navy, a pair each of Chipmunks and Ansons, and an Oxford. The Mk 13 Sycamores were reserved for new crew training (four of the seven available crews were held in readiness for overseas duty with the Middle East or Far East Air Forces).

In August, the Sycamores flew only three sorties, the Hillers 21, Ansons 13, Auster 15,

Chipmunks nine and the sole Oxford three. The Hillers were used for land rescue and the Ansons for sea search. No sea rescue was possible for most of the latter part of 1954, although rudimentary standby was maintained as it had been since the squadron re-formed, perhaps prematurely, in April 1953.

The squadron headquarters and basic standby capability moved to Thornaby in November 1954. During 1955, the Yorkshire station saw 275 Squadron working up on the Sycamore Mk 14 and, by May, both Hillers had been returned to the Royal Navy. Now, the squadron began assuming the operational posture that it would maintain until 1959 and which would

stand its successors in good stead for the future. The first permanent, detached flight had been formed at North Coates in February, with Leuchars following in June and Horsham St Faith in September. Another flight was established alongside the Thornaby headquarters.

Yet these were still pioneering days and aside from the serious business of establishing SAR techniques and procedures, the helicopter offered a variety of unique possibilities. A loose newspaper cutting in the archives at the Royal Air Force Museum Hendon records an unusual September 1955 event between a 275 Squadron Sycamore crew and a fishing boat. According to legend, the

Whirlwind HAR.Mk 2 XJ766 is loaded onto a 53 Squadron Blackburn Beverley at Abingdon, Oxfordshire. The photograph is believed to date from summer of 1956, when this aircraft is known to have been airlifted from the UK to join the Internal Security Flight on Cyprus.

Sycamore crew spotted *Concord III* at work off the Tyne during a training flight.

> The crew shouted down 'Any white fish?' Skipper Alan Morse and his brother Norman yelled back 'Plenty'. The boat was rolling heavily in a strong westerly wind, but the skipper reported on docking at North Shields next day: 'A bucket was lowered and the operation carried out as smoothly as though it was being let down from a quayside. The helicopter was about 25 feet above us. After they drew up their fish, they sent us a bottle of beer and a newspaper as a "swap"'.

During 1956, the unit's establishment of 16 Sycamores was reduced to seven as it lost aircraft and crews to the build-up of a Sycamore force in Cyprus, where British forces were fighting a Greek National Organisation of Cypriot Fighters insurgency. This situation began to improve by the end of the year, so much so that in June and July 1957, new flights were established at Chivenor and Aldergrove, respectively. Squadron headquarters transferred to Leconfield in September, where the North Coates flight joined it; in October, the Thornaby flight moved to Acklington.

By the end of 1957, the full complement of six flights had been established, with the squadron strength of 15 Sycamores divided between Leuchars, Acklington, Leconfield, Coltishall, Chivenor and Aldergrove. These provided SAR cover for much of the east and west coasts. The squadron was also ordered to paint its helicopters in a bright yellow (specifically BS381C:356 Golden Yellow), with 'RESCUE' marked prominently on their sides; giving rise to the RAF rescue helicopter scheme that subsequently became so familiar.

Transfer to Coastal Command

In May 1958, Coastal Command assumed responsibility for RAF SAR. Number 275 Squadron therefore transferred to 18 Group and, in an unrelated move, the unit's Chivenor flight transferred to 22 Squadron during November.

The large proportion of land rescues continued despite the move to Coastal Command. In July 1958, for example, the squadron was called out to 24 incidents. They involved an Auster, a Provost, a US Air Force B-66 bail-out, a Sea Venom short of fuel and a parachute sighting, as well as a submarine search, a range incident, several medevacs and responses to bathers in difficulty.

Whirlwind HAR.Mk 2s began replacing 275 Squadron's Sycamores in early 1959, and a mixture of Whirlwinds and Sycamores remained until December. On 1 September, however, the unit stood down by renumbering as 228 Squadron.

As early as February or April 1959, work had begun for a redesignation and re-role of 275 Squadron's Aldergrove flight, a change which seems to have finally taken place on 1 September as the flight became 118 Squadron; now assigned to Transport Command, its primary mission no longer included SAR.

The last UK SAR Sycamore operation, a medevac from Colonsay to Oban, was completed during May 1960. With 11 Whirlwinds established, 228 Squadron's SAR operations continued unabated with flights at Leuchars, Acklington, Leconfield (co-located with the squadron headquarters) and Coltishall, Norfolk.

Elsewhere the Sycamore soldiered on for just a little longer, however; 103 Squadron

Above left: Dragonfly HC.Mk 2 was among three Dragonflys used by the Far East Air Force on trials in Malaya between 1950 and 1952. Here the aircraft was landing in a jungle clearing marked with pieces of white cloth during a casevac demonstration on 30 June 1951.

Above right: Hoverfly, Dragonfly and Sycamore, all were limited in practical capacity. The Dragonfly was useful in the casevac and SAR roles, but its low power and limited cabin space restricted its utility. Casualties were carried in external panniers, as demonstrated in this Operation Firedog Far East Casualty Evacuation Flight sortie at night.

on Cyprus using it with mixed fortunes on 7 December 1960 after the freighter *Snjeznik* ran aground. Having been posted to 284 Squadron on Cyprus early in March 1959 (it became 103 Squadron on 1 August that year), its then second youngest aircrew member, Group Captain John Price, recalled his involvement in the *Snjeznik* operation in an article for the *Royal Air Force Historical Society Journal* (No. 25, published in 2001):

The ship ran aground at night in a strong gale and, no longer able to use his boats, the captain called for assistance. By first light three helicopters were positioned at Famagusta with fuel, ground crews, a doctor and an ambulance. OC Flying was in charge of the operation. He also arranged for PR from Nicosia to take pictures.

Harvey Thompson was winched onto the ship to control deck operations. This was useful, because he spoke French, as did the captain. There was a strong wind blowing from the stern, which had a very high mast, so Harvey Thompson was winched onto the bow.

However there was no bow deck, and all the survivors were on the poop. Cables were cut away on the poop to provide a very small winching area. The main problem was that in the only possible winching position in the strong and gusty wind conditions, with the winch cable fully extended to reach the survivors, the rotor had to be over the top of the mast, with only four feet clearance.

During the operation one of the helicopters hit the mast and fell into the sea. The navigator got out quickly, but the helicopter sank immediately. The pilot's dinghy lead caught under the collective, so he went to the bottom. When he eventually got out, he was unable to operate the inflation bottle of his life saving jacket. He went under three more times, pushing up from the bottom for his last attempt. As his arm came out of the sea, the third helicopter crew skilfully put the strop over him. It was not possible to get him fully into the helicopter, so he was held in the doorway and flown to a small island, then pulled in and flown directly to the doctor and the ambulance. Had they not been there it is unlikely that he would have survived. It took four days for the base hospital to get the last of the water out of the pilot's lungs and he never flew again. My navigator and I rescued the other survivor.

After the accident the handful of sailors still on board the *Snjeznik* decided to stay put, so Harvey Thompson was winched off, but we remained at immediate readiness thereafter until boats were able to get alongside the ship again. AFCs were awarded to Harvey Thompson and to the pilot who had rescued our pilot survivor, and Queens Commendations went to the two navigators who had winched the survivors up. My logbook has a Green Endorsement.

Other units stationed overseas were also making good use of helicopters to save lives and deliver assistance, among them 66 and 225 Squadrons. Traditionally a fighter unit, 66 Squadron re-formed in 1961 on another Bristol helicopter, the Belvedere, a twin-rotor machine not unlike the modern Chinook in configuration. Based in the Far East, it employed the unusual craft on jungle SAR for almost a decade.

Number 225 Squadron's dip into helicopter SAR marked its return to rescue duties, Lysander ASR had been among its roles soon after the outbreak of World War II. Latterly a Spitfire fighter unit, it reappeared out of the Joint Experimental Helicopter Unit in 1960 and flew SAR with the Sycamore and Whirlwind in Borneo for a year or so from 1964.

Back in the UK, the process of replacing 228 Squadron's piston-engined Whirlwind Mk 2 and 4 helicopters with the turboshaft-engined Mk 10 began in October 1962; a handful were placed on SAR standby in November and by December the changeover was complete. In April 1963, 228 Squadron's 'D' Flight relocated just a few miles from Horsham St Faith to Coltishall.

Thus, 228 Squadron was a Whirlwind HAR.Mk 10 operator when it renumbered as 202 Squadron on 1 September 1964. The Leconfield headquarters was maintained, as were 'A' Flight at Acklington, 'B' Flight at Leconfield, 'C' Flight at Leuchars and Coltishall's 'D' Flight.

Number 22 Squadron

Number 22 Squadron re-formed as a 19 Group SAR helicopter squadron at Thorney Island, on 15 February 1955. Tasked primarily with sea SAR over a 60nm range, it had an initial establishment of eight Whirlwind Mk 2s and was planned to operate as four detached flights providing SAR cover over the English south and south-east coasts, and Wales. One flight was located alongside the Thorney Island squadron headquarters, along with operational training facilities and second-line servicing.

The standard Whirlwind crew comprised pilot, navigator and crewman. A specific crewman trade did not exist and in Malaya these positions had been filled by technical ground tradesman, who assisted with servicing

XG511 was among the three 103 Squadron Sycamore HR.Mk 14s that came to the aid of the grounded Snjeznik *off Cyprus on 7 December 1960. The perilous rescue attempt saw one helicopter crash, exposing weaknesses in both the Sycamore and standard SAR equipment.*

away from base. The issue was less pressing for 22 Squadron and in July 1955 three administrative orderlies were identified for crewman duties, receiving an additional 1s 6d (one shilling and sixpence) per day for the privilege. The squadron's *Operations Record Book*, also known as a Form 540, F540 or simply '540', records the crewman's 'main duties' as being to 'operate the winch and to render first aid to rescued personnel when necessary'.

It is interesting to note that the technical emphasis continued in support helicopters with the introduction of the Loadmaster trade. Crewmen in support helicopters were required to gain a significantly high level of technical knowledge of their aircraft whereas those posted to SAR helicopters needed only a general understanding of technical subjects.

In August 1955, there were well-founded rumours of imminent disbandment, since no aircraft had arrived and all postings to the squadron had been suspended. However, two Sycamores were allocated from the Air Sea Warfare Development Unit and 22 Squadron was able to continue forming. Capability was restricted, however; a 14 March 1955 F540 entry recorded that with three Sycamore pilots available 'the Squadron has with effect from this date to be available for SAR operations between the times: 0900 – 1700 Monday to Friday; 0900 – 1100 Saturday; Nil flying on Sundays'.

On 26 April 1955, the squadron recorded its first live SAR sortie, a somewhat peculiar scramble flown in response to a Vickers Varsity crash at Vicq in France. An airman took the twin-propeller training aircraft from RAF Thorney Island 'unlawfully', reportedly flying it over London for some hours before turning for France. There he lost control, crashing into a house and killing himself, along with four people on the ground.

By May, 22 Squadron had two Sycamores and an Avro Anson and was looking and functioning very much like a flight of 275 Squadron during its early days. It flew 13 hours on more conventional SAR operations during the month. Four Whirlwinds arrived in June, the first being collected from 9 Maintenance Unit (MU) at Cosford on 3 June, and the units first two flights were established, 'A' Flight at Thorney Island and 'B' at Martlesham Heath. A Whirlwind and a Sycamore responded to a Sunderland crash next day, recovering ten of the 13 crew.

A third flight was formed at Valley in September and became operational the following month. Providing cover for the west coast, it was also the first SAR flight to have a navigator as its flight commander.

A Sycamore had once again to be borrowed from the Air Sea Warfare Development Unit when the squadron lost two Whirlwinds. One was sent to the Far East Air Force and the second found to be suffering from corrosion. This remained a significant problem for these magnesium alloy-built helicopters in the maritime environment; the later Wessex HC.Mk 2s were re-skinned with aluminium to reduce the problem.

By April 1956, all four of 22 Squadron's flights were operational, the last of them formed at St Mawgan, to where the squadron headquarters moved in June. The Martlesham Heath flight moved to Felixstowe in April. The Southern Rescue Co-ordination Centre (SRCC) at Plymouth controlled the Thorney Island, St Mawgan and Felixstowe flights, while Valley's flight fell under Northern RCC, at Pitreavie Castle, Fife.

Aircraftman 2nd class Raymond Martin was among those posted to Thorney Island as crewmen or winchmen very early on in 22 Squadron's helicopter tenure. On 5 June 1956, he was involved in rescuing a husband and wife from their sinking yacht, an effort that earned him the George Medal. *The London Gazette* of Friday, 21 September 1956, recorded the following:

GEORGE MEDAL

Aircraftman 2 Raymond MARTIN, Royal Air Force

Aircraftman 2 Martin is a National Service Airman who entered the Royal Air Force in January 1956. He has served with helicopters since April, 1956, and is at present employed as winchman of a helicopter of 22 Rescue Squadron. On the 5th June, 1956, the helicopter was called out from Royal Air Force Station, Thorney Island to the assistance of a yacht reported sinking off Hayling Island. At the time, the winds were of gale force and the yacht was foundering in heavy seas. When he arrived at the scene of the wreck, Aircraftman Martin was aware that there had just been an unsuccessful attempt to rescue the crew of the yacht by another helicopter of his Squadron. This attempt had failed because the rescue strop from the helicopter had fouled the yacht's rigging, tearing the winch out of the helicopter, which had perforce to return to land. Aircraftman Martin, having complete disregard for his own safety, was lowered to the deck of the yacht, which was being battered by heavy seas, and of whose crew of two, one was unconscious and the other, a woman, in dire straits. He placed the unconscious man in the rescue strop and superintended his being hauled to safety. While the helicopter was taking the man to the nearest land and returning to the yacht, Aircraftman Martin remained with the woman on the sinking yacht, where he had to cling to the rigging and at the same time support the woman in order to prevent their being washed overboard. On the return of the helicopter, he placed the woman in the rescue strop and was then hauled with her into the aircraft. By his calm efficiency in the most testing circumstances, this young airman was able to rescue two people. His courage and bearing in most dangerous conditions were of the highest order and reflected great credit upon him.

In October 1956, a flight was formed at St Mawgan and prepared to provide SAR cover and communications for Operation Grapple, the British nuclear tests on Christmas Island. The 'Grapple Flight' sailed aboard HMS *Warrior* on 2 February 1957 and arrived at Christmas Island on 4 March, commencing SAR standby on 6 March. Characteristically, the helicopter facility became indispensable and consequently grew, mainly with communications flying, to the extent that 217 Squadron was formed at St Mawgan out of 1360 Flight to replace it from February 1958. Subsequently equipped with the Whirlwind HAR.Mk 4, 217 Squadron disbanded back in the UK the following November.

With hindsight, the depth of involvement of 22 Squadron's crews in Operation Grapple is surprising. An Atomic Weapons Research Establishment document, dated 17 October 1985, includes elements of a detailed weapons test chronology prepared in November 1957. It includes the ominous phrase 'WEAPON DROPPED' under the heading 'Event', with 'ZERO' noted under the 'Hour H+ or H-' heading, at 08.10.

The plan appears to have included as many as five 22 Squadron Whirlwinds primarily moving

66 SQUADRON

Established on 30 June 1916 as a scout unit, 66 Squadron continued in the role until disbanding in October 1919. Famously re-formed at RAF Duxford, now an Imperial War Museum site, on 20 July 1936, 66 Squadron was among the first Spitfire squadrons. It flew various marks throughout World War II, before disbanding on 30 April 1945.

It returned to Duxford on 1 September 1946 by a renumbering of 165 Squadron, flying the Spitfire, Meteor, Sabre and Hunter in succession, then disbanding on 30 September 1960. When it returned in 1961, 66 was a very different unit indeed.

On 15 September 1961, a new 66 Squadron stood up at RAF Odiham, absorbing the Belvedere Trials Unit in the process. It pioneered the large helicopter's operational use, subsequently employing it in the Far East, where jungle SAR was among its important duties. The squadron disbanded in March 1969.

202 SQUADRON

Established as 2 Squadron, RNAS at Eastchurch on 17 October 1914, 202 Squadron initially flew as a home and coastal defence unit, before taking on a bombing role and moving to France. It disbanded on 22 January 1920.

Like 201 Squadron, it soon returned, operating for a little over 12 months between April 1920 and April 1921, then from 1 January 1929 as a redesignation of 481 Flight at Kalafrana, Malta. Equipped with the Fairey IIID, it mainly flew general reconnaissance. The longer-ranged Fairey IIIF arrived in 1930, enabling the unit to fly further afield and begin ASR operations – the Dornier Wal flying boats operated by Italian airline Società Anonima di Navigazione Aerea (SANA) were fairly regular 'customers'. In 1935, the Supermarine Scapa flying boat replaced 202 Squadron's Fairey floatplanes.

The squadron remained busy monitoring Italian activity during the attack on Abyssinia and, even as it re-equipped with the Saro London in 1937, operations associated with the Spanish Civil War. In September 1939, the unit took up its first wartime base, moving to Gibraltar. On 24 October, a squadron aircraft rescued survivors from a torpedoed ship, but sea conditions prevented the Saro London from taking off and HMS *Douglas* took it under tow.

Regular patrols became the norm, with the Fairey Swordfish joining the squadron for short-range

work from October 1940. Re-equipment with the Catalina from May 1941 brought a serious increase in capability, while a four-month flirtation with the Sunderland in 1942 came to nothing. With the Catalina, 202 Squadron continued its patrol, ASW and ASR work until war's end, disbanding on 27 June 1945.

A unit with considerable history, 202 was resurrected by the renumbering of 518 Squadron on 1 October 1946, taking over its predecessor's Halifax Met Mk 6 aircraft and meteorological reconnaissance mission. Regular meteorological flights became the new norm, on the Handley Page Hastings from 1950, until the squadron disbanded again, on 31 July 1964.

On 1 September it rose again, this time as a renumbering of 228 Squadron, equipped with the Whirlwind HAR.Mk 10 at Leconfield. A dedicated SAR unit, 202 Squadron now also maintained flights at Acklington, Leuchars and Coltishall. After a squadron headquarters move to Finningley, the Sea King HAR.Mk 3 came on strength in May 1978, 22 and 202 Squadrons rearranging their flights to concentrate the Sea King operators under one number plate. Thus, 202 Squadron took responsibility for the SAR flights at Boulmer, Brawdy, Coltishall and Lossiemouth.

In 1982, the unit took an apparently retrograde step in taking the Wessex HAR.Mk 2 on strength, but the older type covered a deficiency in home-based aircraft as 'C' Flight deployed with its Sea Kings to the Falkland Islands, immediately after the conflict, to form 1564 Flight.

When Finningley closed in 1989, 202 Squadron moved its headquarters to Boulmer, relocating it again in 2008, this time to Valley, where it remained until disbanding in 2016. Again, 202 proved a difficult unit to put down, returning later that year as 202 (Reserve) Squadron, a redesignation of the Valley-based Search And Rescue Training Squadron, a Defence Helicopter Flying School unit.

Equipped with the Griffin HT1, 202 (Reserve) Squadron's primary duty was the delivery of maritime and mountain flying training to new UK military helicopter crews and to experienced personnel serving on the front line. The work continues, albeit after a return to the simple 202 Squadron designation, with the Airbus Helicopters Jupiter HT1 having replaced the Griffin in 2018.

217 SQUADRON

On 1 April 1918, 17 Squadron, RNAS became 217 Squadron, RAF. Flying Airco DH.4 bombers, it disbanded on 19 October 1919. Equipped with the Avro Anson, it re-formed on 15 March 1937 as a general reconnaissance unit. It used these on anti-submarine patrols after the outbreak of war, subsequently beginning attacks on French

ports while re-equipping with Beauforts. In August 1942 the unit transferred to Ceylon, first operating Beauforts and then Beaufighters, before disbanding on 30 September 1945.

Number 217 Squadron's next appearance was at St Eval, where it brought the Neptune into RAF service simultaneously with a move to Kinloss. It disbanded again on 31 March 1957.

The unit's final iteration was as a Whirlwind HAR.Mk 2 SAR squadron. It formed at St Mawgan on 1 February 1958 when 1360 Flight was redesignated and provided SAR cover for the Operation Grapple trials on Christmas Island. It disbanded back in the UK on 13 November 1959.

225 SQUADRON

Number 225 Squadron was unusual in serving two separate periods of rescue duty in conflicts more than two decades apart. As with 224 Squadron, 225 Squadron formed on 1 April 1918 through the amalgamation of units previously with 6 Wing, RNAS in Italy. It also flew primarily as a bombing squadron, before disbanding in December 1918.

On 3 October 1939, 'B' Flight, 614 Squadron became 614A Squadron and, almost immediately after, the new 225 Squadron. It began by delivering Lysanders to France, then operated anti-invasion patrols, before establishing an ASR detachment at Pembrey. This offshoot flew its initial mission on 6 May 1941 and was transferred to Fighter Command later that month.

The arrival of Hurricanes and then Mustangs saw 225 Squadron focus on armed reconnaissance and it continued this role, with various types, into North Africa and then Italy, disbanding there as a Spitfire operator on 21 January 1947.

It re-formed as an expansion of the Joint Experimental Helicopter Unit on 1 January 1960, taking on the army support role with the Sycamore and Whirlwind. In 1964, 225 Squadron joined combat in Borneo, adding SAR and casevac to its duties, before disbanding back in the UK during November 1965.

228 SQUADRON

Created as a flying-boat unit at Great Yarmouth, Norfolk, on 20 August 1918, 228 Squadron flew anti-submarine and anti-shipping missions, disbanding after World War I at Killingholme, Lincolnshire, on 30 June 1919. It re-formed at Pembroke Dock, Pembrokeshire, on 15 December 1936, again as a flying-boat unit, initially with the Supermarine Stranraer and then the Short Sunderland. It flew anti-submarine and transport work throughout World War II before disbanding again, at Lough Erne, County Fermanagh, on 4 June 1945.

It re-formed, out of 224 Squadron, as a transport unit at St Eval, Cornwall, on 1 June 1946, but disbanded again on 30 September. It returned to service at the same station on 1 July 1954, now equipped with the Shackleton, which it flew until 6 May 1959, when it stood down again.

On 1 September 1959 it began a five-year association with helicopter SAR by a renumbering of 275 Squadron. Thus, 228 became a Sycamore HAR.Mk 14 and Whirlwind HAR.Mk 4 operator, with detachments at Acklington, Northumberland; Coltishall, Norfolk; and Leuchars, Fife, covering the east coast. It took the Whirlwind HAR.Mk 10 in 1961 and continued with the type until its final stand down, at Leconfield, East Riding of Yorkshire, on 31 August 1964.

1360 FLIGHT

A Whirlwind HAR.Mk 2 operator, 1360 Flight disbanded into 217 Squadron at St Mawgan on 1 February 1959.

SEARCH AND RESCUE WING

From the outset in 1953, it was envisaged that the two separate RAF SAR helicopter squadrons would operate independently. 275 Squadron was established in 13 Group of Fighter Command and 22 Squadron in 19 Group, Coastal Command, each with its own training and engineering organisations.

The two squadrons became closer in May 1958 when 275 Squadron was transferred to 18 Group, Coastal Command. However, not until the introduction of the Whirlwind HAR.Mk 2 to both squadrons was their training combined; 22 Squadron's Training Flight at St Mawgan achieving Operational Training Unit (OTU) status in July 1959.

In 1962, the Central Flying School (Helicopters) took over SAR training at its Valley detachment. The OTU was closed and the QHIs from St Mawgan formed the helicopter element of the Coastal Command Categorisation Board. On 27 November 1969, Coastal Command was disbanded at St Mawgan and the following day 19 Group was titled Southern Maritime Air Region (SOUMAR). From then on, both SAR squadrons fell under 18 Group, Strike Command control.

From October 1957 the headquarters of 275, 228 and 202 Squadrons had been at Leconfield, with 22 Squadron's headquarters established at St Mawgan in June 1956, before moving to Thorney Island in April 1974. In January 1976, 22 and 202 Squadrons were brought together under the Search and Rescue Wing at Finningley. The 18 Group Standardisation Unit (Helicopters) (18 GSU(H)) also moved in, from Northwood.

The Search And Rescue Wing headquarters were established in the 'Green Shed', an apt description for a series of pre-fabricated offices

and corridors, housing the Officer Commanding, Wing Adjutant and secretarial staff, the Officers Commanding 22 and 202 Squadrons, with their training officers (pilot, navigator and winchman) and 18 GSU(H). Second-line servicing of all RAF SAR helicopters was performed at the SAR Engineering Wing Headquarters across the road from the Green Shed. At last, the whole front-line RAF SAR force organisation was at one location.

The squadron training officers and 18 GSU(H) worked closely together to improve flying and operational standards, standard operating procedures and equipment. The Wessex was introduced to SAR Wing in 1976 and the Sea King in 1978. In September 1976, 22 and 202 Squadrons lost their autonomous engineering capability as resources were merged into the SAR Engineering Squadron, a move met with 'mixed feelings' according to 22 Squadron's F540.

In December 1992, Finningley was closed and the SAR Wing disbanded. The Wing's headquarters element moved to St Mawgan under the command of the Station Commander RAF St Mawgan, who became SAR Force Commander. Number 22 Squadron's HQ returned to St Mawgan and 202 Squadron's moved to Boulmer. Eighteen GSU(H) moved back to Northwood until February 1997, when it joined the SAR Force headquarters at St Mawgan.

The squadron training officers, although posted to their respective squadron HQs, tended to operate and travel from their dispersed flight locations in an attempt to reduce the inevitable disruption to family life that the nomadic existence of a training officer entailed.

In September 1997, 22 Squadron's headquarters moved to Chivenor. The SAR Helicopter Force was again dispersed, but retained the ethos of a coherent SAR organisation.

Number 228 Squadron responded on 8 December 1959 after the North Carr lightship broke its moorings. The vessel was eventually brought under control but although its crew remained unharmed, the Broughty Ferry lifeboat, also in attendance, capsized with the loss of all eight crew.

A Central Flying School Whirlwind HAR.Mk 10 provided this SAR demonstration flight on 8 February 1972.

personnel between observation and monitoring sites. One crew, however, was tasked with surface water sampling at ground zero, only 55 minutes after detonation. A 'passenger' and special equipment were picked up for the collection procedure, with the helicopter permitted to land and deliver its sample should it be discovered to be of 'low radioactivity', before continuing to the airfield decontamination area.

In the case of the sample testing 'highly radioactive', it was to be 'delivered without landing', the helicopter flown to a 'dirty area' to drop off the passenger and then on for decontamination. The sample Whirlwind's crew were to wear 'protective clothing', but those of another operating in the 'forward area' were expected to don their protective kit only if instructed to do so during a radiological survey after the detonation.

Meanwhile, 22 Squadron's residual Grapple Flight personnel returned to be reabsorbed into the unit's main formation. Aircraftman Raymond Martin GM had been among those detached to Christmas Island and, on his return to the UK, he was posted to St Mawgan as a 'Staff' Winchman on the Training Flight, until his discharge from National Service.

In November 1958, 'A' Flight, 22 Squadron moved from St Mawgan to replace the 275 Squadron flight at Chivenor, under a geographical rationalisation of responsibility. The HQ Flight also moved to St Mawgan, mainly taking a crew training role, but also having a SAR standby facility.

The squadron Training Flight acquired the status of Operational Training Unit (OTU)

in July 1959 but continued to maintain a limited operational capability. It also provided operational training for new pilots arriving from the Central Flying School Helicopter (CFS(H)) Training School and navigators/signallers arriving directly.

In December 1959, the Thorney Island flight had to be withdrawn, much against the wishes of local residents, temporarily leaving south coast SAR cover to the Royal Navy on an ad-hoc basis. The situation was partly rectified in May 1961, when the Felixstowe flight moved to Tangmere, and fully restored in July when 22 Squadron replaced the Thorney Island flight with a newly re-formed fourth flight at Manston.

Situated on the island of Anglesey, RAF Valley was an ideal base for SAR helicopters, enabling rapid transit out into the Irish Sea and inland to Snowdonia. Yet sometime around 1960, 'C' Flight, 22 Squadron, found time and facility to add additional duties to its regular routine. The unit had taken to using the small landing pad on a flat rock alongside the Skerries lighthouse, 25 minutes' flying time from Valley, for practice in the vital skill of setting the helicopter down in a confined space. These 'touch and go' landings had become commonplace, when a period of bad weather denied the lighthouse keepers their usual resupply by boat.

It added little to the training task for the Whirlwinds to touch down and remain just a few minutes while food and newspapers were delivered, and mail exchanged. According to a contemporary report, 'A toolbox, painted Post Office red, waterproofed and erected on a pole on the flat rock, serves as postbox. Seldom do

Number 22 Squadron Whirlwind HAR.Mk 2s under maintenance at RAF Valley in 1956.

the keepers and airmen meet each other, or talk except by radio.' A 15 December 1961 report further notes:

Twice a week throughout the year the yellow helicopters from a detachment at RAF Valley, Anglesey, land at the Skerries Rock a few miles away.

Apart from talks on the radio the helicopter crews never meet the lighthouse men. But on Christmas Eve, the duty pilot, Flight Sergeant Ian McArthur, will invite one of the lighthouse men to come down to the tiny landing ground marked out on the rock and exchange greetings.

Mail for the lighthouse is now always addressed 'c/o 22 Squadron, RAF Valley'.

By now, the 22 Squadron OTU was also in a position to provide standardisation for

Sergeant Eric Smith descends to Jeanne Gougy, *which ran aground off Land's End in November 1962.*

228 Squadron, since the whole SAR force was equipped with Whirlwind HAR.Mk 2s. Conversion to the Whirlwind HAR.Mk 10 began in May 1962 and was complete by September. One of the early Whirlwind HAR.Mk 10 rescues resulted in the second award of a George Medal to a winchman. Flying with Flight Lieutenant JG Egginton as captain and navigator Flight Lieutenant J Canham, Air Signaller and winchman Sergeant Eric Smith volunteered to be lowered to the stricken French fishing vessel *Jeanne Gougy*, to rescue two trawlermen from inside the wheelhouse. *FLIGHT International* reported on the award in its 14 March 1963 edition:

GEORGE MEDAL

Sergeant Eric SMITH, Royal Air Force

The George Medal has been awarded to a sergeant signaller with one of the search and rescue squadrons, Sgt Eric Smith of the 22 Squadron detachment at Chivenor, North Devon. He receives the award for his courage and disregard of his own safety in rescuing French fishermen from the trawler *Jeanne Gougy*, which had gone aground at Land's End. Sgt Smith was lowered into the sea and succeeded in securing the body of one of the French fishermen and brought it to the aircraft, although he was repeatedly submerged in breaking waves 12–15ft high and swallowed considerable amounts of sea water and oil.

Four men were taken off by means of cliff rescue gear but the fifth – too weak and exhausted – remained in the wheelhouse. Sgt Smith was lowered through the wheelhouse door, succeeded in reaching the seaman and dragged him into a position from which he was winched to safety. Lowered again, he extracted another exhausted seaman; then, despite exhaustion and nausea, made two further descents to see if there were any more survivors. All the time he was in great danger from the heavy seas.

Training and Techniques

In the absence of an OTU, SAR training was initially carried out on the squadrons, with 275 Squadron instructing its own crews and those destined for the Sycamore units being formed at Sylt, Aden and Cyprus. The CFS provided initial pilot training on the Sycamore and in April 1956 a Sycamore Qualified Helicopter Instructor (QHI) arrived to fill 275 Squadron's Training Officer position. Prior to his appointment, pilots were generally ignorant of many aspects of helicopter flight, including engine-off landings. The situation was rectified just in time for the squadron's first engine failure over the sea, which occurred without injury to the crew.

A crew of pilot and navigator flew the Sycamore. For SAR purposes, the initial intention was for the navigator to double up as winch operator, lowering a strop to the survivor. But the scheme was clearly unsatisfactory from the outset; it required the survivor not only to be sufficiently fit but also sufficiently competent to position the strop for a safe lift.

The next idea was to employ the Sproule Net, developed by Lieutenant Commander John Sproule RN, in which the survivor could be scooped from the water without being required to take an active part in the rescue. The device had been designed for use with the Dragonfly and although some satisfactory results were obtained with the Sycamore, the position of the aircraft's engine exhaust caused a serious problem – it tended to burn the net and, on occasion, the casualty too. Furthermore, inaccurate net delivery could cause it to strike the survivor, with disastrous results, and it could not be used on land. The Sproule Net was therefore not adopted as standard RAF rescue equipment, although it was employed in training, for the recovery of bodies from the water, into the late 1970s.

By July 1955, it had been concluded that a winchman was required, lowered on the winch cable to rescue the survivor. With only two crew aboard the Sycamore, the pilot, operating the winch controls from his cyclic stick, lowered the navigator on the winch cable. Communication between the two was maintained by a long intercom lead, the winchman providing instructions so the pilot could place him with the survivor. The system worked until the winchman entered the water, causing the system to short-circuit and his instructions to abruptly cease. A polished convex hubcap, from a Hillman staff car, was placed on the winch arm to provide the pilot with a view of the winchman on the cable below the aircraft. It was seen via the addition of an ordinary rear-view mirror mounted ahead of the cockpit.

During a practice lift in December 1955, a Sycamore struck the Bell Rock Lighthouse on the Angus coast, killing both crew. It was impossible to recover the bodies by helicopter since the Sproule Net could not be used on land, while issues with the long intercom lead prevented a double lift being used.

The accident, and problems associated with recovering the crew, reinforced the need for a satisfactory, long-term solution to the problem of safely flying and manoeuvring the helicopter and employing the winch. Notwithstanding the loss of range and cabin space, it was realised the way ahead lay in adding a third crewmember, a winch operator, to operate the winch while the winchman was on the cable.

By January 1956, the Sycamore squadron was reluctantly beginning to accept the third crewman; it had been adopted at the outset for the Whirlwinds of 22 Squadron with their much larger cabin volume. Nevertheless, the weight penalty incurred by carrying the third man was regarded as such a disadvantage that experiments with the long intercom lead and mirrors continued until August 1957, when 275 Squadron began training crewmen purely as winch operators, increasing the standard crew complement to pilot, winch operator and winchman.

The Sector Control system, originally established to control fighter aircraft, provided VHF fixes to aid SAR helicopter navigation until the introduction of Decca after 1958. Homing equipment was first installed on 275 Squadron aircraft in 1954, initially to the unit's Anson and later to the Sycamores, enabling crews to home on aircrew survivors. By April 1958, all 275 Squadron crews were fully trained for night and instrument flying, and practised in engine-off landings; by May they were officially cleared for night transit flying and rescue sorties over land.

The essentials of the winchman's basic rescue equipment changed little from the early Whirlwind days. It included an immersion suit, a bosun's chair and quick release fastener, NATO strop and a Grabbit hook. The flexible, semi-rigid Neil Robertson rescue stretcher became standard for lifting immobilised casualties from 1956 onwards, while a first-aid

Above left: Winching into the Sycamore was a cumbersome procedure that required the navigator to move into the cabin. There he operated the winch, relying either on the casualty, or assistance on the ground, to safely complete the rescue.

Above right: Corporal D McNamee inspects a 275 Squadron Sproule Net, or scoop net, at Thornaby on 1 September 1955.

Below: A 22 Squadron Whirlwind HAR.Mk 2 from St Mawgan demonstrates the Sproule Net in use.

kit was also available. Additional equipment over the years included an intercom system that enabled constant communication between the winchman and crew, while the scope and quality of training was also improved.

WHIRLWIND SAR

By the late 1950s, the public had come to place great value on its 'local' rescue helicopters and any move by the RAF to close or move a SAR helicopter flight was resisted with great vigour. The drama that ensued after the closure of 'D' Flight, 22 Squadron's Thorney Island detachment, in December 1959, had shown that the public outcry and lobbying by local officials could force deployment plans to change, however well the RAF justified them.

Thus, in May 1961, when the Felixstowe flight was due to move to Manston, it was diverted instead to Tangmere, close to Thorney Island. A further flight then had to

A Khormaksar-based Aden Search and Rescue Flight Sycamore HR.Mk 14 exercises with an Aden Marine Craft Unit 60ft General Service Pinnace in the Gulf during 1963.

be established at Manston to close a gap in SAR cover. An additional motivation for the change rested with Air Staff annoyance that during the summer holidays, the Solent and south coast were treated to regular views of rescue helicopters bearing the legend 'ROYAL NAVY' in large letters.

These naval aircraft were generally equipped for anti-submarine warfare and tended to operate only during normal working hours. They were therefore not held at readiness like the regular seven-days-a-week SAR service the RAF was obliged to maintain. With flying operations at the airfield winding down, in May 1964, 22 Squadron's 'B' Flight left Tangmere and returned to Thorney Island, returning the south coast helicopter flight to the home from where its withdrawal in 1959/60 had caused such public angst.

In March 1969, the Manston flight was selected for closure. Its aircraft and crews were briefly required to deploy and re-form as 1564 Flight at El Adem, following an Argosy crash in Libya. A reduction in fighter activity over southern England and, therefore, SAR requirement, coupled with a shortage of crews, led to the judgement that the Manston area could be covered by Coltishall to the north and east, and Thorney Island to the south and west. The newspaper and vocal outcry caused the Department of Trade to contract Bristow Helicopters to provide SAR coverage. Operated under Coastguard control, it employed the Whirlwind Series 3 helicopter, the civilian equivalent of the RAF's Mk 10.

During its three-year tenure from 1 June 1971 to 30 September 1974, the Bristow establishment flew 668 rescue sorties, preserving 108 lives. In 1972, the Manston crew of pilot Lee Smith (also

Among 275 Squadron's instructional responsibilities, it trained crews for the Aden Sycamore detachment. Here a casualty, wounded during operations near the Aden-Yemeni frontier, is carried from a Sycamore at the Dhala airstrip in February 1957. Note the 'RESCUE' title in English and Arabic.

the pilot during the *Sea Gem* drilling barge/ oil rig rescue, for which Sergeant John Reeson was awarded the George Medal), navigator Peter Redshore and winchman Pat Ingoldsby, was awarded the Department of Trade and Industry's Wreck Shield for the 'Most Meritorious Rescue in 1972'.

Introduced from late 1962, the Whirlwind Mk 10 significantly expanded the RAF's SAR helicopter capability. The type was operated in the manner established with its piston-engined forebears, but with up to 30 per cent more fuel/ payload, for greater weight-carrying ability or much enhanced range, and it could respond more successfully to a wider range of tasks. As a result, the public became progressively more aware of the rescue service the helicopters provided, while placing great faith in their availability. A general comparison of incidents responded to over in 1961/62 compared with 1965/66 demonstrates just how far the service had progressed.

Category of Incident	User	Incidents 1961/62	Incidents 1965/66
Aviation emergencies	Military and civilian	61	219
Shipping		19	67
Civilians	Bathers, yachtsmen	190	938
Air ambulance/casevac	DHSS*	141	162

*DHSS = Department of Health and Social Security

Of course, an individual call-out may have resulted in more than one casualty rescued, or in none at all. For example, in 1966, 22 Squadron recorded 34 aviation incidents, resulting in 14 persons rescued; 69 air ambulance/casevac sorties; 70 responses to swimming incidents resulting in the rescue of 16 bathers; 252 calls to small boats/yachts in trouble, from which 137 people were rescued; 59 missions to persons stuck on cliffs, with 61 individuals rescued; 56 operations described as miscellaneous and resulting in 42 rescues; and 27 false alarms.

Air Ministry News Letter 779, dated 22 December 1961, provides a snapshot not only of the increasing importance of helicopter SAR, but also of other RAF assets. It reports: 'RAF high-speed search and rescue surface launches, whose work is now largely taken over by helicopters, answered 17 calls during the year, saved three lives and spent 71 operational hours at sea. Long-range maritime reconnaissance Shackleton aircraft of Coastal Command were called upon several times to escort civilian airliners on fire or in other difficulties over the Atlantic.'

The document goes on to record an incident where a 228 Squadron Whirlwind let down a rope to a dinghy whose occupants were in trouble, then towed them to shore, plus another in which a Whirlwind winched a dinghy crew to safety, then left its winchman behind to sail the boat home.

Sea Gem Disaster

Unlike their fighter pilot brethren for whom the majority of flights were training missions, every SAR call-out was the equivalent of an interceptor's quick reaction alert; it was an operational sortie, a true call into action and, quite often, the unknown. Acts of bravery and skilful flying were commonplace, although the majority of sorties might be regarded simply as 'doing the job'. But there were exceptions, through individual or crew heroism, the difficulty of rescue or scale of the disaster.

Launching in appalling weather from Valley on 3 March 1965, Flight Lieutenant Huggett and crew demonstrated the SAR crews' dedication to those in distress as they set off in search of a vessel aboard which a seaman was in urgent need of medical evacuation. Flight Lieutenant Huggett received an Air Force Cross (AFC) for the mission, gazetted in the Tuesday, 15 June 1965 supplement to *The London Gazette* of Friday, 11 June 1965:

AIR FORCE CROSS

Flight Lieutenant Donald Frederick HUGGETT, Royal Air Force

On 3rd March 1965, a call for assistance was received at Royal Air Force Valley, from the Motor Vessel *Rolfe*, which had on board a seaman suffering from acute appendicitis and requiring urgent medical attention. Flight Lieutenant Huggett immediately took off with his crew in a Whirlwind Mark 10 helicopter. The exact position of the vessel was not known but he set off to find it in spite of a blizzard with gale force winds, visibility down to 400 yards and conditions in which there was a severe risk of icing. After take-off Flight Lieutenant Huggett lost sight of the ground above 100 feet and thereafter was restricted to carrying out his flight below this height. The vessel was sighted after 15 minutes but with a sea running at State 8, a pitching vessel and no horizon to guide him he was committed to a high hover to avoid the masts and had to rely entirely on the directions of his navigator to lower the winchman to the deck and eventually hoist the seaman on board. On the return flight to Bangor hospital Flight Lieutenant Huggett had to follow the coastline at a very low height and eventually landed in a foot of snow. The patient was handed over and the helicopter returned to base. On landing it was found that so much damage had been caused to the engine due to icing that it is doubtful whether the helicopter could have remained airborne for many more minutes. The seaman was operated on within one hour of being picked up while the lifeboat, which had been launched had to spend several hours trying vainly to regain the harbour in the blizzard. During the whole of this operation Flight Lieutenant Huggett showed calmness, determination and courage of the highest order. His prompt action and complete disregard for personal safety possibly saved the life of the seaman.

On 27 December 1965, a 202 Squadron Whirlwind Mk 10 crew of pilot Sergeant Leon Smith, navigator Flight Lieutenant John Hill and winchman Sergeant John Reeson drew on their deepest reserves of courage and resolve to rescue three men after the drilling barge *Sea Gem* collapsed into the North Sea.

In May 1964, exploratory drilling began after geological studies provided strong evidence for the presence of oil and gas deposits in the region. The first 'hole', sunk in German waters, yielded nothing but an explosive nitrogen discharge. Four holes had soon been drilled in British waters, apparently without success, and by 17 September 1965, a further four rigs were drilling. On that day *Sea Gem*, responsible for the fourth 'British' exploration, reached 8,500ft depth without result. Undeterred, its drilling crews pushed on, soon noticing bubbles beyond those normally expected from the small pockets of gas commonly encountered. Two days later it became clear this was a major find; *Sea Gem* had discovered the first of the North Sea's natural gas – methane – reserves.

Built as a work barge, *Sea Gem* had been modified with ten extending legs, a drilling derrick, helipad and other fittings to create a 5,600-ton drilling barge, or 'oil rig'. Its configuration enabled the legs to be raised, the rig moved, and the legs extended again once the rig was positioned. On 27 December 1965, the crew was busy extending the legs again after moving the rig two miles from its previous, history-making position.

Men were working at various of the rig's levels, while others were sleeping or at recreation, when eight of the legs failed, tipping the rig sideways with such force that men on the upper deck were cast into the sea. Others fell from bunks or were hit by dislodged and flying equipment and debris; adding to the crisis, the radio cabin was swept into the sea before any distress call could be sent. Fourteen men made it into a liferaft, from where they watched as the rig went down in just 30 minutes.

Sailing close by, the crew of the cargo vessel *Baltover* had watched in horror as the tragedy unfolded. At 14.09, *Baltover* broadcast: 'Oil Rig *Sea Gem* has just collapsed and sinking. Am sending a boat across to her. Require further assistance.' Some of those who hadn't made it into the liferaft – a second raft had proven impossible to launch – had been clinging on to the sinking rig's highest point but were now lost as it capsized. Meanwhile, as the freezing water claimed more casualties, *Baltover's* crew was picking up the majority of the survivors when the 'B' Flight, 202 Squadron Whirlwind arrived.

Flying in appalling weather, the crew was greeted by floating wreckage and one of the rig's legs jutting from the water. Speaking to the *Daily Mirror*, 24-year-old pilot Sergeant Smith described the scene as 'pandemonium'. Winchman Sergeant Reeson went down twice, recovering two men to *Baltover*, before succumbing to exhaustion. With men still in the water and clinging to debris, Flight Lieutenant Hill, the navigator, volunteered to go down. He located a large man entangled in wreckage and, unable to free him, went with the casualty, debris and all, on the winch cable back up to the helicopter. The crew then attempted to recover two bodies that appeared within reach but were too exhausted to continue; they flew safely back to base at Leconfield.

In recognition of their extreme efforts, Sergeants Reeson and Smith were awarded a Queen's Commendation for Valuable Service in the Air and the George Medal, respectively, while Flight Lieutenant Hill received an Air Force Cross. All were gazetted in the 3 May 1966 second supplement to *The London Gazette* of 29 April 1966:

GEORGE MEDAL

Flight Sergeant John REESON, Royal Air Force
Sergeant (now Flight Sergeant) Reeson, a winchman of 202 Squadron, Leconfield, was a member of the crew of a search and rescue helicopter called to the assistance of the British Petroleum Company's oil drilling rig, "*Sea Gem*," which had collapsed in heavy seas forty miles off the Lincolnshire coast on 27th December 1965. The air temperature at the time was below freezing, with gale-force winds and heavy seas with waves up to twenty feet high. A thick layer of oil covered the sea, the surface of which was strewn with debris. On arrival in the area, three survivors were seen by the crew of the helicopter and Sergeant Reeson was immediately lowered to one of them. Despite the appalling conditions and the struggles of the survivor, the Sergeant managed to secure him to the winch hook and together they were lifted to the helicopter. Whilst the helicopter then hovered over a nearby ship, both were lowered to the deck. At the time the ship was hove-to and pitching wildly and, during the latter part of the descent, Sergeant Reeson was struck on the head whilst protecting the survivor from the ship's rigging. When winched back to the helicopter the Sergeant was in a state of exhaustion and had swallowed both sea water and oil, but, despite his condition, he insisted on being lowered to the second survivor. After a prolonged struggle, and with mounting fatigue, he managed to secure the second survivor and, partially supporting him with his legs, they were winched up to the helicopter, taken to the nearby ship and lowered to the deck. When he returned to the helicopter after this second rescue, Sergeant Reeson was in a state of collapse and the navigator insisted on taking his place for the rescue of the third survivor. Despite his state of exhaustion, the Sergeant continued to take part in the rescue by manning the winch control and, by his commentary, guided the pilot during the prolonged operation. During the return flight to base, although in pain himself and sick from swallowing oil and sea water, Sergeant Reeson helped to give first aid and artificial respiration to the third survivor, continuing

From left to right, Sergeant Leon Smith, Flight Sergeant John Reeson and Flight Lieutenant John Hill, the 'B' Flight, 202 Squadron crew that responded to the Sea Gem collapse on 27 December 1965.

to do so until the rescued man was taken over by a doctor. In the prevailing circumstances Sergeant Reeson would have known immediately that any rescue attempt necessitating a descent into the water would seriously endanger his life. His total disregard to the hazards confronting him during both rescues and particularly during the second, when he was himself injured and nearing exhaustion, was an act of the greatest valour. His exploit stands out as one of the most courageous and determined rescues carried out by Coastal Command in recent years.

AIR FORCE CROSS

Flight Lieutenant John Raymond HILL, Royal Air Force

Flight Lieutenant Hill of 202 Squadron, Leconfield, was navigator of the helicopter called to the assistance of the British Petroleum Company's oil drilling rig, "*Sea Gem*," which had collapsed in heavy seas forty miles off the Lincolnshire coast on 27th December 1965. On arrival at the scene the helicopter crew saw three survivors amongst the debris and wreckage, and by his commentary, Flight Lieutenant Hill guided the pilot whilst the winchman made two difficult rescues from the sea. On completion of the second rescue the winchman was so exhausted, injured and unfit to make a third descent, that Flight Lieutenant Hill instantly volunteered to take his place for the third rescue attempt. He did this with complete disregard for his own safety, well knowing the appalling conditions and risk involved. The third survivor was heavily built and in too exhausted a condition to assist in his own rescue. He was entangled in floating debris and his life jacket hampered the rescue operation. Flight Lieutenant Hill struggled to secure

the drowning man whilst icy seas broke over them and the presence of oil made a firm grasp impossible. He was able to secure the survivor only partially to the winch hook before they were both recovered to the helicopter. In the process of being lifted, he retained the heavy man on the winch hook by his own strength although still entangled in debris. During the return flight to base, despite intense fatigue, Flight Lieutenant Hill not only navigated the aircraft but also helped to administer first aid to the rescued man. Having witnessed the manner in which the winchman became injured and exhausted during two hazardous descents into the water, and being unfamiliar with the task, Flight Lieutenant Hill was under no illusions as to the difficulties facing him when he decided to undertake the rescue of the almost helpless third survivor. His refusal to be deterred in the face of such odds and his subsequent handling of the rescue attempt was an act of the greatest fortitude.

QUEEN'S COMMENDATION FOR VALUABLE SERVICE IN THE AIR

Sergeant Leon George SMITH, Royal Air Force

For his action as pilot of the helicopter which was called to the assistance of the survivors of the capsized oil drilling rig, "*Sea Gem*," in the North Sea, on 27th December 1965. Although he had completed only the minimum of training since his recent return to flying duties and despite extremely adverse conditions, Sergeant Smith maintained an accurate hover for prolonged periods whilst his crewmen effected the rescues. During the latter part of the operation he received diminishing assistance from his crew as they in turn became exhausted and this called for added resourcefulness on his part.

The four flights of 202 Squadron covering Britain's east coast had generally longer ranges to fly than those of 22 Squadron, which, being deployed in the more highly populated south, dealt with a higher rate of incidents. Whereas 14 per cent of 22 Squadron's flying time was classed as operational, the corresponding figure for 202 Squadron was 10 per cent. Year by year, from 1964 to 1969, these figures and the total annual flying rate, which averaged 3,877 hours for 22 Squadron and 3,458 for 202 Squadron, remained more or less constant. Both squadrons flew at a similar intensity as far as monthly hours were concerned, about 30 hours per established aircraft regardless of the number of SAR scrambles. This left around 15 hours per pilot for SAR training, instrument and night flying and engine-off landing practice. The table below indicates the overall flying rate and operational achievement for both squadrons between 1964 and 1969.

A 22 Squadron operating off Valley in 1956 demonstrates winching with a cooperative casualty. Note the Shackleton also in attendance.

Flying rates for 22 Squadron, 1964–1969

Year	Total hours	Operational hours	Operational sorties	Casualties lifted
1964	4,227	551	352	46
1965	3,651	536	304	45
1966	4,228	748	352	62
1967	4,085	508	340	42
1968	4,153	617	346	51
1969	3,553	457	296	38

Flying rates for 228 and 202 Squadrons, 1964–1969

Year	Total hours	Operational hours	Operational sorties	Casualties lifted
1964	2,647	268	294	30
1965	3,032	270	303	27
1966	3,332	366	333	37
1967	3,714	334	338	30
1968	3,855	404	321	34
1969	4,170	430	347	36

There was no commitment to night SAR because the Whirlwind lacked the equipment for safe operations in complete darkness. The policy was therefore to maintain 15-minute readiness throughout the hours of daylight and one-hour readiness at night. In practice, most calls for nocturnal sorties were responded to.

Risks and Recoveries

The piston-powered Whirlwinds were relatively underpowered and in its early days, the type was not particularly reliable. Several ditched or crashed, among them a very prominent incident on 30 August 1955, when XJ436 flown by Officer Commanding (OC) 22 Squadron, Squadron Leader Powry, ditched during a national press demonstration with a Marine Craft Launch.

One month later, Flying Officer Cox ditched XJ434, veteran of the unit's first live Whirlwind scramble, during wet winching training.

The entire Whirlwind fleet was temporarily grounded after a Queen's Flight aircraft crashed fatally in December 1967, by which time 22 Squadron alone had lost seven more of the helicopters. The accident rate diminished greatly as the aircraft matured in service, its crews, as with all RAF helicopter crews, operating to an exceptionally high standard. Through the ongoing development of SAR techniques and equipment, sound training, hard work, dedication and, often, sheer personal courage, the RAF's SAR Whirlwind crews overcame the limitations of its range, power and lifting capacity, as well as the shortness of its winch cable.

Setting aside the risks associated with bad weather, poor visibility and equipment failures, threats to life and limb were also posed from unexpected quarters. On 31 January 1965 for example, the crew of Whirlwind XP351 reported being shot at over Sandwich, Kent. Inspection on the ground revealed a bullet hole in the aircraft's tail.

An extraordinary number of gallantry and professional awards was made to RAF SAR helicopter crews. These included the George Medal (GM), Air Force Cross (AFC) and Air Force Medal (AFM), plus the Queen's Commendation for Valuable Service in the Air (QCVSA) and Queen's Commendation for Bravery in the Air (QCBA), and AOC-in-C's and AOC's Commendations (these latter awarded to ground crew as well as aircrew). Many civil and foreign awards were also presented.

In general, pilots (aircraft captains) were recognised for their outstanding perseverance and aircraft handling skills in atrocious flying conditions. Winchmen were awarded medals and otherwise noted for courage and fortitude, often at great risk to their personal safety. Navigators were recognised for their role in making the rescue possible by their calm professionalism and ingenuity, without which the SAR helicopter team could not operate. It is believed that the highest number of awards for a single RAF SAR helicopter operation was for the rescue of 16 seamen from the deck of

By contrast with the photograph on page 88, a CFS(H) Whirlwind HAR.Mk 10 employs a winchman in the preferred manner, during the unit's October 1969 exercise.

A 22 Squadron Whirlwind HAR.Mk 10 in October 1973.

the sinking Motor Vessel (MV) *Amberley* on 2 April 1973.

A Whirlwind from Leconfield joined two from Coltishall, flying through heavy snowstorms and 70-knot winds. Flight Lieutenant Bernard Braithwaite, the Leconfield pilot, was awarded the AFC for the rescue, all three winchmen (Master Air Electronics Operator Dinty More, Master Signaller Ken Meagher and Flight Sergeant Dick Amor) received the AFC or AFM, and Queen's Commendations for Valuable Service in the Air went to the winch operators (Master

Navigator Ron Dedmen, Flight Lieutenant Tony Cass and Flight Lieutenant Don Arnold); Flight Lieutenants Jim Ross and Ian Christie-Miller, Coltishall's pilots, were not recognised.

In general this apparent inequality in the issue of awards has been accepted, but in some cases, disparities have caused consternation and disquiet among the crews. Those receiving higher awards typically supported the call for increased recognition of crewmembers receiving lesser awards or no recognition at all.

Winchmen in particular placed their personal safety, and often lives, at risk every time they left the aircraft on the winch cable. Training minimised these risks, however, and, where possible, the aircraft was hovered at low altitude over a flat surface before the winchman was eased out. The helicopter then climbed to its operating altitude as the cable was winched out, maintaining the winchman at a safe height above the ground. The pilot manoeuvred the aircraft to a point overhead the incident under direction from the winch operator, who also used the winch to keep the winchman close to the ground as he was carried to the survivor.

Recovery of the winchman and survivor was effected by a reverse of this method, the aircraft being lowered as the winchman and survivor were winched in. This mode of operation provided a degree of reassurance in the event of a mishap; even in training it was

not unknown for the winchman to fall from the cable through equipment or procedural failure.

Serious consideration was also given to the ever-present possibility of engine failure or the inability to hold a hover in turbulent or windy conditions. With the winchman at a safe height, the winch operator could cut the cable, releasing the winchman from the stricken helicopter and perhaps reducing the risk of serious injury while the pilot crash landed or ditched the aircraft. These winching procedures were followed as closely as possible throughout the Whirlwind and Wessex eras.

Nonetheless, some notable rescues deemed to merit the award of the AFC/AFM to winchmen could not be completed through these procedures. Flight Sergeant John

An 84 Squadron Whirlwind HAR 10 exercises with an 1153 MCU RTTL.

Flight Lieutenant Harvey Spirit, an instructor with 234 (Reserve) Squadron at RAF Brawdy, was forced to eject from Hunter T.Mk 7 XL571 after its engine failed just off the Pembrokeshire coast on 8 September 1977. A 'D' Flight, 22 Squadron Whirlwind HAR.Mk 10, also out of Brawdy, was quickly on the scene, winchman Flight Sergeant Eric Ainslie descending into St George's Channel to reach Spirit's liferaft.

Donnelly won the first of his two AFMs for a rescue on 19 May 1974. Suspended on a 200ft rope extension attached to the winch cable, 800ft above the cliff floor at Clogwyn on Snowdon, he was swung pendulum-fashion to reach an injured survivor below an overhang.

His second AFM was awarded for a night rescue from a yacht in heavy seas, during which he used a rope to help move the survivors, enabling the Whirlwind to winch safely away from the yacht's mast. It was an improvisation of the hi-line that later became standard equipment on the Sea King, assisting in rescues from ships and dinghies. Unfortunately, it is impossible to tell the tale of every significant rescue, especially given that to the rescuer or rescuees every operation was significant.

THE MODERN ERA

Wessex HC2

Numbers 18 and 72 Squadrons introduced the Wessex HC2 into front-line service at Odiham in 1964. The aircraft was employed in the Support Helicopter role, but provided SAR cover during the Whirlwind grounding in December 1967. In 1974, two 72 Squadron Wessex HC.Mk 2s were modified for the SAR role at Fleetlands. The crew sent to collect the first aircraft (XT602) struggled to identify it, since it had been finished in the squadron's usual camouflage, rather than the SAR yellow, an issue soon rectified.

Equipped with SAR-modified HC.Mk 2s, 'D' Flight, 72 Squadron was assigned to replace the Bristow Helicopters Whirlwind Series 3 aircraft contracted to the Coastguard at Manston. The local population was again concerned at the prospect of change,

WESTLAND WESSEX HAR.MK 2

Again beginning with a US design, Westland took Sikorsky's S-58 as the basis of the Wessex HAS.Mk 1 for the Royal Navy. From this anti-submarine aircraft it then developed the Wessex HC.Mk 2 assault transport and HAR.Mk 2 SAR helicopters for the RAF.

Both Mk 2 variants featured the unusual coupled Gnome powerplant, effectively two engines working in unison, but with the possibility of shutting one down for cruising flight. The HAR.Mk 2 served flights of 22 Squadron at Chivenor, Leconfield, Leuchars, Manston and Valley from May 1976, while the HC.Mk 2 joined 84 Squadron on Cyprus from March 1982, where its various duties included SAR.

A variety of Wessex variants, including the HAR.Mk 2, subsequently served 84 Squadron, which retired the type, in favour of the Bell Griffin HAR.Mk 2, on 1 April 2003. By this time, the Wessex had long since left 22 Squadron service, the Sea King having replaced it from 1994.

• •

SPECIFICATION

WESTLAND WESSEX HAR.MK 2

Powerplant coupled 1,350shp Bristol Siddeley Gnome Mk 110 and Mk 111 turboshaft engines

Length (overall) 65ft 9in (20.09m)

Height 16ft 2in (4.94m)

Main rotor diameter 56ft (17.07m)

Maximum speed at sea level 132mph (212km/h)

Service ceiling 12,000ft (3,660m)

Normal range 310 miles (499km)

'A' Flight, 22 Squadron at Chivenor, Devon, took the Wessex HAR.Mk 2 in 1976. This image dates from a 9 April 1985 training exercise.

but the Ministry of Defence provided assurance that the station's SAR flight would become a permanent detachment. It actually remained at Manston for a further 20 years, before moving to Wattisham, simultaneous with Coltishall's closure. The 72 Squadron crews trained with the Search and Rescue Training Squadron at RAF Valley, before assuming SAR standby in October 1974.

The Wessex had many advantages over the Whirlwind but also bore similarities – in configuration it was much like a large Whirlwind, with the cockpit mounted separately above the spacious main cabin. But it was also a far more robust aircraft, with a heavy-duty tricycle tailwheel undercarriage. It featured powerful Gnome coupled engines and good single-engine capability as a result. It was also significantly faster, with much improved payload and enhanced radius of action.

The only perceived disadvantage resulted from the new aircraft's greater weight, which required that it be hovered at higher altitudes over the sea and made it not quite as manoeuvrable as the Whirlwind. Conversely, it had a good auto-stabilisation system, making it a stable winching platform and improving its ability to transit in cloud. A radar altimeter improved the Wessex's ability to operate in poor visibility and at night, but without a full autopilot it was still not designed for nocturnal operations over the sea.

Almost two years passed before more Wessex HC.Mk 2s were modified for SAR duties, gaining the designation HAR.Mk 2 in the process. 22 Squadron partly re-equipped in 1976, with a cascade effect of flight redesignations: 'C' Flight, 202 Squadron at Leuchars became 'B' Flight, 22 Squadron in April; 'D' Flight,

72 Squadron at Manston became 'E' Flight, 22 Squadron in June, while 'C' Flight, 22 Squadron's Whirlwind 10s gave way to the Wessex at Valley that same month. 'A' and 'D' Flights, 22 Squadron remained at Chivenor and Brawdy, respectively, with the Whirlwind 10.

Number 202 Squadron continued with the Whirlwind 10 as 'A' Flight at Boulmer, 'B' Flight at Leconfield, 'C' Flight at Coltishall and 'D' Flight at Lossiemouth. The Wessex crews exploited the aircraft's advantages to the full and it became a capable and versatile SAR helicopter, yet always limited by its inability to operate routinely over the sea at night.

The Wessex was initially provided with a 100ft winch cable but subsequently, rather than employing a rope extension, as on the Whirlwind, a formal 120ft tape (attributed to Flight Lieutenant Mike Ramshaw) was introduced and greater used on both Wessexes and Whirlwinds. In 1977, a 300ft cable was fitted to the Wessex, replacing the tape.

Weather has been a constant feature of SAR operations and the RAF has always been ready to support those hit by its worst excesses. Those include heavy snowfall – blizzards hit Scotland on 29 January 1978 and 22 Squadron went into action, moving its effort south as the winter weather transferring into England.

An RAF Odiham Wessex, Army Air Corps Lynx and Royal Navy Sea Kings supported the effort and 22 Squadron's F540 sums up the intense period thus:

The rescue and subsequent recovery operations continued until 4 February and during that time 354 people were evacuated; 18 medevac missions were flown, 400+ food drops were made; and countless isolated vehicles and houses

Although the Wessex was only modified for SAR from 1974, the Muharraq Search and Rescue Flight had already operated the type in the role, as this October 1970 image proves. It shows Arabic script added under the aircraft's 'RESCUE' title.

were checked. Thirty-two hours of the total 61 hours operations flown by the Squadron Wessex were flown on 29, 30 and 31 January.

'B' Flight at Leuchars and 'C' Flight at Valley flew snow relief operations throughout January, only standing down on 4 February. Two weeks later, it was the turn of Chivenor's 'A' Flight and Brawdy's 'D' Flight to take on snow relief when blizzards hit south-west England and south Wales. Additional Wessex and a Whirlwind were brought in before the operation ceased on 28 February.

Always among the UK's busiest SAR stations, Valley scrambled its Wessex on 20 July 1980 after casualties were spotted in the sea. The subsequent rescue resulted in the winchman, Master Air Loadmaster Robert Danes, being awarded the AFC. The award was gazetted in the Tuesday, 30 September 1980 second supplement to *The London Gazette* of Monday, 29 September 1980:

A 22 Squadron Wessex crew practises cliff rescue along Anglesey's rugged coastline in October 1980.

AIR FORCE CROSS

Master Air Loadmaster Robert Brian DANES,
Royal Air Force

On the evening of 20th July 1980, Master Air Loadmaster Danes was the Duty Search and Rescue Winchman of 'C' Flight, 22 Squadron, Royal Air Force Valley. Her Majesty's Coastguard reported that four people had been sighted in the sea to the west of North Stack, Holyhead Island. Within three minutes the Wessex helicopter was airborne and shortly afterwards a number of seamen from an overturned fishing boat were sighted clinging to a liferaft. On recovering the first survivor a further eleven were seen around the raft, which was drifting rapidly towards the treacherous Gorgarsh cliffs, some 400 yards away. It soon became apparent that unless these men were recovered immediately, they would be dashed against the rocks and killed. The rescue was complicated by the weight of the aircraft and the captain jettisoned much of his fuel to leave sufficient payload available to accommodate the unexpected number of survivors. Master Air Loadmaster Danes commenced a desperate battle to save the seamen. Time after time he was lowered into the heavy swell that was being whipped up by a 30 knot wind. With every man he rescued the situation below deteriorated as the liferaft drifted closer to the cliffs. Besides being almost continually submerged in the sea, Master Air Loadmaster Danes began to suffer from the effects of the aviation fuel that had been jettisoned into the water. If time had allowed, he would have alternated roles with the winch operator, but as every second was vital he could not afford to rest. By the time the last man had been rescued the raft was only 30 yards from the rocks and Master Air Loadmaster Danes was totally exhausted and requiring urgent medical attention, having swallowed saltwater and aviation fuel. Throughout this extremely demanding operation, Master Air Loadmaster Danes's outstanding courage and cool determination, coupled with the highest professional competence, were the vital factors that made possible the rescue of these 12 lives from the sea.

Remarkably, Danes was again on board a Wessex, this time operating from the opposite side of the UK, when he became involved in a rescue that might have won him the AFC had he not already been a recipient. Instead, he was awarded a 'bar' to his existing medal, as gazetted in the Tuesday, 19 April 1983 second supplement to *The London Gazette* of Monday, 18 April 1983:

Number 84 Squadron withdrew the RAF's final operational Wessex from service in 2003. This example was winch training in June 2002.

BAR TO AIR FORCE CROSS

Master Air Loadmaster Robert Brian DANES, AFC, Royal Air Force

Master Air Loadmaster Danes was the winchman of a Search and Rescue Wessex helicopter scrambled from Royal Air Force Coltishall on the evening of 19th November 1982 to assist in transferring 3 seriously injured seamen aboard the Chinese People's Republic vessel *Kungming*, to hospital. The weather conditions were poor with mean winds of 60 knots, sea state 9 and severe turbulence and dense spray at low level. On arrival it was apparent that the conditions would be hazardous for the winchman; waves of between 30 and 50 feet in height were rolling along the length of the 14,000 ton ship,

Number 22 Squadron put this Sea King (leading) and Wessex formation up in February 1989.

breaking over the bows and sweeping the deck to the stern, the only place from which to carry out the winching operation, although it was rising and falling through 50 feet and was alternately clear of the water, and then awash. Despite this and many hazardous projections and wires near the winching area, Master Air Loadmaster Danes volunteered to be winched down to the pitching deck. After releasing himself from the winch cable he was waist deep in flowing seawater and but for safety lines positioned by the ship's crew would have been swept overboard. On regaining a foothold he was led along the continually awash deck to the main superstructure of the ship where the three injured seamen were located. Working alone and unable to communicate with the Chinese crew except by sign language, he applied first aid to the casualties and then prepared the most seriously injured seaman for recovery to the helicopter. With great risk to his own life and little assistance he manoeuvred the stretcher back along the deck to the winching area where both he and the casualty were recovered to the

aircraft. Undaunted, he then repeated the operation and successfully recovered a second casualty to the aircraft. By this time the aircraft was short of fuel and the rescue had to be abandoned. Under the guidance of a doctor who was on board the aircraft Master Air Loadmaster Danes continued to apply medical aid to the casualties until they were transferred to an ambulance in Holland. Throughout this extremely hazardous and difficult rescue, Master Air Loadmaster Danes displayed exceptional courage and devotion to duty saving those in need. In the face of grave personal danger his actions were in the highest tradition of the Service.

The beginning of the end for the SAR Wessex came after the Bell Griffin was introduced when the Search and Rescue Training Unit at Valley transferred from 18 Group to the Defence Helicopter Flying School on 1 April 1997. The type remained in the SAR front line until the Sea King Mk 3 finally replaced it, also at Valley, that June.

CHAPTER 4

SEA KING SUPERLATIVE

SEA KING HAR.MK 3

By the mid-1970s it had become apparent that a new helicopter was required to take the SAR Wing confidently towards the end of the century. An all-weather, long-range aircraft was needed and to that end, 16 Sea King HAR.Mk 3 helicopters were ordered from Westland Helicopters. The type came into service in 1978; 202 Squadron was re-equipping while 22 Squadron continued with a mixed Wessex and Whirlwind fleet. 'D' Flight at Lossiemouth became the first Sea King flight, taking a pair of aircraft on 22 August 1978, followed by 'A' Flight at Boulmer, 'C' Flight at Coltishall and 'B' Flight at Brawdy. Each flight's crews trained on the new aircraft as a unit, at the RAF Sea King Training Unit, stationed at RNAS Culdrose.

The Sea King brought a major enhancement in SAR capability. Larger than the Wessex, its fuel load was sufficient for an operational endurance of about six hours. Its maximum speed varied with all-up weight, but to a maximum 125 knots.

The Sea King's most significant operating improvement was in its all-weather and night capability over the sea, however. It equipped the co-pilot with a Decca Doppler Tactical Air Navigation System (TANS) computer and a full range of radio navigation aids. The radar operator employed a lightweight search radar used for obstacle clearance during transit over the sea, while a radar/TANS interface used the radar plot to drive the radar operator's moving radar map for close tactical navigation. Where a known feature could verify the radar position it was used in the control of search patterns.

The aircraft featured auto-stabilisation and a simplex autopilot, comprising a height hold and automatic transition system, capable of automatically flying it to and from the hover over the sea. An auxiliary hover trim system, operated by the winch/radar operator, was used for final detailed manoeuvring the hover.

The Sea King's limited icing clearance was sufficient for icing to be encountered and

Sea King HAR.Mk 3 XZ597 had been on strength with 'D' Flight, 202 Squadron only a matter of days when this image was captured over its Lossiemouth base in September 1978.

then avoided. It also had a larger passenger-carrying capacity than the Wessex, with sufficient space in the cabin for the carriage and use of modern first aid and life-support systems. It even had a small galley, with a water heater and space for holding snack meals and drinks.

Operating the Sea King was significantly different to the Whirlwind and Wessex. The new aircraft's four-person crew comprised pilot, co-pilot, radar/winch operator and winchman. Traditionally, the captain occupied the right-hand seat as first pilot responsible for flying the aircraft. The co-pilot was responsible for normal navigation and aircraft systems management; he was also responsible for operating the radios and for general coordination during rescue operations. However, in the Sea King the aircraft captain had the opportunity to

choose from which seat he was to operate and there were many occasions when the captain occupied the left-hand seat after an airborne diversion to a SAR mission.

Questions were asked during the Sea King's first year of operations as to whether a single pilot and a navigator, in the co-pilot's seat, could operate the aircraft. The idea was quashed after the squadron commander invited the Air Officer Commanding 18 Group (a navigator) to handle the flying controls after an auto-stabilisation failure. The equipment system had been trimmed away from the central position, causing a large attitude change in pitch and roll when auto-stabilisation was disengaged and making the aircraft difficult for a non-pilot operator to handle.

In the cabin, a senior non-commissioned officer air electronics operator radar/winch operator replaced the traditional navigator/winch operator. His duties were to guide the aircraft safely during transit over the sea and place it in a position from where a transition down to the target could be made. At the rescue scene he left the 'radar shack' to become the winch operator. Additionally, with the auxiliary hover trim joystick, he could fine tune the aircraft's position should the pilot have insufficient references to maintain an accurate hover over a target in the sea.

The winchman's duties remained largely unaltered, except that the Sea King's larger cabin enabled a greater range of first aid and life-support equipment to be carried; over the years, the winchman's expertise in first aid increased to paramedic standard. Previously, winchmen had done their best to stabilise casualties sufficient for them to be winched and carried a short distance to hospital.

A RadOp/winch operator looks back from his curtained cubicle, or 'radar shack'. The curtain could be drawn to protect the radar and, later, video screens from glare; the equipment was installed behind the cockpit on the aircraft's port side.

Now, with the possibility of being well over two hours from medical assistance, the winchman might spend more time with the casualty before winching into the aircraft and then tend to their medical needs during longer transits. Additionally, with easy access between the Sea King's cabin and cockpit, the winchman was able to assist the pilots with detailed navigation, radio management and situational awareness, while also making good use of the galley.

Although the Sea King was capable of carrying out the full gamut of Whirlwind and Wessex SAR missions, its size and increased rotor downwash meant it needed to be hovered over the sea at about twice the normal operating altitude of a Wessex and three times that of the Whirlwind, making precise hovering more difficult. Its mass and inertia made for a stable winching platform, however,

provided the auto-stabilisation authorities were trimmed to the central position and the pilot made small control inputs.

Outside these parameters the aircraft was more difficult to control smoothly. In the first year of operation different operating heights were tried. Experience quickly showed that when the Sea King was hovering at its usual 40ft above the sea on a calm day, its downwash was sufficient to blow a single-person dinghy upside down, with its occupant still inside. Conversely, the Sea King still had to be flown at Whirlwind altitudes when operating with small RNLI lifeboats.

Eventually a standard operating altitude of 50ft over the sea evolved; it also had the major benefit of keeping the aircraft clear of most of the sea spray raised by its downwash. Salt ingestion into the engines could reduce their performance and lead to engine failure, while pilots tried to avoid using the aircraft's windscreen wipers when turning out of the hover into the sun; the resulting smears could badly obscure visibility.

For mountain operations it quickly became accepted practice to fuel the aircraft to relatively low fuel states to ensure an adequate thrust margin, crews preferring to refuel, if necessary, for longer-range operations. Moreover, despite claims by Wessex crews to the contrary, the Sea King was just as effective in the mountains. Indeed, operating at fuel weights for an equivalent patrol time to the Wessex, the Sea King had a greater power margin.

Static Solution

Static electricity builds up in helicopters as a result of the movement of the rotor blades through the air and friction in other moving components, including the engines and gearboxes. The voltage generated is largely a factor of the aircraft's altitude while the static charge held, and its rate of generation depends on the environment the aircraft is operating in. On a dry day, the level and rate of static charge generated is relatively small and generally creates no major problems. However, when a helicopter operates under cumulonimbus clouds the magnitude and rate of charge is very high and potentially lethal.

The Sea King was usually flown with the captain in the right-hand seat and co-pilot to port.

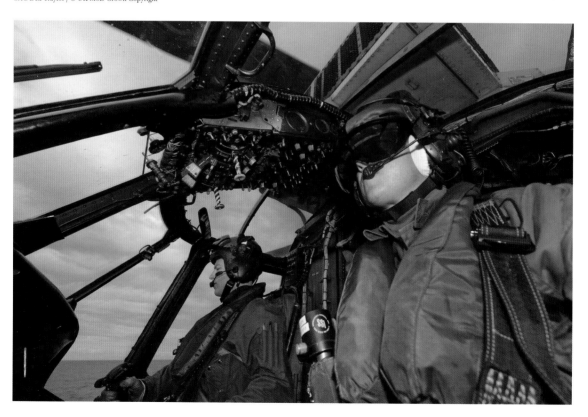

Static electricity emerged as a problem early on in the Sea King HAR.Mk 3's career. Static discharges had been encountered from the Whirlwind; indeed Flight Sergeant Eric Smith GM had suffered the effects while struggling to gain a handhold on *Jeanne Gougy*. The level of static electricity generated by the Wessex was greater than that of the Whirlwind but generally remained within tolerable limits. However, the Sea King generated a significantly larger charge.

Nevertheless, on an average day the effects of static electricity discharges through Sea King winchmen were generally regarded as a normal operating hazard. Cases of serious injury caused by electrical burns were still recorded by the Royal Navy and other Sea King operators. At first, RAF Sea King winchmen attempted to manage the problem, but after several serious electric shocks to winchmen and lifeboat crews, who latterly refused to go anywhere near the winchman until he had released himself from the winch cable, the issue was investigated.

A team of scientists visited Coltishall to make a practical assessment of the problem. Winchmen were invited to wear various items of equipment, including Faraday Cages and immersion suits, and boots and gloves with copper wire attached to electricity away from the body and discharge it on contact with the surface. None of these proved practical.

The crews suggested fitting static discharge wicks to the aircraft as a means of reducing the overall charge, an idea the scientists initially discounted because it would reduce the time taken for the voltage to build to its previous level after discharging. Eventually a trial installation of wicks to the main rotor

Safely secured via a long strap and harness to a fixing point inside the cabin, the RadOp/winch operator spent long periods at the open door during a rescue.

SAC Chris Davidson / © UK MoD Crown Copyright

blades and horizontal stabiliser was tried, subsequently authorised and proved to be effective in reducing the overall problem.

At the same time, the 'zapper snapper' static discharge lead was created and tried at Coltishall. Attached to the winch hook, it dangled below the hook or winchman, touching down first and effectively earthing the hook and or crewmember. It proved very effective, but its use was initially prohibited because it had not been cleared by the engineering authority. This was soon rectified and the 'zapper snapper' remained standard winchman equipment. The Sea King's static electricity problem thus became manageable, although whenever possible, crews avoided winching under cumulonimbus clouds or in other areas of probable atmospheric electrical activity.

The Sea King winchman took on much the same role as with the Wessex and Whirlwind, but provided enhanced medical care inside and outside the aircraft.

© UK MoD Crown Copyright

Sea King Tested

The Sea King had been in service only months when 'A' Flight at Boulmer launched an aircraft in response to a major disaster, once again involving the North Sea oil industry. Reports were received of a capsized accommodation vessel, and 'A' Flight's reaction to the crisis led to aircraft captain Flight Lieutenant Robert Neville receiving the AFC and winchman Flight Sergeant Charles Yarwood the AFM, while pilot Flight Lieutenant Michael Lakey and radar/winch operator Flight Sergeant John Moody received Queen's Commendations

for Valuable Service in the Air. All four were gazetted in the Tuesday, 20 May 1980 second supplement to *The London Gazette* of Monday, 19 May 1980:

AIR FORCE CROSS

Flight Lieutenant Robert Edwin NEVILLE, Royal Air Force

On the evening of 27th March 1980 Flight Lieutenant Neville was the duty captain on the Sea King Flight of 202 Squadron at Royal Air Force Boulmer. At 1800 hours a call was received from the Rescue Co-ordination Centre at Pitreavie Castle reporting that the accommodation platform *Alexander Kielland* had capsized in the Ekofisk oil field with over 200 people on board. Within eight minutes the standby aircraft was airborne and en route to the scene of the disaster, some 170 miles north-east of Boulmer. The weather deteriorated rapidly as the aircraft neared the search area, with low cloud, driving rain and winds gusting to over 55 knots. Flight Lieutenant Neville immediately set up a low level search pattern and, despite the very poor visibility, soon located a liferaft with 10 survivors on board. Initial attempts to place the winchman onto the liferaft by means of the auxiliary hover trim were frustrated by the mountainous 30 feet waves. Flight Lieutenant Neville elected to maintain the hover himself under the direction of the winch operator and despite the appalling operating conditions all ten seamen were successfully recovered into the aircraft. After landing these survivors on an adjacent oil rig the captain went back to the search area and found a lifeboat by means of the locator beacon. The weather by now had deteriorated still further and it was necessary to carry out an automatic transition to the hover in order to make contact with the boat. The winchman was lowered and found 26 survivors

Above left: An 'A' Flight, 202 Squadron Sea King out of Boulmer demonstrates an over-sea hover during winch drills.

Above right: Increased power, compared to the Wessex, enabled the Sea King to perform well in the mountains. This 'C' Flight, 22 Squadron aircraft was on exercise from Valley in 2015. SAC Gina Edgcumbe / © UK MoD Crown Copyright

Below: Close cooperation with the RNLI was a feature of RAF SAR operations. This 22 Squadron Sea King HAR3A was training with a lifeboat in 2006.

WESTLAND SEA KING

Based on the Westland development of the Sikorsky S-61 Sea King, the Sea King HAR.Mk 3 and 3A served as the RAF's definitive SAR helicopters. The first British Sea King, actually a US-supplied SH-3D, completed its maiden flight in the UK on 11 October 1966, and the Royal Navy's initial production Sea King HAS.Mk 1 flew for the first time on 7 May 1969.

Based on the HAS.Mk 2 with uprated Gnome engines and a six-bladed tail rotor, the Sea King HAR.Mk 3 flew for the first time on 6 September 1977. Compared with the Sea King HAS.Mk 2, the Mk 3 included tankage for an additional 113 imperial gallons of fuel, for a range of 690 miles. Such figures easily mislead, however, and a more useful handle on the aircraft's capability is gained by comparing its 270-mile radius of action – how far from base it could fly, perform a rescue and then return to base – with those of the Wessex (95 miles) and Whirlwind (85 miles).

The Sea King Training Unit began preparing RAF crews for the new aircraft during 1978 and by August 1979 the type had replaced 202 Squadron's Whirlwinds. Not until July 1994 did the Sea King oust 22 Squadron's Wessex, although the squadron then also took the Sea King HAR.Mk 3A from May 1997.

Ordered in 1992, the six Mk 3As featured an advanced auto-hover facility designed to bring the aircraft accurately into a hovering position at the pilot's command. The system initially proved problematic, but work to rectify the issues ultimately produced a superior SAR aircraft.

Among the most important Sea King enhancements, the STAR-Q Multi Sensor System (MMS) was introduced across the fleet from 2003. Mounted in a turret under the port sponson support (stub wing) via a bracket attached to the fuselage side, STAR-Q generated still images and video via infrared (IR) and daytime TV cameras.

Controlled by a keyboard at the radar operator's station, STAR-Q could be rotated through 360 degrees in azimuth, look 'up' 20 degrees and 'down' 120 degrees. It was reportedly capable of detecting a swimmer's head in the water at 0.6 miles in favourable conditions and thermal imaging (IR) mode. The RadOp was equipped with a viewing screen for real-time STAR-Q imagery, but the footage was also digitally recorded and of broadcast quality.

Meanwhile, a detachment of two HAR.Mk 3s had been established on the Falkland Islands after the 1982 conflict. Assigned to 1564 Flight, painted in a grey 'combat' colour scheme and equipped with radar warning receivers and chaff dispensers, they were combined with 1310 Flight's Chinooks to form 78 Squadron in April 1986. In November 2007, 1564 Flight was resurrected after the Chinooks were withdrawn, now flying traditionally painted yellow Sea Kings. It continued in the role until standing down on 31 March 2016, as the final RAF Sea King operator.

SPECIFICATION

WESTLAND SEA KING HAR.MK 3

Powerplant two 1,660shp Rolls-Royce Gnome H1400-1 turboshaft engines
Length (overall) 72ft 8in (22.19m)
Height 16ft 10in (5.13m)
Main rotor diameter 62ft (18.90m)
Maximum speed at sea level 143mph (230km/h)
Service ceiling 14,000ft (4,270m)
Normal range 690 miles (1,110km)

but as none was injured, a surface vessel was homed in to the lifeboat and they were taken aboard. After nearly 6 hours operating in the area the helicopter was landed on a nearby oil rig and the crew was able to take a much deserved rest. The search was then resumed for a further period of three and a quarter hours. During the entire mission, in the most appalling conditions Flight Lieutenant Neville displayed the highest standards of flying skill and leadership of his crew. His actions throughout were in the highest traditions of the Royal Air Force.

AIR FORCE MEDAL

Flight Sergeant Charles Michael YARWOOD, Royal Air Force

On the evening of 27th March 1980 Flight Sergeant Yarwood was the duty winchman of the stand-by Search and Rescue Sea King of 202 Squadron at Royal Air Force Boulmer. At 1800 hours the helicopter was tasked to investigate reports that the *Alexander Kielland*, an accommodation platform in the Ekofisk oil field, had capsized in heavy weather. The platform, used as a floating hotel, was thought to have some 200 oil men on board and was situated 170 miles north-east of Boulmer. As the aircraft approached the area the weather deteriorated rapidly and by the time the search began the wind was gusting at more than 55 knots with heavy driving rain, low cloud and very poor visibility. A liferaft with 10 men on board was located but attempts to establish a hover with the auxiliary hover trim proved impossible due to the mountainous 30 feet high waves and the rapid gyrations of the raft. However, the aircraft captain finally succeeded in establishing a hover on voice directions and Flight Sergeant Yarwood was lowered to the raft. Several attempts were made to place him onto the raft but these were frustrated by its rapid movement and

The STAR-Q turret was a prominent addition below the port sponson support.

SAC Scott Ferguson / © UK MoD Crown Copyright

Flight Sergeant Yarwood sustained severe bruising of his legs from being smashed against its side by the heavy seas. Undeterred, he volunteered to be placed in the water near the raft and then, with complete disregard for his own safety, detached himself from the hook, swam to the raft and climbed aboard. With the hi-line still connecting him with the aircraft he was able to recover the winch cable and assist the ten survivors to safety before himself being recovered to the aircraft. Having landed the survivors on a nearby oil rig, the helicopter was returned to the search area and a further 26 men in a lifeboat were located. Although suffering from exhaustion and pain from the battering he had received Flight Sergeant Yarwood volunteered again to be winched down to attempt a rescue. After having satisfied himself that all in the lifeboat were

uninjured he allowed himself to be winched back aboard the helicopter and the survivors were taken aboard a surface vessel. Flight Sergeant Yarwood was undeterred by the inherent personal danger of winching in such hazardous conditions and displayed outstanding courage, professional skill and pertinacity in the course of a well-directed and successful air-sea rescue operation.

The new helicopter was soon showing its mettle in further incidents. On the night of 1 October 1980, after Lossiemouth's first standby aircraft and a Coastguard S-61 helicopter had been unable to effect a rescue from the stricken motor vessel *Finneagle*, a scratch second standby crew, comprising pilot and captain Flight Lieutenant Mike Lakey, veteran of the *Alexander*

Kielland operation, co-pilot Flight Lieutenant Dave Simpson, radar/winch operator Flight Lieutenant Bill Campbell, winchman Sergeant Rick Bragg and doctor Squadron Leader Hamish Grant, scrambled to assist the vessel's crew. They rescued 22 people from the burning, exploding ship.

For this act of gallantry, Lakey was awarded the George Medal, Simpson received a Queen's Commendation for Valuable Service in the Air, Campbell was awarded the Air Force Cross, Bragg the Air Force Medal and Grant the Queen's Commendation for Brave Conduct. All were gazetted in the supplement to *The London Gazette* of 14 April 1981:

GEORGE MEDAL

Flight Lieutenant Michael Julian LAKEY

Flight Lieutenant Lakey is the deputy Flight Commander and a search and rescue helicopter captain of 'D' Flight Number 202 Squadron at Royal Air Force Lossiemouth. During the night of the 2nd October 1980 the Motor Vessel *Finneagle* transmitted a Mayday message from its position fifty miles north west of Orkney. The vessel had suffered an explosion and was on fire amidships, with twenty-two persons including three women and two children on board. The first standby had already been scrambled and although 'D' Flight has no requirement to maintain a second standby helicopter

Close examination of XZ595's tailplane, or horizontal stabiliser, might just reveal two tiny static discharge wicks. The aircraft was photographed after completing 'C' Flight, 22 Squadron's 9,000th rescue, of a man suffering a head injury, on 5 August 2012.

SAC Gina Edgcumbe / © UK MoD Crown Copyright

during the hours of darkness, it was decided to assemble an off duty crew to assist. Flight Lieutenant Lakey volunteered to captain the second crew and took off at 2350 hours to go to the assistance of the stricken vessel. The conditions at the scene of the incident were appalling, with a mean wind speed of fifty knots gusting to seventy knots and a very high sea state giving wave heights of sixty feet. The first Sea King had been forced to abandon its attempts to put a line on the vessel's deck and a civilian S61 helicopter, after making several similar attempts, was also forced to withdraw from the scene. The *Finneagle's* captain had assembled the crew and passengers on the vessel's foredeck. He was forced to maintain an into wind course because of the severe weather conditions and to prevent the fire and resulting fumes from reaching those on board. Flight Lieutenant Lakey had no choice other than to attempt to position his helicopter for winching from the vessel's port bow despite the fact that this would require him to manoeuvre very close to a foremast and a high forward superstructure. The *Finneagle* had lost electrical power and the only illumination available was from the helicopter's own lights and the glow of the fire. An attempt was made to lower the winchman on to the foredeck but because the vessel was pitching and rolling extremely violently, Flight Lieutenant Lakey's efforts to maintain a steady hover caused the winchman to swing through a dangerously wide arc. Flight Lieutenant Lakey therefore decided to employ the Hi-line winching technique which obviates the necessity for the helicopter to maintain an absolutely precise overhead position. The prevailing conditions were so bad that it took twenty minutes to achieve an accurate positioning of the Hi-line on the *Finneagle's* deck. Two rescue strops were attached to the winch hook and as the first survivors were about to be lifted a massive wave pitched the

ship so close to the aircraft that immediate evasive action was necessary. By his exceptional skill not only the aircraft but also two female survivors, each clutching a child, were saved. After lifting eight survivors Flight Lieutenant Lakey learned that the vessel's cargo was highly dangerous and included a consignment of carbide. The vessel was well on fire, with intermittent explosions taking place, and the remaining fourteen survivors were experiencing difficulty in breathing due to the fumes from the burning cargo. At this moment the *Finneagle's* captain radioed that he considered the vessel to be in imminent danger of sinking. Flight Lieutenant Lakey rapidly assessed the situation and having discussed it together with his crew decided to carry on with the rescue, undeterred by the obvious dangers. The remaining fourteen crew members were then successfully winched to safety, despite the necessity of renewing and repositioning the Hi-line twice during the winching period. Continuing to display inestimable skill, Flight Lieutenant Lakey flew his aircraft to safety with twenty seven persons on board. Although he had been on duty for over nineteen hours Flight Lieutenant Lakey, with outstanding coolness, courage and exceptional flying skill remained in a close hover position with the violently pitching and rolling vessel for a period of one and three quarter hours. He inspired and led his crew by his magnificent example throughout the operation, displaying personal gallantry in the very highest traditions of the Service.

AIR FORCE CROSS

Flight Lieutenant Thomas William McRoberts CAMPBELL
(Much of Flight Lieutenant Campbell's entry repeats that for Flight Lieutenant Lakey above and the extract here is therefore abridged to avoid repetition.)

The 'zapper snapper' can be seen extending below the winchman's feet during this 2012 training exercise from Leconfield.

Flight Lieutenant Campbell is a radar and winch Operator of 'D' Flight 202 Squadron at Royal Air Force Lossiemouth. During the night of the 2 October 1980 the captain of the Motor Vessel *Finneagle* broadcast a Mayday message... the 'D' Flight first standby helicopter was scrambled... Realising the seriousness of the incident and considering the likely number of people to be rescued, Flight Lieutenant Campbell assembled a second helicopter crew from off-duty personnel and volunteered to join it himself as the Radar and Winch Operator. At the scene of the incident, the crew were advised that the first Sea King had been forced to abandon its rescue attempt, due to the prevailing conditions... A civilian S61 helicopter, which had been scrambled from its Sumburgh base in an attempt to make winching contact with the vessel had also been forced to abandon its rescue attempts. Together with his aircraft captain and other crew members, Flight Lieutenant Campbell decided to try to lower the winchman on to the stricken vessel. The only feasible winching position was off the vessel's port bow requiring a constant and highly accurate hover to be maintained in accordance with Flight Lieutenant Campbell's verbal directions.

Because of the very close proximity of the vessel's high forward superstructure and foremast and the vessel's violent motion, it proved impossible to place the winchman on deck and he was recovered to the cabin. The helicopter crew then decided to adopt the Hi-line winching technique which does not require the helicopter to maintain a precise overhead position. From his position at the rear of the helicopter Flight Lieutenant Campbell was fully aware of the hazardous nature of this undertaking. Below and slightly to his right the vessel continued to burn fiercely with intermittent explosions, whilst the foremast followed an erratic path close to, and frequently at the same height, as the rear fuselage of the helicopter. Flight Lieutenant Campbell directed his captain with unflagging determination for twenty minutes before it was possible to position the Hi-line on the *Finneagle's* deck. With two rescue strops on the winch hook the first survivors were just about to be winched up when a huge wave pitched the ship perilously close to the aircraft. Whilst calling to his captain to take evasive action he skilfully operated the winch thereby saving the first survivors, both women, each of whom was clutching a child. Winching continued until eight survivors had been lifted safely from the vessel. Then it was learned that the *Finneagle's* cargo was highly dangerous and included a consignment of carbide... However, the rescue was continued, regardless of the obvious dangers, and Flight Lieutenant Campbell resumed his tasks of talking his pilot into the overhead position and supervising the stowage of survivors. The remaining fourteen survivors were successfully winched to safety... With complete disregard for his personal safety Flight Lieutenant Campbell ignored the effects of the fire's intense heat, the intermittent explosions and the possibility that he was breathing dangerous fumes during the entire winching operation which lasted for a period of one and three quarter hours.

Regardless of the imminent danger to his own life and by his skill, courage and determination, Flight Lieutenant Campbell carried out a vital role in the rescuing of twenty-two people from a perilous situation. His gallantry was in the highest traditions of the Service.

AIR FORCE MEDAL

Sergeant Richard John BRAGG
(Much of Sergeant Bragg's entry repeats that for Flight Lieutenants Lakey and Campbell above and the extract here is therefore abridged to avoid repetition.)

Showing exceptional courage in the face of great danger and in weather conditions more hazardous than any he had previously experienced Sergeant Bragg was lowered from the helicopter in an attempt to position him on the vessel's foredeck. The *Finneagle* was pitching and rolling extremely violently and the pilot's efforts at maintaining a steady hover caused Sergeant Bragg to swing through a dangerously wide arc. In view of the very real danger to Sergeant Bragg's life the helicopter captain ordered him to be recovered to the cabin. The helicopter crew then decided to adopt the Hi-line winching technique, which obviates the necessity for the helicopter to maintain an absolutely precise overhead position. Sergeant Bragg positioned himself to assist the Winch Operator for the duration of the winching operation. From his station at the rear of the helicopter he was fully aware of the hazardous nature of this undertaking. Below and slightly to his right, the vessel's amidships continued to burn fiercely with intermittent explosions, whilst the foremast followed an erratic path close to and frequently at the same height as the rear fuselage of the helicopter. With two rescue strops on the winch hook, the first eight survivors were safely lifted from the vessel… The rescue was continued regardless of the obvious dangers and Sergeant Bragg continued with his tasks of assisting with the positioning of the rescue strops and getting survivors on board the helicopter… With complete disregard for his personal safety, Sergeant Bragg ignored the effects of the fire's intense heat, the intermittent explosions and the possibility that he was breathing dangerous fumes during the entire winching operation, which lasted for a period of one and three quarter hours. In addition to his great coolness, courage and determination in attempting to board the vessel, his subsequent efforts while assisting the Winch Operator undoubtedly prevented the total winching time being perilously extended.

Six weeks later, on 18 November 1980, two US Air Forces Europe (USAFE) A-10 'Warthogs' collided in mid-air, eight miles north-west of Coltishall. One pilot ejected immediately and was picked up by the station's second standby aircraft and taken to Norwich. The other jet remained airborne for a short time before the pilot ejected into the sea off the North Norfolk coast. The first standby aircraft diverted to help him.

On arrival at the scene, the Sea King crew discovered that the pilot had failed to separate himself from his parachute and was being dragged through the sea in the 45-knot wind. Without consideration for his personal safety, Master Air Loadmaster Dave Bullock attempted a rescue. During the attempt the parachute inflated, lifting the pilot and Bullock from the water. The winch cable snapped. Rather than save himself from an impossible rescue, Bullock continued to support the pilot until he became exhausted. He died alongside the US serviceman. For his supreme sacrifice in this tragic rescue, Dave Bullock was posthumously awarded the George Medal. He was gazetted in the 4 August 1981 second supplement to *The London Gazette* of 3 August 1981:

GEORGE MEDAL

Master Air Loadmaster David Edward BULLOCK

Master Air Loadmaster David Edward Bullock was posted to Royal Air Force Coltishall as a Search and Rescue helicopter winchman with 'C' Flight Number 202 Squadron on 17th February 1978. On the morning of 18th November 1980, he was a member of a Search and Rescue Sea King helicopter crew alerted at 0930 hours following a mid-air collision between two A10 fighter aircraft of the United States Air Force. Once airborne, the Sea King was directed to help one of the American pilots who had ejected from his aircraft over the sea. He was found still attached to his parachute, which was deployed and dragging him through the water. Weather conditions at the scene were extremely hazardous with gale force winds raising fifteen foot waves in an icy sea. The Sea King hovered over the A10 pilot and, undeterred by the obvious dangers, Master Air Loadmaster Bullock elected to be lowered by cable into the sea so that he could directly assist the pilot who was unconscious but judged to be alive. On entering the water, Master Air Loadmaster Bullock was seen immediately to attach himself to the A10 pilot's harness with a 'Grabbit Hook' so that they would not become separated in the extreme conditions. Meanwhile, the survivor was being dragged at high speed through the waves by his parachute, which periodically was being re-inflated by vicious gusts of wind. In these appalling conditions, Master Air Loadmaster Bullock was observed calmly to set about the task of attempting to save the life of the unconscious pilot. Unable to release the parachute, he attempted

in the face of great difficulty to cut the numerous shroud lines, some of which were entangled around the pilot's arms. He persisted in these efforts, despite the numbing cold and buffeting waves, for several minutes during which both men remained attached to each other and the helicopter. Eventually, however, a particularly strong gust of wind caught the parachute canopy and dramatically increased the tension on the rescue cable, which snapped under the unusual load. The unrestrained parachute then continued to tow both men erratically through the numbing sea and, periodically, below its surface. Initially, Master Air Loadmaster Bullock could be seen keeping the A10 pilot's head above the water. Then, progressively, he lost strength and his ability to control the survivor's position correspondingly diminished until, after three or four minutes, he too lost consciousness. Subsequently, both men were dragged through the water for some time and were dead when finally recovered. In the most appalling weather conditions, more hazardous than any he had previously encountered during his 2 years in the Search and Rescue role, Master Air Loadmaster Bullock was winched down to a helpless pilot. Despite the unique and considerable difficulties, created by the inflated parachute, he calmly went about the business of attempting to recover the pilot to the helicopter as quickly and as safely as possible. He was close to success when the cable broke. Well aware of the very dangerous situation created by this catastrophic turn of events, he had every opportunity over a period of three or four minutes, to disconnect himself from the pilot and save his own life. However, consciously and with conspicuous courage he chose to remain with the pilot in the hope of saving him. The selfless sacrifice of his own life while trying to save another totally accords with the very highest traditions of the Royal Air Force.

In May 1982, a Sea King was shipped to Ascension Island to assist in moving passengers and stores between the island and the ships travelling to and from the Falkland Islands, under Officer Commanding Naval Party 1222, as part of Operation Corporate. The detachment lasted until September, by which time 'C' Flight, 202 Squadron had been detached from Coltishall bound for the Falkland Islands.

The deployment posed a strain on RAF SAR resources. Back at Coltishall, 22 Squadron, flying the Wessex, replaced 'C' Flight, 202 Squadron; for the first year, crews were taken on detachment from Leconfield and Manston. In August 1983, 'F' Flight, 22 Squadron formed at Coltishall, remaining there until 'C' Flight, 202 Squadron returned with its Sea Kings in September 1985, the permanent Falkland Islands detachment having been renumbered as 1564 Flight.

In mid-June 1985, the first of three new Mk 3s arrived to augment the Sea King fleet, which returned to its previous UK strength. Additional crews were posted to 202 Squadron to ease the burden of the Falkland Islands detachment, which was manned on rotation from the UK. However, a general shortage of aircrew in the RAF as a whole, and the helicopter force in particular, caused manning shortfalls, reducing the effectiveness of the additional establishment of Sea King crews.

Further redistributions of RAF SAR helicopter assets continued to meet station closures and SAR cover requirements. Over 31 August/1 September 1988, 'E' Flight, 22 Squadron (Wessex) moved from Manston to Coltishall as 'C' Flight, 202 Squadron (Sea King) moved in the opposite direction. In April 1993, 'B' Flight, 22 Squadron at Leuchars (Wessex) was disbanded, despite significant opposition from the local community. In July 1994, 'B' Flight, 202 Squadron at Brawdy (Sea King) also disbanded, but 'B' Flight, 22 Squadron reformed at Wattisham with Sea Kings. At the same time, 'E' Flight, 22 Squadron at Coltishall and 'C' Flight, 202 Squadron at Manston disbanded. The latter's departure was marked by a congratulatory demonstration of support and thanks from the local population.

Overseas Detachments

Although a few RAF squadrons and miscellaneous units were either established overseas for ASR or helicopter SAR, or took it on as a regular task, major detachments of UK-based SAR helicopters to overseas theatres of operation were few. Two of these unusual deployments fell to 22 Squadron, which deployed personnel and aircraft from St Mawgan to Christmas Island in January 1957, maintaining a detachment there until the following January. It deployed again, this time from Manston, to reform 1564 Flight at El Adem in March 1969; the detachment stood down that October.

By far the most significant post-war overseas SAR operation, the RAF's provision of helicopter search and rescue to the Falkland Islands, began in August 1982, when 202 Squadron deployed its Coltishall flight to the South Atlantic.

The Falkland Islands

After the Falkland War it was decided that the UK would maintain a deterrent force in the South Atlantic against the potential of renewed Argentine aggression. The RAF established a forward operating base at Port Stanley, enabling a regular airbridge service and providing for the islands' defence by fighter aircraft. Chinook helicopters from 18 Squadron were deployed to assist with troop and load carrying, particularly for the building of radar stations. Bristow Helicopters was contracted to provide S-61 helicopters for passenger and internal load carrying, while 'C' Flight, 202 Squadron deployed from Coltishall to provide SAR cover as its primary role and to assist the Chinooks and S-61s in their utility work as a secondary task. While the SAR helicopters could and frequently did respond to civilian and military incidents on the islands and at sea, the detachment's raison d'être was to standby should one of the based fighters suffer a failure that obliged its pilot to eject.

Sea King Mk 3s XZ591, XZ592 and ZA105 were painted overall in Dark Sea Grey for the initial deployment and nicknamed 'Grey Whales' as a result. Various equipment was also added, including radar warning receivers, Omega navigation systems, night-vision goggle compatibility and an 8,000lb underslung load beam. In August 1982 the aircraft were loaded aboard the container vessel *Contender Bezant* at Southampton and, stowed in a hangar fabricated from shipping containers, shipped along with their ground crew to Port Stanley.

They arrived on 27 August, preceded by their aircrew, who had flown by VC10 to Ascension Island and then boarded the *Norland* for the Falkland Islands, arriving on the 24th. The permanent detachment of

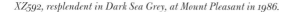

XZ592, resplendent in Dark Sea Grey, at Mount Pleasant in 1986.

Sea Kings and crews for Falklands' SAR and logistics duties had begun.

The SAR flight was established at Port Stanley airfield but in March 1983, moved to Navy Point, across the harbour from the town of Port Stanley. The unit worked from Portakabins and the aircraft from tent hangars; the dispersals were fabricated from pierced steel planking. The domestic quarters were also in Portakabins, just a few hundred yards from the working accommodation, but access between the two was via a peat bog and a large number of wooden pallets was soon acquired and laid end to end, forming the 'pallet path' between the two.

The flight continued to operate as closely as possible to the way it had in the UK, but although many notable rescues were completed, the secondary utility role consumed almost all of its resources and aircraft availability soon became the limit on the flight's activity due to this high rate of tasking and the completion of routine servicing.

The Aircraft Servicing Flight at Port Stanley Airfield carried out second-line Sea King servicing up to and including minor servicing. A further maintenance challenge emerged as the deployed aircraft became the first RAF Sea Kings to suffer cracks in the so-called '290 frame'. A standard fatigue cracking issue in a primary structural frame that held part of the main gearbox supports, the fault required rectification and monitoring.

One aircraft required further repair following an August 1983 heavy landing at Port Stanley Airfield's refuelling site. The helicopter set down tail rotor first, followed by a heavy descent on to the main wheels, which broke off an undercarriage sponson. The pilot recovered

to the hover, despite the seriously damaged tail rotor. Successfully selecting the wheels up, he landed the aircraft safely on the underfuselage load beam without further damage.

Nevertheless, the rate of secondary tasking continued to the extent that the support role took a higher priority than SAR. With the exception of actual 'live' missions that required nothing other than a dedicated SAR helicopter, essential medical evacuation tasks were passed to the Army Air Corps and its helicopters.

Meanwhile, servicing schedules were extended to keep aircraft available for support tasks. At one stage the flight had only one serviceable helicopter, but with only ten flying hours remaining to the end of an extension of a previously approved command extension to a scheduled servicing. Of those ten hours, six were reserved for SAR operations to allow for the possibility that a rescue mission might take the Sea King to the edge of the Falkland Islands Protection Zone. This left four hours for utility flying over the four days before another Sea King returned from servicing at Port Stanley.

In August 1983, the detachment was entitled 1564 (Tactical Support) Flight (reusing the numerical designation assumed by 'D' Flight, 22 Squadron on arrival at El Adem in March 1969). Its crews, wishing to remain loyal to 202 Squadron, HQ SAR Wing and HQ 18 Group, which 'understood' SAR helicopter operations, initially resisted the change, fearing they would become a support helicopter unit with a SAR commitment. But they bowed to the inevitable and became 1564 Flight, a directly administered overseas Strike Command unit.

In a brief moment of respite to 1564 Flight's availability woes, on the bright Sunday morning of 27 November 1983, all three Sea Kings were serviceable and the opportunity taken for two of them to escort the third on the short flight to Port Stanley for scheduled servicing. But the tasking continued unabated and the flight remained short of hours and typically with only one airworthy helicopter available until March 1984.

Adding further to the burden, the Royal Navy was unable to take the additional task of helicopter maritime radar reconnaissance (MRR) of the Falkland Islands Protection Zone, because of a shortage of Sea King engines. The flight was therefore given the daily MRR task as a priority mission over SAR. It involved a lengthy sweep search over the sea using the aircraft's radar, with the Royal Navy holding SAR standby with its shipborne Sea Kings while the RAF helicopter was airborne. However, on two occasions the Royal Navy was unable to scramble within the required timescale.

The first occurred when a Sea King was required to come to immediate readiness for four fighter aircraft on local sorties but unable to land because of a sudden advection of fog over Port Stanley Airfield. The second was for 1564 Flight's MRR helicopter, which suffered an auxiliary hydraulic failure and force-landed on an inaccessible part of the southern shore of Berkeley Sound.

Still, though, 1564 Flight completed several rescues. By the beginning of March 1984, the servicing backlog had been cleared and the flight returned to its full operating strength. By then the previous importance of supporting radar station construction was also coming to an end and the flight returned to a more normal rate of tasking.

Mount Pleasant Airfield

In April 1986, 1564 Flight moved to Mount Pleasant Airfield (MPA), with 1310 Flight (previously the 18 Squadron Chinook detachment at Kelly's Garden) joining it in May 1986 to reform 78 Squadron.

The squadron took its Sea King crews on detachment from 202 Squadron and 'C' Flight, 22 Squadron on rotation; Mk 3A crews, other than winchmen, were not detached to 78 Squadron since the time and cost of re-training was considered inefficient. The length of individual detachments varied over the years from four months during the first few years, to two months for most of the Sea Kings' time on the islands. In late 2000, aircrew detachments were reduced to just six weeks.

The original Grey Whales were replaced on rotation with other Mk 3 Sea Kings, similarly painted grey and modified before departure from the UK. This resulted in the UK fleet comprising a mix of grey and yellow helicopters until, in 1999, it was decided that 78 Squadron no longer needed grey Sea Kings and the standard SAR scheme was adopted. By now, all RAF Sea King Mk 3s also had a majority of the modifications originally needed for Falkland Islands operations.

Among the unusual capabilities practised regularly in the South Atlantic, 78 Squadron and the re-formed 1564 Flight that succeeded it regularly refuelled from Royal Navy ships, either by alighting or using the helicopter inflight refuelling, or hover inflight refuelling (HIFR) method. A 78 Squadron Sea King used RFA *Grey Rover* as a refuelling stop during an extreme 600-mile long-range rescue of a sailor from HMS *Southampton*, south of the Falkland Islands, in April 2000.

SEA KING HAR.MK 3A

The last major enhancement to the RAF's SAR helicopter force came with the purchase of six Sea King HAR.Mk 3As, the Sea King OCU at St Mawgan embarking upon its first Mk 3A course in May 1996. But it was abandoned after three weeks because of problems with the height programmes of the flight-path control computer. After further system development, that first course was completed in May 1997 and its graduates took the new aircraft to Chivenor on 12 May to establish SAR standby.

The Sea King 3A also deployed to Wattisham, in July 1997, displacing the incumbent Sea King Mk 3s to Valley, where they replaced the RAF's final SAR Wessex. Now the SAR helicopter force comprised 22 Squadron with Mk 3As at Chivenor and Wattisham, and Mk 3s at Valley, and 202 Squadron with Mk 3s at Boulmer, Lossiemouth and Leconfield.

The Mk 3A was designed to deliver a quantum leap in autopilot-controlled SAR procedures. It featured a duplicated auto-stabilisation and autopilot system, increasing the options available to the flying pilot. In the Mk 3, the pilot needed to fly the aircraft manually to a suitable point to let-down to the target. A rudimentary height hold was available down to 200ft and from there, with the helicopter facing into wind, an autopilot programme could be engaged for descent down to an altitude of between 60 and 30ft. With the Sea King hovering, the pilot would hand fly to the target before re-engaging auto-hover mode.

In the Mk 3A the auto-stabilisation system was improved, and a flight-path computer and advanced autopilot were added, capable

A 1564 Flight Sea King practises HIFR with HMS Clyde *on 1 May 2013.*

© Paul E Eden

of a range of functions beyond auto-hover. Improving the system still further, a new sophisticated navigation suite could be tied into the flight-path computer. Redundancy was built into the navigation system, which employed four independent navigation methods and compared their derived positions. The co-pilot, as system operator, could decide which had the best information and therefore influence navigation accuracy.

With all systems online, the flying pilot could engage the flight-path computer, which then managed the aircraft's speed, height and heading. It might simply maintain them or be selected to adjust heading according to the navigation suite. A flight plan of different landmarks could be programmed from an extensive 3,500-entry database. With the computer engaged and appropriately set up, the aircraft followed the prescribed route without the pilot having to touch the controls. The pilot was still required to fly the landing, but it was a major enhancement in reducing crew fatigue during long overwater rescues.

Automatic modes for overwater flight in poor weather or at night were also enhanced. An easily used radar altimeter hold could be employed below 1,000ft and once at or below 750ft, if a target was overflown, the aircraft could be let down automatically to a 50ft hover at a single button push. After the button had been pushed, the aircraft took control, flying a pattern that ended in a hover adjacent to the target.

Improvements were also made to the regular methods of establishing a 50ft hover. The aircraft could automatically be let down from any altitude below 750ft, increasing the flexibility of the modes of operation. The capability provided for hands-off flight from any airspeed down to zero ground speed at 50ft. In the Mk 3 such an approach to the hover needed to be a straight line approach, into the wind. In the Mk 3A, not only could the system accept the aircraft being slightly off the wind, but it could manoeuvre the aircraft laterally during let-down for a closer arrival at the target.

Should a straight approach be impractical, a curving let-down was possible for both variants. The Mk 3 pilot needed to control the aircraft's direction and speed until the timed altitude programme had finished; in the Mk 3A, the pilot controlled the speed and direction, but once he had finished manoeuvring control could be returned to the flight-path computer to complete the let-down.

Unfortunately, the Mk 3A's improvements came at a price. Pilots regarded the Mk 3 a joy to hover in any situation. Its controls were light and sensitive, allowing the aircraft to be placed with precision. The Mk 3A was less easy to hover, however, the new variant's 'Gucci kit' interfaced with the helicopter through 'gaps'

in the control runs, where computer inputs could be differentiated from pilot inputs. The controls became less sensitive as a result and the aircraft tended to wander in the hover. The issue could be overcome with practice but tarnished the model with a poor reputation during its early years. Only later, as early Mk 3A 'pioneers' were posted back on to the Mk 3 was it realised that reduced control sensitivity was a small price to pay for the Mk 3A's enhanced safety and reliability.

TRAINING EVOLUTION

Search and rescue training was initially delivered ad hoc on the squadrons. Pilots were trained in aircraft handling, but winch operators and winchmen were left largely to their own devices as they developed procedures and skills. In November 1958, with the departure of 'A' Flight, 22 Squadron to Chivenor, a Training Flight was formed as part of the HQ Flight at St Mawgan. In July 1959 the Training Flight became an OTU and provided training and standardisation for 228 and 22 Squadrons.

In 1962, 3 Squadron, CFS(H), was established at RAF Valley, as a permanent detachment from Ternhill. It was tasked to deliver SAR training for helicopter students in general, and SAR crews in particular, on the Whirlwind Mk 10. It also trained its own Qualified Crewman Instructors (QCIs). Also playing a vital role in helicopter crew training but primarily in standards assurance, the helicopter element of the Coastal Command Categorisation Board was formed around the same time as 3 Squadron, CFS(H). A small unit, it transferred to 18 Group in November 1969 with the disbandment of Coastal Command, becoming the 18 Group Standardisation Unit (Helicopters) (18 GSU(H)).

With the move of CFS(H) from Ternhill to Shawbury in September 1977 and the formation of 2 Flying Training School (2 FTS) for basic helicopter flying training, 3 Squadron, CFS(H) was redesignated as the Search and Rescue Training Squadron (SARTS) of 2 FTS. In December 1979, responsibility for SAR training at RAF Valley was transferred to 18 Group and SARTS became the Search and Rescue Training Unit (SARTU, pronounced 'SAR-too'). In February 1981, Wessex Mk 2s replaced the Whirlwind Mk 10s, SARTU delivering training to all helicopter students, SAR QCIs and operational SAR crews.

On 1 April 1997, 2 FTS disbanded at Shawbury and the Defence Helicopter Flying School (DHFS) was formed to train helicopter pilots for all three services. SARTU was transferred to the DHFS and equipped with the Bell Griffin, the RAF's new advanced rotary-wing training aircraft. Its role remained largely unchanged, notwithstanding the fact that all Qualified Helicopter Crewman Instructor (QHCI) training had been transferred to CFS(H) in 1994.

Sea King Training

Until the introduction of the Sea King in 1978, all new SAR crews had been posted directly from Valley to their operational flights. With the new type's arrival, crews destined to fly it operationally received their full SAR

A 'B' Flight, 22 Squadron Sea King HAR.Mk 3A training at RAF Wattisham in January 2010.

SAC Andrew Morris / © UK MoD Crown Copyright

training at Valley before going to the RAF Sea King Training Unit (RAF SKTU) for type conversion. The latter had been established at RNAS Culdrose in February 1978, initially formed as a Royal Navy squadron under a Royal Navy commander and staffed by a mix of RN and RAF instructors. Its first course had commenced in February 1978, training its QHIs and QCIs on Sea King operations. Its primary task was then to train operational crews for the four Sea King SAR flights at Lossiemouth, Boulmer, Coltishall and Brawdy.

The comprehensive Sea King conversion course lasted approximately four months and, for the first time for RAF helicopter crews, flight simulators formed an important element of the training. By October 1979, all four Sea King flights were operational, and the size of the courses dropped from four full crews to just a pair of pilots and rear crew. The RAF SKTU then became the RAF Sea King Training Flight of 706 Naval Air Squadron (NAS) before separating from it in January 1982 to become

a small independent lodger unit at RNAS Culdrose; it moved to St Mawgan in April 1993. On 1 April 1996, in keeping with the new policy of giving OCUs and training squadrons Reserve status, the RAF SKTU became 203 (Reserve) Squadron. In December a Sea King simulator opened at St Mawgan, enhancing the training of both 203(R) Squadron's students and operational aircrew.

Routine training on the SAR flights was the responsibility of the squadron training officers. They were required to raise individual aircrew abilities to an acceptable operational standard and then improve those skills to the highest possible level. For many years an individual was awarded a category that reflected his flying and operational ability. These categories ranged from D (a probationary category), which had to be upgraded to a C (average) within six to nine months.

After a longer period of time, above average crews were encouraged to upgrade to the B category. Those very few individuals who

displayed the highest, exceptional ability were nominated an A category, for which they were entitled to wear a 'Command Crew' and, later, A category badge on their flying suits.

The hierarchical categorisation system had the positive effect of encouraging individuals to work to achieve higher standards. Moreover, during a period in the mid-1980s when the categorisation system was abolished and replaced by an operational/non-operational rating, it was noticed that the general standard of training and operational ability fell, for some individuals to just the minimum required to maintain their operational status. Fortunately, the categorisation system was subsequently restored and with it the overall standard of training and operational effectiveness.

In 1996, to bring the SAR helicopter force in line with the Nimrod Force, the more direct D to A labelling of categories for flying and operational ability was replaced by a system related to an individual's operational status and ability – Limited Combat Ready, Combat Ready, Combat Ready (Advanced) and Combat Ready (Select). In many respects the systems were similar, but the term 'Limited Combat Ready' had no effective meaning among the SAR flights, since Limited Combat Ready crew were placed on operational SAR standby in exactly the same manner as Combat Ready personnel. The new system also lost some of the element of encouragement for crews to achieve higher standards.

Fortunately the generally high calibre of the SAR crews overcame the anomaly and there was typically a healthy ethos of achievement among the RAF's SAR helicopter operators.

Standardisation is an important element in maintaining the highest professional standards, regularly assessing units and personnel to ensure safety and operational standards are met. Within the RAF SAR helicopter community, the standardisation units were responsible for the formulation and writing of Standard Operating Procedures (SOPs) as well as the standardisation and categorisation of crews, in the UK and, by request, overseas RAF, foreign and Commonwealth SAR helicopter units.

In 1995, elements of 11 and 18 Groups combined at Northwood to form 11/18 Group, and 18 GSU(H) became part of the 11/18 Group Helicopter Standardisation Unit (11/18 HSU). After the failure of the Sea King Mk 3A's initial service introduction, 11/18 HSU's Sea King element stood down for a six-month period in 1996/97 to assist in the formation of the Mk 3A Operational Evaluation Unit (OEU) at St Mawgan.

A further major reorganisation of Strike Command, on 1 April 1999, saw the disbandment of 11/18 Group and the formation of 3 Group. The RAF's SAR helicopter force was transferred to the new group and 11/18 HSU's Sea King component redesignated as 3 Group Helicopter Standardisation Unit (3 Group HSU).

The HAR.Mk 3A reached 'B' Flight, 22 Squadron at Wattisham in July 1997. ZH544 was based there in May 2012.

Cpl Pete Devine / © UK MoD Crown Copyright

THE MAGNIFICENT SEVEN

Proof of the quality of the RAF's SAR crews was demonstrated every time they launched for a 'job'. Some missions were little more than routine, others more testing, but every standby scramble had the potential to be life changing. Many particularly courageous or skilful operations resulted in the award of medals and commendations, but several did not. Among the latter, on 14 December 2001, RESCUE 131, an 'A' Flight, 202 Squadron Sea King from Boulmer, was directed away from one job to attend a second emergency, off the Northumberland coast. Flight Lieutenants Bill Sasser and Andy Smith, Flight Sergeant Al Hegerty and Sergeant Neil Finch were flying into mortal danger.

Loaded with a potentially explosive mix of fertiliser and diesel, MV *Rosebank* suffered a fire in its domestic quarters. The vessel's master reported the fire to the Coastguard at 22.32, explaining that he believed it to be under control. Very soon after, he called again, reporting that the fire had worsened. The Coastguard called a 'Mayday' and the Boulmer helicopter was diverted to assist.

When RESCUE 131 arrived on scene, its crew found the vessel partially obscured by smoke. The master had been speaking to

Capable though the Mk 3A's systems were, there was no substitute for crew skill when the helicopter was obliged to work close to the cliff line.

them by radio from the bridge, but with the helicopter's downwash worsening the smoke, he had been forced to abandon it. An attempt to communicate with the Sea King by lamp failed and when the fire continued burning out of control, at around 23.25 the chief officer used protective equipment to enter the bridge and retrieve a handheld VHF radio. At 23.33 with communication regained, the master requested evacuation from the vessel's open deck. With dense smoke over the deck, however, the helicopter gave instructions for the five-man crew to muster on the focsle.

Sergeant Finch winched down and successfully recovered four crew, but then smoke began filling RESCUE 131's cabin and a series of explosions forced the aircraft away from the ship. Finch remained on board with *Rosebank*'s master in a rapidly worsening situation, since even the liferafts were burning. Protected by his flying equipment, Finch might easily have decided a leap into the sea offered him a better chance of survival than remaining on board, but the master would surely have perished. As radio communication between the winchman and the Sea King failed, the helicopter attempted to close in again, twice narrowly avoiding a tall mast.

Eventually, the crew managed to bring the Sea King directly overhead Finch; the winch operator, Hegerty, assuming they were in position because the cable appeared to be almost vertical. The visibility was so bad that none of the crew had clear sight of the winchman until a brief moment of clarity allowed both men to be lifted from the conflagration at 23.38. As RESCUE 131 turned away, a vast fireball engulfed the bridge. The helicopter touched down at

BELL GRIFFIN

In 1955, the US Army chose Bell's Model 204 to satisfy its requirement for a casualty evacuation (casevac) and utility transport helicopter. The first of three XH-40 prototypes of the Model 204 completed its maiden flight on 23 October 1956. Six YH-40 development aircraft followed before the first of the HU-1A production aircraft, which quickly gained the nickname 'Huey'.

HU-1 became UH-1 under the 1962 consolidation of US military aircraft designation systems and a plethora of improved models followed, especially in response to the demands of the war in Vietnam. The Model 205 introduced a longer fuselage from 1963, initially as the UH-1D, and the model became the basis of the Model 212, delivered to the US Air Force (USAF) from 1970 as the UH-1N.

The Model 212 featured the unusual PT6T, a combination of two turbines driving a single shaft for much increased power reserves. With the revised powerplant there was clearly more performance to be extracted from the airframe and Bell achieved this by installing an uprated engine and four-bladed main rotor to create the Bell 412, which first flew in 1979. The type was delivered from 1981, and in 1992 the Canadian Armed Forces ordered 100 of the CH-146 Griffon variant. Variations of the name stuck with the type, which remains in production.

Two distinct Griffin variants entered RAF service, the HT.Mk 1 trainer having been withdrawn from the Defence Helicopter Flying School in 2018. Meanwhile, the Griffin HAR.Mk 2 serves 84 Squadron as a multi-role helicopter from RAF Akrotiri, Cyprus. Among its many missions, the Griffin provides an essential SAR mission and employs underslung Bambi Buckets for firefighting. The aircraft is equipped for night-vision goggles and features a FLIR/TV turret, affording its crews a relevant night capability.

• •

SPECIFICATION

BELL GRIFFIN HAR.MK 2

Powerplant one 1,800shp Pratt & Whitney Canada PT6T-3D Turbo Twin Pac turboshaft

Length overall, rotors turning 56ft 1¾in (17.1m)

Height 11ft 5in (3.50m)

Main rotor diameter 46ft (14.02m)

Main rotor disc area 1,661.90sq ft (154.39m²)

Never exceed speed 140kt (259km/h)

Maximum altitude 20,000ft (6,100m)

Range with maximum payload around 375nm (695km)

As well as serving 60(R) Squadron, DHFS, the Griffin HT1 equipped SARTU and, later, 202(R) Squadron, for maritime and mountain flying training.

Number 203(R) Squadron took this Sea King aboard HMS Illustrious *for deck landing practices in February 2013.*

Wansbeck Hospital at 00.10 on 15 December, all its occupants requiring treatment for smoke inhalation.

There were also occasions when a relatively simple rescue was complicated by nothing more than ill fortune. On 24 September 2000, for example, 'A' Flight, 22 Squadron at Chivenor launched its standby aircraft to assist a climber who had fallen 120ft down the Baggy Point cliffs near Croyde, Devon. He came to rest severely injured on a narrow ledge just above the breaking waves.

Winchman Flight Sergeant Tim Thompson and crew had little time to prepare for the mission as they completed the mere three-minute transit time between Chivenor and the accident site. On the scene, Thompson requested that he be winched to the casualty with a stretcher and successfully strapped the injured man into the device. With the sea state worsening, a number of his fellow climbers descended to lend assistance, only to hear Thompson's shouted warning of a rogue wave.

The group was unharmed, but Thompson and his charge were washed off the ledge. The winchman dived underneath the stretcher in order that he might keep the casualty's head out of the water but trapped his foot in some rocks. Struggling to free himself, Thompson succeeded not only in keeping the stretcher afloat, but in passing it to the climbers.

He then attached himself and the stretcher to the winch cable and both were recovered to the helicopter. Thompson administered medical assistance throughout the flight to North Devon District Hospital, without regard to his own injuries. He was awarded the Air Force Cross.

By their nature, SAR missions tend to happen away from the media and public eye, out at sea or on a mountaintop, usually in poor weather and all too often at night. But Boscastle was different. The weather was, indeed, very poor, but much of the action occurred during the afternoon and into the evening, the drama unfolding even as the TV news crews set up their cameras.

Heavy rainfall hit north Cornwall on Monday, 16 August 2004, some locations recording in excess of 200mm between 11.00 and 18.00. Rain began falling at Boscastle, a small picturesque fishing village, around 12.30. At 14.33, the emergency services received a first call related to the emerging crisis, reporting flooding on the A39 road at Otterham Station, a few miles inland of Boscastle. At 15.09 it became clear that members of the public were trapped in their vehicles at the same location and at 15.31 the Cornwall County Fire Brigade learned of three people trapped in the woods above Boscastle, and dispatched an appliance to assist.

At 15.46 an auxiliary Coastguard member living in the vicinity of Boscastle alerted the Maritime Rescue Co-ordination Centre (MRCC) at Falmouth of a dangerous rise in water levels in the River Valency, which flowed to the sea through Boscastle. Two Royal Navy SAR helicopters, RESCUE 169 and RESCUE 193, launched from RNAS Culdrose and, based on their crews' observations, HM Coastguard declared a Major Incident at 16.35.

At 17.10 the crew of RESCUE 193 reported: 'Pass to all emergency services, this is a Major Incident. We request all the standby aircraft available and all available land-based emergency services as we are in danger of losing Boscastle and all the people in it.'

Further helicopters were immediately requested from the ARCC at RAF Kinloss,

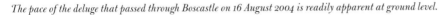

The pace of the deluge that passed through Boscastle on 16 August 2004 is readily apparent at ground level.

Culdrose launching a third, while two 'A' Flight 22 Squadron Sea Kings lifted from RMB Chivenor and a third from St Mawgan. The Coastguard S-61 from Portland also joined, along with a local air ambulance helicopter. Between them, the Royal Navy and RAF Sea Kings recovered 97 people as flood water devastated the village; three RNLI lifeboats stood just off Boscastle harbour entrance should anyone be swept out to sea. Between the S-61 and ground emergency services, a further 103 people were rescued. There were no fatalities and only eight minor injuries recorded. The people of Boscastle reportedly remember the rescue helicopter fleet assembled on 16 August as the Magnificent Seven.

Appalling weather was again the enemy in July 2007, after floods inundated parts of Gloucestershire and the south-west Midlands. The RAF responded with personnel and helicopters and of the 250 people rescued by helicopter, 88 were lifted by just one 'E' Flight, 202 Squadron Sea King over multiple sorties over 22 and 23 July.

Those whose jobs expose them to crisis, injury and even death on a regular basis frequently adopt an unusual sense of camaraderie and humour to help manage their own well-being. Royal Air Force squadrons have always been and will remain hotbeds for 'banter', which becomes a useful coping mechanism in difficult situations. This lighter take found its way into 202 Squadron's annual report for 2006, in the description of a sortie flown by RESCUE 131, veteran of the *Rosebank* mission.

The annual report provides an interesting snapshot of SAR operations and, in its 2 February 2006 entry for 'A' Flight at Boulmer, notes: 'Scrambled to a golfer who had fallen and broken his leg at Slaley Hall Golf Club. R131 landed on the course and was thus declared an immovable obstacle in accordance with rule 14(c), allowing relief, without penalty, of two club lengths not nearer the hole. Then casualty was placed on a stretcher and flown to Newcastle.'

On 12 February, 'E' Flight, 202 Squadron at Leconfield completed a seemingly easy job, collecting a woman with a broken leg from Flamborough Head and delivering her safely to hospital in Scarborough. But the mission was flown through dense fog, the Sea King letting down under radar control and the crew only spotting the casualty at 100m. They flew north to Scarborough along the cliff line, employing radar navigation, and recovered to Leconfield using the aircraft's navigation suite under instrument meteorological conditions.

The Sea King was a relatively large, robust helicopter and there was a general agreement among its RAF crews that if a life were in the balance and they could launch safely, then they would get underway and assess as the situation developed. Should conditions deteriorate sufficiently to make a crash seem inevitable, then the crew would land and wait. Otherwise, they might progress very slowly, watching for obstacles as they brought salvation ever closer to the injured or distressed party.

On 15 March 2006, 'D' Flight despatched Flight Lieutenant Elstow and crew from

Chivenor and St Mawgan sent RAF Sea Kings to assist over Boscastle.

A Royal Navy Sea King leads an RAF colleague over Boscastle, as seen from the electro-optical turret on a third aircraft. RAF crews considered the disaster's winching operations relatively straightforward, but complex coordination of airborne assets in tightly confined airspace was also required.

Lossiemouth in RESCUE 137, bound to fly a medical team from Dundee to Tingwall, Shetland, to medevac a premature baby. Transiting at low level in difficult weather, the Sea King landed at Sumburgh for fuel. There it was tasked out to sea to assist with an oil rig fire.

Returning to Sumburgh, it collected the medical team and baby, flying them to Aberdeen, from where it was again tasked to assist a rig, this time the *Tern*, upon which a generator fire was creating dense smoke. Arriving first, RESCUE 137 assumed the role of on-scene commander and, with a Nimrod overhead, proceeded to manage various helicopters during the rig's evacuation. Finally, the crew flew two approaches themselves, taking 22 workers off the *Tern*.

Task complete, they returned to complete the medevac mission, before landing back at 'Lossie' on 16 March, after exactly 12 hours in the air.

Back at Leconfield, on 12 August, 'E' Flight, 202 Squadron scrambled RESCUE 128, comprising pilot Squadron Leader Paul Coleman, co-pilot Flight Lieutenant Iain Robertson, radar/winch operator Sergeant Adrian Cooper and winchman Sergeant David Standbridge, to assist the yacht *Molly Louise*. The lengthy report reads:

Rig Support Vessel *Putford Provider* had intercepted incomplete distress messages from the yacht, indicating that crew had been washed overboard in heavy seas. When R128 arrived on scene, the *Putford Provider* had just located the yacht and was alongside her, and was attempting to communicate, with little success, with the one remaining crew of the yacht. By now, the *Putford Provider* had established that 3 persons had fallen overboard approximately 45 minutes earlier, so R128, armed with a logical search position worked out by the Rig Support Vessel, departed to search this datum. Within 30 seconds of arrival at this position, 3 persons were sighted in the water. Two were tied together and waving; the third, however, was face down. He was winched first into the aircraft. At this point, the co-pilot, Flt Lt Robertson, left his seat and commenced CPR on the man, while the other two were winched aboard. Given the requirement to provide continuous CPR to one casualty and to carefully monitor 2 others that were hypothermic, Flt Lt Robertson continued to provide assistance to the rear crew for the 40 min transfer to Hull RI [Royal Infirmary]. At this point, Humber lifeboat indicated from the yacht's position that the remaining crewman had been transferred from the yacht, and appeared to be in a state of deep mental shock. This, allied to a long medical history that made interesting reading, called for helicopter assistance, and R128 returned to the scene, following a refuel at Leconfield, to recover this final crewman, using a hi-line and he was flown to Hull Royal Infirmary.

The crew of R128 remarked that the *Putford Provider's* crew deserve great credit for the outcome of this incident.

The squadron's 2007 annual report added further detail. A considerable volume of seawater had been shipped during the initial winching operations, causing the VHF radios and intercom to fail even as Squadron Leader Coleman sat alone in the cockpit, increasing the difficulty of flying solo in poor weather. Coleman reckoned previous experience flying the Whirlwind solo had been instrumental.

Among many non-military accolades awarded to SAR crews, the RESCUE 128 crew received the 2007 Vodafone Lifesavers' Award for the *Molly Louise* mission, while Sergeant Standbridge was presented with the Commander-in-Chief Air Command Commendation and Billy Deacon Helicopter Rescue Award for his part in the rescue.

The outcome of RESCUE 131's two-day mission over 27 and 28 October 2006 was less happy than its 2 February 'golfing' sortie. The 'A' Flight aircraft launched to search for the fishing vessel *Meridian*, 180nm north-east of Boulmer. Working with an RAF Nimrod and Royal Norwegian Air Force Sea King, plus five vessels, RESCUE 131 twice landed on oil rigs for fuel. The search team had only discovered floating debris by the time the Boulmer helicopter returned home after eight hours' flying.

It launched again at first light the next day, but only debris was found, despite a Royal Norwegian Air Force P-3 Orion joining the search effort. Again taking fuel from two rigs, RESCUE 131 recovered to Boulmer after ten hours' flying.

The annals of RAF SAR are rich with tales of rescue at sea, but equally important and courageous work was done among the peaks of Britain's high ground. It should never be forgotten that Arctic conditions in the mountains of Wales and Scotland are common; even the best prepared climber may be caught on the mountainside by suddenly changing weather or an ankle-breaking stumble. A series of four sorties, flown by

'D' Flight, 202 Squadron out of Lossiemouth in response to a single incident on 20 November 2006 demonstrated the difficulties of winter mountain flying, frustrations of equipment failure, courage and ingenuity of the RAF crews and typically close cooperation with other emergency agencies. The drama unfolded little more than 20 minutes' flying time from Lossie.

RESCUE 137 scrambled in dreadful weather to search for two missing climbers in Coire an t-Sneachda, Cairngorms. The wind was gusting 80 knots and snow showers reduced visibility to 100m as the helicopter landed a mountain rescue team (MRT) as close as possible to the incident area. It then lifted for an infrared search, but to no avail, the crew

Conditions over Cockermouth were appalling when five RAF Sea Kings launched in response to flooding on 19 November 2009.

© Paul Kingston / North News

electing to return to base at 04.55 ready for a visual search at first light.

Airborne again around 07.00, RESCUE 137 dropped more MRT personnel, along with search dogs. The handlers held tightly on to their animals, for fear of them being blown from the mountainside.

RESCUE 138 arrived on scene to relieve RESCUE 137. The search continued and a casualty was located. The winchman descended and an attempt was made to lower a stretcher to him. But the winch lost hydraulic power, causing a delay as the radar/winch operator unboxed the emergency electrical hoist. Thanks to an incorrect plug assembly, this failed to work. Unthwarted, the crew opted to 'land on', the co-pilot and RadOp walking the stretcher to the casualty in waist-deep snow. Walking back to the helicopter with the casualty in place was even more difficult. Having dropped the casualty at Raigmore Hospital in Inverness, the RESCUE 138 crew returned to Lossie for a helicopter with a serviceable winch.

Lifting from base, RESCUE 138 flew directly to a rendezvous with a MRT, which had located the second casualty, a young university student. An MRT medic accompanied the casualty into the Sea King and CPR was administered en route, but the climber was declared dead on arrival at Raigmore.

Responding to a major emergency on 19 November 2009, Sea Kings launched from 'A' Flight, 202 Squadron at Boulmer, 'A' Flight, 22 Squadron at Chivenor, 'E' Flight, 202 Squadron at Leconfield, 'D' Flight, 202 Squadron at Lossiemouth and 'C' Flight, 22 Squadron at Valley. The five helicopters converged on the Cumbrian town of Cockermouth, at the confluence of the Rivers Cocker and Derwent. Heavy rain – 12.5in in 24 hours – caused the rivers to swell and by 15.00 Cockermouth's main street was under about one foot of water. The crisis continued to worsen as water levels rose, to 5ft and 8ft in places, and by midnight the flood was flowing in a torrent through the town.

Joined by civilian and RAF mountain rescue teams from Leeming and Valley, plus the RNLI, Coastguard and other emergency services, the Sea Kings began winching victims to safety as soon as they arrived on scene. First into the fray was the Valley crew of pilot Officer Commanding 22 Squadron Wing Commander Steve Bentley, co-pilot Flight Lieutenant Giles Ratcliffe, radar/winch operator Squadron Leader Ian Wright and winchman Sergeant Keith Best.

In the 12 hours they were away from base, the crew recovered 27 people, among them eight from the Black Bull pub in the town centre. Their final rescue of the day saw Best punch his way through a double-glazed window to evacuate people trapped in a flooded building. The helicopters took fuel from Carlisle Airport, which, along with the SAR crews, operated throughout the night.

It was 202 Squadron's good or, perhaps, ill fortune to accept a call to one of the SAR communities' more bizarre rescues. The story appeared in *The Daily Telegraph*, dated Wednesday, 10 August 2005. Leconfield's 'E' Flight was scrambled to assist after the Coastguard and other emergency services were unable to find a man reportedly trapped in gorse bushes and brambles at Filey, North Yorkshire. The victim subsequently revealed that his predicament came about when he decided to take a conciliatory cycle ride after losing £100 on gaming machines. Spotting familiar undergrowth, the unemployed 34-year old left the coastal path in search of a BMX track he remembered from his youth.

He told the press he'd encountered a fence and some water but had decided to continue. The water quickly turned to ankle-deep mud and he became trapped. Initially claiming to have been tangled in the bushes for two days, the man later recalculated that it had been closer to seven hours.

Unable to raise a signal on his mobile phone, he remained trapped overnight, before waving his cigarette lighter and catching the attention of an early-morning walker. The Sea King crew spotted his hand emerging from the bushes, winchman Flight Sergeant Colin Yorke plucking him to safety. At Scarborough Hospital the man was treated for mild hypothermia, dehydration and lacerations.

A 21-year RAF veteran, Flight Sergeant Yorke said of the mission: 'It was certainly one of our stranger rescues. He was right in the middle of the gorse. It was as if he had been dropped there by a spaceship.' The man's bicycle was never found.

FLIGHT LIEUTENANT WILLIAM WALES

Just a few weeks prior to 202 Squadron's gorse bush rescue, in June 2005, His Royal Highness the Duke of Cambridge graduated from the University of St Andrews with a 2:1 MA (Hons) in Geography. Joining the Royal Military Academy Sandhurst, he then completed 44 weeks of training before being commissioned into the Household Cavalry (Blues and Royals) as a Second Lieutenant in December 2006. Promoted Lieutenant in 2007, the Duke continued his British Army career for only another year or so, having elected to train as a pilot.

After completing the standard RAF selection procedures and training, he began specialist SAR helicopter pilot training early in 2009. In September 2010 he joined 'C' Flight, 22 Squadron at Valley, in the process drawing considerable media attention to the station while he and his wife-to-be made every effort to fit into air force life. The Duke flew his first operational mission on 2 October 2010 as part of a crew that airlifted a suspected sufferer of a heart attack off a gas rig in Morecambe Bay.

Stationed at Valley throughout his three-year operational tour, Flight Lieutenant William Wales took on the flying and other duties expected of any pilot of similar rank, and endured teasing from his squadron mates, which included using a specially purchased 'Royal Wedding' tea towel in the crew room prior to his 29 April 2011 marriage to Catherine Middleton.

Looking back on Flight Lieutenant Wales's tour from outside SAR Force, it would be easy to dismiss his service as a token placement. But that would be deeply unfair. He flew 156 SAR operations, served a detachment on the Falklands Islands and qualified as an aircraft captain, in June 2012. That qualification ought to be enough to cement his reputation as an excellent pilot. Captaincy was awarded after a tough training sortie, typically with the squadron commander flying as co-pilot.

It was not unusual for SAR helicopters to be retasked on to actual missions during training events and such was the case on Flight Lieutenant Wales's qualifying sortie, he and his crew swiftly changing mindset from training and examination to saving lives. The rescue was a success, but the Duke also saw his fair share of danger and tragedy, no more so than in the *Swanland* disaster of November 2011.

There is no place in a SAR helicopter crew for fools or crew who do not make the grade. Asked for their candid opinion of him as a pilot and squadron mate, Flight Lieutenant Wales's colleagues were unanimous in describing him as an exceptional aviator. His achievement was perhaps all the more impressive for the fact that on occasion, royal duties forced his removal from the regular crew roster. That created a headache for the squadron planners but also asked a great deal of the Duke. Safe flying is about constant learning, currency, regular practice in the air, flying and training for the mission.

Flight Lieutenant Wales managed to balance his public duties with the demands placed on every professional aviator and still excelled in a difficult, unpredictable and often dangerous role. He took those qualities with him into a two-year stint of air ambulance flying, helping raise public awareness of both search and rescue and the vital work done by air ambulance crews nationwide, a fitting testament to a brief but bright career.

TOWARDS THE END

Botched Privatisation

For many years serving personnel and Ministry of Defence (MoD) documents had referred to the RAF's SAR organisation as 'SAR Force', but the RAF's formal force structure really only came into effect around the time of a structural reorganisation that created Air Command out of Strike Command and Personnel and Training Command on 1 April 2007. Joint Force Harrier had been created in 2000, but the practice of grouping aircraft in 'Forces' according to role or type – Typhoon Force and Air Mobility Force, for example – originated with Air Command. Elsewhere, the former SAR Wing of 3 Group, comprising 22 and 202 Squadrons as its front-line units, became SAR Force (SARF) alongside 84 Squadron and 1564 Flight under 2 Group in April 2008. As such, it was formally SAR Force, headquartered at RAF Valley, that moved forward into the last few years of RAF helicopter SAR.

Ironically, two years prior to SARF headquarters moving into RAF Valley, in May 2006, Minister for Defence Procurement Lord Drayson and Shipping Minister Stephen Ladyman announced the government's intention to provide SAR helicopter cover through a private finance initiative (PFI) from 2012. The PFI was considered an excellent method for satisfying many of the second-line roles performed by the military by effectively putting contracts out to tender with civilian organisations. A contract of up to 30 years, worth around £1 billion was envisaged, enabling industry to replace the Sea King fleet with the latest equipment, while maintaining the current levels of service cost effectively. The government expected that no SAR stations would be closed and no SAR crews lost, since the military personnel would continue working alongside civilian colleagues.

RAF Lossiemouth experiences its fair share of wintry weather and has extensive mountains close by. This 202 Squadron crew was training at the station on 5 January 2010.

Canada's CHC was thought likely to be among those bidding, since it already had a five-year contract to take over SAR provision from the Maritime and Coastguard Agency (MCA) at Sumburgh, Stornoway, Lee-on-Solent and Portland beginning in 2007. John Astbury, the MCA chief executive, expected any new SAR helicopter to be 50 per cent faster than the Sea King and claimed that the amalgamation of services then supplied by the RAF, MCA and Royal Navy under one contract would 'help save more lives'.

On 9 February 2010, the MoD and Department for Transport (DfT) chose Soteria as its preferred bidder for what by then had become the Search and Rescue – Helicopter (SAR – H) contract. A 25-year deal, the contract envisaged a partnership with the DfT and MoD in which military and civilian crews worked side by side, the military personnel rotating back into the RAF's Support Helicopter force and ensuring SAR expertise was nurtured and expanded, rather than lost. As far as the RAF was concerned, it was almost business as usual, at least in terms of crewing, but with shiny new helicopters.

The Soteria consortium comprised CHC; the Royal Bank of Scotland as a trusted PFI equity investor; Thales UK, a proven provider of training and equipment to the MoD and experienced PFI provider; and Sikorsky, which would supply its S-92 helicopter.

A Soteria press release quoted its bid director David Rae as saying:

> SAR-H is a very important programme for the UK and this decision is a strong vote of confidence in Soteria and our ability to provide this vital public service. Soteria will work in partnership with the MoD and DfT and other SAR and civil resilience stakeholders to ensure that the UK's history of providing a world-leading SAR service is assured and enhanced through the introduction of modern technology in the form of the Sikorsky S-92.

Contract signature was scheduled for February 2011. By now its value had risen to £6 billion. On 8 February news of shocking 'irregularities' emerged, causing the government to call an immediate halt. Transport Secretary Philip Hammond explained the situation in a damning Commons statement:

> The irregularities included access by one of the consortium members, CHC Helicopters, to commercially sensitive information regarding the joint Ministry of Defence – Department for Transport project team's evaluations of industry bids and evidence that a former member of that project team had assisted the consortium in its bid preparation, contrary to explicit assurances given to the project team.
>
> Ministry of Defence police are investigating how the commercially sensitive information came to be in the possession of the bidder.

Emotions were already running high over the prospect of SAR passing to a preferred bidder from a military provider and in response to the 8 February news, Bob Crow, general secretary of the Rail, Maritime and Transport Union, stated: 'This whole sordid and botched episode shows that the raw greed of the private sector should never be allowed anywhere near life or death rescue services on the high seas. Millions of pounds of taxpayers' money has been wasted and the whole plan should now be scrapped, not shelved.'

When CHC took responsibility for the MCA SAR services out of Sumburgh, Stornoway, Lee-on-Solent and Portland in 2007, it replaced Bristow Helicopters, which had established the services with S-61 helicopters in 1983 at the UK's first civilian SAR bases. But the company's UK SAR history went back even further, to the Whirlwind Series 3 flight it provided at RAF Manston from June 1971 to September 1974.

In 2012, CHC's MCA contract expired and Bristow was chosen over the incumbent to take over under the so-called UK Gap SAR contract, flying S-92s out of Sumburgh and Stornoway, from summer 2013. With a long record of excellence in SAR provision, Bristow was well placed to benefit from the government's continued attempts to privatise the whole of UK SAR helicopter coverage. In 2013, DfT did indeed award a new contract and Bristow began establishing ten SAR bases, operating an even mix of 22 S-92 and AgustaWestland (now Leonardo) AW189 helicopters, from 1 April 2015. The ten-year deal was worth £1.6 billion, escalating to £1.9 billion, and scheduled to end on 31 March 2026.

Four years into the contract, the UK defence and services company QinetiQ reviewed UK SAR provision in a 23 July 2019 report. It discovered that the transition from military governance had been successful. Nonetheless, none of the RAF's final SAR bases remained in use and mountain rescue teams in particular had reported that not only could the increased downwash of the new helicopters compared with the Sea King prove hazardous, but helicopter assistance was refused more often under Bristow's jurisdiction.

QinetiQ's major concerns were over resilience. It applauded the choice of a two-type fleet that avoids the potential of losing SAR cover in the event of a grounding, but flagged the single-operator model as potentially problematic should the company encounter commercial issues.

Ironically, the US-owned Bristow Group had voluntarily filed for Chapter 11 bankruptcy protection in the US Bankruptcy Court for the Southern District of Texas on 11 May 2019, with £1.1 billion in debt. UK SAR coverage was assured, however. In July, Simon Tye, Bristow Helicopter's SAR Business Manager, told FlightGlobal.com that Chapter 11 'is nothing to do with this company. It has not and does not affect this operation.'

Continued SAR provision seemed secure at the time of writing in early 2020, but QinetiQ's stark warning will resonate in any future contract: 'The introduction of a review process to manage the financial risks to MCA associated with a single commercial operator would be prudent given lessons from the Carillion collapse and recent reports regarding the financial performance of the [SAR] service provider's parent company [Bristow Group].'

Speaking at the Royal International Air Tattoo in July 2019, the MCA's Aviation Technical Lead Maritime Operations, Michael King, provided some indication of its SAR requirements from 2026. Commercial SAR had been established very much along the lines of its military forebear, but four years of MCA operations had enabled a reassessment of requirements. Some 60 per cent of calls were to overland casualties, for example, while drones were also seen as providing useful search functions that helicopters might otherwise be called upon to perform.

SAR Force adopted a modern logo.

© UK MoD Crown Copyright

King suggested that the next SAR contract would be awarded on the basis of how well it satisfied the MCA's desired results, rather than on technicalities. There would be no official preference for helicopter types, so long as two different models were employed, while base changes and reductions would be considered. The contract's duration had yet to be decided, but Bristow was expected to bid, alongside Babcock and, ironically, CHC Helicopters.

Falkland Islands' SAR is managed under a separate contract, awarded to a team comprising AAR Airlift, British International Helicopters (BIH) and Air Rescue Systems. BIH had been operating a pair of S-61N helicopters alongside the RAF's Sea Kings on the islands for many years, providing logistics and utility flying. Under the April 2016 combined SAR and Support Helicopter contract, this provision continued, but with the addition of two dedicated AW189 SAR aircraft. Valued at £180 million, the contract runs until 2026.

Continuing Under a Cloud

Plans for the withdrawal of UK military helicopter SAR in favour of civilian contracted provision were already well underway on Sunday, 25 March 2012, when a Sea King crew from 202 Squadron's 'A' Flight, operating out of RAF Boulmer, launched in response to a gas leak and fire on the Elgin wellhead platform. Royal Air Force SAR crews had been a constant reassurance to North Sea rig workers since the *Sea Gem* catastrophe in December 1965 and now they were launching for a very different mission.

Decommissioning work was in hand when a gas leak erupted just after noon and personnel aboard the stricken *Elgin* well platform, plus those on the *Rowan Viking* rig, located alongside for the work, needed to be evacuated. The rigs were some 150 miles off Aberdeen. With other helicopters and the rigs' helipads available, the Boulmer Sea King took charge of the evacuation as rescue co-ordinator, a task rarely undertaken by any SAR helicopter.

The Elgin *(on the left) and conjoined* Rowan Viking *platforms, seen from RESCUE 131's electro-optical turret.*

© UK MoD Crown Copyright

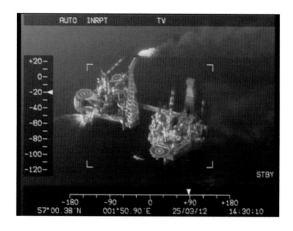

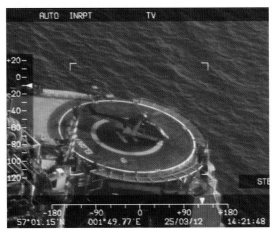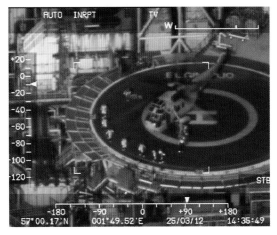

Above left: Unable to winch, the civilian helicopters – this is a Super Puma – had no alternative but to land-on. © UK MoD Crown Copyright

Above right: With conditions suitable for landing, the Lossie Sea King also set down for speedier boarding. Rig workers follow strict procedures for safe helicopter operations. © UK MoD Crown Copyright

Top: The Aeronautical Rescue Coordination Centre, at RAF Kinloss coordinated all UK aerial SAR assets. This photograph was taken 13 months before the Elgin *incident.* SAC Ben Lees / © UK MoD Crown Copyright

With Flight Lieutenant Iain Cuthbertson flying as captain, the crew of Sea King RESCUE 131 included Flight Lieutenant Gareth Dore, co-pilot, RadOp Flight Sergeant Nigel Mortimer and winchman Flight Sergeant Andrew Rowland. All four were passing their time on duty when the call came in. Flight Lieutenant Cuthbertson remembered:

I was sitting in the ops room, checking email. The initial call informed us that an oil rig had suffered a major incident and required complete down-manning. We were asked to get underway ASAP.

I quickly made the decision to increase the fuel load for around a one-hour loiter time on scene, but still ensuring that we'd have the performance to conduct an extraction from the platform. I asked the ARCC

[Aeronautical Rescue Coordination Centre, at RAF Kinloss] to find out what fuel options were available and the details of any other assets attending the scene, then walked to the aircraft. My main concern was whether any of the other platforms in the area were going to be able to provide fuel and, if not, did we have enough endurance to extract everyone?

Departing Boulmer, the weather conditions were good, but over the sea it appeared quite hazy. The task itself – extract the personnel from one rig to another – was pretty simple as long as fuel was available nearby and the situation on the rig didn't escalate any further.

But then ARCC told us we would be acting as air coordination officer [ACO] for the rescue. This meant that we would be responsible for the coordination of all the air assets on scene – I was lucky to have an experienced crew and we quickly discussed how we could achieve the mission.

For Flight Lieutenant Dore, the mission had taken an unexpected turn:

When the ARCC told us we were to assume the role of ACO I couldn't quite believe it. This was a capability rarely put to use, but one for which I had completed a training course in Denmark the previous October. Coordinating a number of aircraft can be very busy, with radio calls made and received on numerous frequencies – all within a time critical and dynamic situation.

As we approached the scene, we had eight helicopters tasked to attend, including two RAF Sea Kings (the other from RAF Lossiemouth) and a Norwegian rescue helicopter, with the remainder from the offshore transportation companies. During the initial rescue phase, we had five helicopters evacuating the *Elgin* platform. We could see the gas leaking and the condensate trail spreading on to the sea. We decided to use the larger helicopters first, in order to make the most from each lift.

Visibility was quite poor and when we were offloading personnel at the nearby *Noble Hans Duel* platform, we couldn't see the *Elgin* platform, just 4nm ahead. We needed a fairly robust plan to ensure helicopters didn't crash into one another

Flight Lieutenant Iain Cuthbertson captained RESCUE 131.

© UK MoD Crown Copyright

Flight Lieutenant Gareth Dore, RESCUE 131's co-pilot.

© Linda Mellor Photography

and we achieved this by directing them to fly at different heights outbound and inbound to the *Elgin* rig. We also directed aircraft not immediately required to hold clear at designated positions.

New Crew

In response to a question in the House of Commons, it was announced on 20 July 1989 that the RAF's policy had been revised to permit female aircrew to be employed in non-combat roles. It was not proposed that women should be accepted for the fast jet, support helicopter or maritime reconnaissance roles. The restrictions on women flying support helicopters and maritime reconnaissance aircraft were finally lifted in 1991 and ironically opened the door for women to become SAR pilots, radar/ winch operators and winchmen, potentially exposing them to greater hazards than those of everyday fast jet flying.

The RAF's first female helicopter pilot, Flight Lieutenant Nicky Smith graduated from 89 Course, 2 FTS at RAF Shawbury on 16 October 1992. Converting on to the Sea King, Smith flew with 202 Squadron at Boulmer and then Lossiemouth, before transferring to 22 Squadron at Valley, from where she completed in excess of 250 sorties. She subsequently converted on to the Wessex, a seemingly backwards step in terms of aircraft capability, but one that equipped her to take command of 84 Squadron on Cyprus in March 2002. Putting her SAR experience to good use, the posting also made her the RAF's first female squadron commander.

Smith and others like her paved the way for women in the Service, among them Sergeant Rachael Robinson, the RAF's only female winchman. As the 1990s became the 2000s, the RAF began demonstrating a particularly forward-thinking attitude to diversity and a 22 Squadron mission out of Chivenor on 21 March 2013 was notable not only for the courage demonstrated by Sergeant Robinson but also for its co-pilot, transgender Flight Lieutenant Ayla Holdom.

With Flight Lieutenant Christian 'Taff' Wilkins flying as captain, the crew of RESCUE 169, from 'A' Flight, 22 Squadron at RMB Chivenor included Flight Lieutenant Ayla Holdom as co-pilot and Master Aircrewman Tim Race as the radar/winch operator and winchman Sergeant Rachael Robinson. Their Sea King was first to reach the French trawler *Alf*, 50nm off Milford Haven, where a crewman with serious head injuries required immediate evacuation in atrocious weather. HMS *Echo*, a Royal Navy hydrographic vessel, and an RNLI lifeboat were also in attendance.

Describing the scene, Wilkins said: 'There was a big swell and the deck was pitching up to 40ft. It was going to be a difficult deck to manoeuvre over and it was obvious that it was going to be difficult to get Rachael on board. The winds were strong, up to 40 knots, so we were restricted in the heading of the aircraft and could only operate in one direction.'

The French trawler crew spoke little English, so a three-way translation was arranged via satellite phone, involving the UK and French Coastguards and RESCUE 169. When the crew decided it was time for Rachael to make her descent, which was every time the aircraft was over the deck, Wilkins lost his hovering references because of the direction the Sea King was facing.

'It got to a point where I was hovering blind over the vessel. I couldn't see what it was doing, I couldn't see how I needed to manoeuvre, I couldn't see if it was going to come up underneath us and hit the bottom of the aircraft. We normally operate with the vessel at a 40 degree angle off the aircraft as that way you have a perfect line to see, allowing you to operate your height and to manoeuvre to get the winchman down safely.'

Robinson made six separate hazardous descents. But the sea was so rough and the boat's movements so severe that she was repeatedly dragged from its deck and battered against its structure.

The options for a safe rescue were becoming limited, and as the Sea King departed for fuel, Wilkins suggested a boat-to-boat transfer to the RNLI lifeboat. This proved impossible. Then a call came reporting the injured man's condition as critical. A helicopter evacuation was the only possibility and RESCUE 169's crew decided to go back for a second attempt.

A revised plan was conveyed to the trawler. The lifeboat would move into position 20m off the vessel's starboard side while HMS *Echo* moved closer to shield the French vessel from the weather. This gave Taff a fixed visual reference for a stable hover and Robinson descended again.

She recalled: 'We managed to get a point of contact with the vessel and I was dangling 20 to 30ft beneath the aircraft. It was a large impact when I made contact due to the vessel moving so quickly over the waves. The French crew cheered when I finally got on board. It was pitching and rolling, with waves coming over the sides; I just thought, right; where's the casualty?'

While Robinson was below decks, Wilkins calculated the lift with Master Aircrew (MACr) Race. Robinson explained: 'If we mistimed the lift I could have been winched up as the deck started to rise; both myself and the casualty could have ended up being hit by the deck.' But Wilkins lifted the Sea King at just the right time, taking Robinson and the French crewman off the deck.

The injured crewman survived. Flight Lieutenant Christian 'Taff' Wilkins was awarded the Air Force Cross and Sergeant

Sergeant Rachael Robinson received the Queen's Gallantry Medal for her part in the Alf *operation.*

SAC Gina Edgcumbe / © UK MoD Crown Copyright

Above: Winchman Sergeant Robinson begins one of several difficult and dangerous descents in an attempt to lift Alf's grievously injured crewman from the rolling and pitching vessel.

© UK MoD Crown Copyright

Top: A small vessel, Alf was moving violently in heavy seas when RESCUE 169 arrived on scene.

© UK MoD Crown Copyright

Rachael Robinson the Queen's Gallantry Medal (QGM) for their actions during the rescue. Later, Robinson also received an Individual Commendation from the Shipwrecked Mariners' Society and a Master Award from the Guild of Air Pilots and Air Navigators for the same mission. Both crew echoed the sentiments of SAR Force in general, Wilkins claiming pride in the AFC, but noting: 'There are a lot of guys out there doing amazing jobs. Tim kept Rachael safe and without Ayla it wouldn't have been achievable.'

Squadron Leader Nicky Smith converted onto the Wessex in 2002, before commanding 84 Squadron in Cyprus.

Sgt Jack Pritchard / © UK MoD Crown Copyright

A particularly unusual incident on 8 October 2013 demonstrated exactly why crews prepared themselves for any eventuality every time they launched. John Wildey, the only passenger in a Cessna 172 light aircraft, found himself flying after his friend and pilot fell unconscious. While an instructor in the control tower at Humberside Airport talked Wildey down to an eventual safe landing, Leconfield scrambled a 202 Squadron Sea King to shadow the Cessna, its crew providing an airborne perspective on the scene and Wildey's impressive attempts at control, as well as using the aircraft's lights to help orientate him for the night-time landing.

Among professional aviators there is an unspoken understanding that the only qualities of any real importance in the air are professionalism and the ability to do the job; gender, creed, sexual orientation and nationality become irrelevant. Except on the evening of 8 October 2013, when the Sea King crew helping guide John Wildey out of danger decided the voice of their captain, Flight Lieutenant Becca Bethell, might well be more calming than that of the male co-pilot who would normally carry out radio communication. Speaking some time after his heroic descent, Wildey said: 'I'm ex-RAF so I knew I was in good hands.' Once again, an RAF SAR crew had used all its ingenuity and experience to achieve a successful outcome.

A Hazardous Business

Search and rescue helicopter operations involve their own particular hazards in addition to those normally associated with military aviation. However much crews attempted to understand

and mitigate risk, they were required to hover their aircraft for extended periods, often in the so-called 'avoid curve', with no immediate safe landing area in the event of an engine or other catastrophic failure. Hovering in close proximity to obstructions that were frequently moving along unpredictable paths was also frequently necessary, in order to carry the winchman to the casualty.

Helicopter rescues tend to occur in extreme weather conditions and at night and, if the incident is inland, quite often on high or mountainous terrain – one seasoned Valley SAR pilot admitted that when the alert phone rang at night in a storm, he always hoped it was a call to sea, not the mountains, because there's less chance of flying into something at sea.

When lives are in peril, SAR crews knowingly fly their aircraft to the limits of their range, endurance and flight envelope to achieve a rescue, while winchmen frequently place their lives at risk. Despite those hazards, the RAF's helicopter SAR crews trained and flew daily and generally without mishap, a major credit not only to their airmanship and dedication of their ground crews, but also to the enthusiastic and unstinting devotion to duty of the wider military organisation that supported them and the Rescue Coordination Centre, which continues to support UK helicopter SAR today.

Fundamentally, the RAF's SAR helicopter crews operated on the basis of mutual trust and exceptional training. Always aware of the dangers they might encounter, they were equipped to make positive assessments of the risks involved before deciding on the most appropriate way forwards. For an outsider flying with an RAF SAR crew, the relationship between personnel was immediately impressive.

Regardless of rank, airmen and women were encouraged to speak up when they believed a decision was poor or when a better alternative might exist, and the opinion of the person best placed to make the call was always respected.

Before new pilots achieved operational captaincy, they needed to gain the trust of their rear crew, a factor taken into account by the flight commander before making a recommendation to the squadron commander. Moreover, there were very few cases when an operational captain was removed from duty for further training and, when no significant improvement had been made, withdrawn from SAR duties after having lost the trust of the rear crew.

There is no better evidence of the trust and mutual respect between a crew than that displayed during any of the more dangerous rescues. One such occurred during the night of 26/27 November 2011. The cargo ship MV *Swanland* was swamped in heavy seas west of Lleyn Peninsula in the Irish Sea. Laden with 3,000 tons of building stone, the vessel broke up and sank, leaving its crew little time to abandon ship. A Sea King HAR.Mk 3 from 'C' Flight, 22 Squadron, RAF Valley, was the first helicopter on scene, effecting a rescue that was dramatic, dangerous and tragic in turn.

Flight Lieutenant Thomas 'Sticky' Bunn was on shift the night of the *Swanland* mission. He fell asleep thinking that he might be disturbed quite soon. The crew related the mission in a series of 2012 interviews. Sticky recalled:

I was the 22 Squadron, 'C' Flt Op Captain that night. Flight Lieutenant William Wales was my co-pilot, Sergeant Graeme 'Livvy' Livingston my RadOp and MACr Richard 'Rich T' Taylor was winchman. The wind was already howling when we went to bed and I half expected the 'job phone' to ring that night, but hoped it wouldn't, since the conditions were going to be nasty.

The phone woke William at 02:20 and we learnt it was an overwater 'wet job', which, from a flying point of view, was preferable to going to the mountains in 40 knots of wind and rain at night. We quickly became aware that this was a serious job, with the Coastguard reporting a ship breaking up 30 miles south-west of RAF Valley. As a crew we knew this wasn't an everyday job and as I got into my immersion suit the adrenaline was flowing. I hoped we could get there in time.

Wales took up the story: 'The call came into my bedroom at Valley – the co-pilot's bedroom had the phone next to the bed; it always woke me with a jump! Collecting all the information I needed and waking the others, I could already hear the wind and rain outside. Then I walked into the ops room and heard Holyhead Coastguard blaring out a Mayday call to all vessels and realised this was a little bigger than I'd first thought.'

As the Sea King got airborne, the crew were hoping they'd find all eight of the ship's crew alive, but the weather was very much against them. 'The wind was gusting 50 knots, with cloud base down to 300ft and heavy rain at times,' Wales recalled. 'The poor weather also made it really dark, so the NVGs [night-vision goggles] were struggling to see much. The sea state was easily a 6, with a lot of white water. Initially, we were hopeful that everyone was in the liferafts, since there was another boat on scene, keeping them visual with its lights.'

In fact, the helicopter was barely out to sea when the true severity of the situation was

confirmed. 'Livvy found a surface contact on the radar, shortly after lifting from Valley. As we got closer and descended, we broke cloud and saw searchlights panning over the water through our NVGs,' said Sticky. 'I think we hoped this would be the Mayday, but it turned out to be the MV *Bro Gazelle*, a large cargo ship rendering assistance. There was no sign of a second ship on radar, which meant we were probably looking for survivors in the water and this was serious. We talked to *Bro Gazelle* on the radio and she reported seeing two dinghies, which was encouraging, since there would be plenty of room for the eight crew.'

Wales described the scene as chaotic:

There was debris everywhere, with reflective strips and lights all over the water. We went to the first liferaft, hoping that all the crew were inside. One person waved to us. The liferaft was fully afloat and being watched by the boat, so we decided to look for other survivors in the water; they were in greater danger. There were lots of lights and reflective strips to check, but we found another liferaft shortly after and put the winchman down, in fierce conditions, to check inside, but there was no one in it. Then the liferaft rolled with Rich T inside.

Taylor remembered thinking initially:

We were just going out to take the people off the boat. But as we walked out to the aircraft, we heard that the ship had sunk very quickly. Our initial plan was to proceed to the liferaft in the *Bro Gazelle's* searchlights. Once we'd seen the guys in that dinghy, we shot off to the other dinghy. That's when we started coming across life rings, nautical equipment, all the stuff that had washed off the top of the boat.

We had to stop and check all the life rings to make sure there was no one clinging to them, all the strobe lights and reflective strips had to be checked too, by hovering over each item and having a really good look at it. We ruled out all the flotsam and proceeded to the second dinghy. There was something hanging out of the side, but no one waving to us. We had to assure ourselves that no one was in it, maybe unconscious or too injured to wave.

We elected to put me down. It was quite challenging. The pilots ended up having to fly manually. After several attempts at getting me inside, I ended up in the water alongside it, then a big wave lifted me up and carried me into the dinghy. I arrived in a heap. It was pitch black inside because the aircraft had moved away quite a bit. I began searching the raft. And that's when it rolled over.

I was under the water for some time and the pilots and winch operator were quite concerned. If they'd just winched in, they could have dragged me through something and injured me, so they had to let the situation develop. Luckily, I popped up, in a bit of a spluttering mess, but on the wrong side of the dinghy. I had to swim underneath to get back to the aircraft side. They recovered me and I was pretty pooped; it was really swim for your life stuff.

Then we went back for the first dinghy, but it had drifted some way and it was difficult to find. Again it was a tricky winch and sadly we found only two people inside. The pilots and winch operator continued searching while I assessed the guys medically. They were cold, shocked and worried for their shipmates, and told me that a 'rogue wave had hit the ship and it just folded in two'. They confirmed that they'd seen other people trying to get into dinghies, so we continued the search.

The pilots had struggled to keep the aircraft stable. Sticky agreed that the Sea King's auto-hover system had been unable to keep them in position over the liferaft:

> The Sea King's auto-hover trim (ATM) was struggling to hold position in the high sea state, so we had to hold the hover over the dinghy 'manually'. This meant things were a bit more difficult than we would have liked.
>
> Livvy reported Rich T swinging towards and entering the water, and then the dinghy flipping with Rich still inside. This wasn't pretty and I feared for him. At some point he came out of the dinghy and we recovered him back to the aircraft. Our hearts sank when Rich told us the dinghy was empty.

From his seat beside Sticky, Flight Lieutenant Wales had an intimate view of his captain in action. 'He remained calm and in control throughout. He had to fly the rescue manually, a tricky procedure for non-SAR crews; normally we would use the RadOp in the back, with a joystick to steer the hovering aircraft over the liferaft, since he has the best references. However, in this case the kit wasn't working because the waves were so big, and Sticky had to fly it with minimal visual cues, because it was so dark and there were walls of water coming at him.'

With Rich T safely back in the cabin, the crew was determined to find the first dinghy. On the way, the helicopter flew over a large debris field and an emergency beacon broke through on the radios. 'We became hopeful this was where we would find survivors and started to search methodically upwind. We saw survival aids, floats, doors and lots of debris ripped from the ship, but no survivors,' Sticky remembered. 'This was when it hit home that a ship really had gone down. Right there. William

78 SQUADRON

After its formation on 1 November 1916, 78 Squadron spent a little over three years on Home Defence, before disbanding on the last day of 1919. It re-formed as a bomber squadron on 1 November 1936, flying with the Heyford, Whitley and Halifax, before becoming a transport unit on 7 May 1945.

Equipped with Dakotas, it moved to Egypt and served in the Middle East, later taking Vickers Valetta transports. After disbanding in 1954, the unit re-formed, on the Scottish Aviation Pioneer, in Aden during 1956. Later it added Twin Pioneers, its close work with local army units perhaps inevitably leading it to become a helicopter operator.

In November 1958, the unit had relinquished its Pioneers and in 1967 the Wessex HC.Mk 2 replaced the last of its 'Twin Pins'. Although its role remained largely unchanged with the helicopters, 78 Squadron moved to the Persian Gulf in 1968 and added SAR to its repertoire. It disbanded in December 1971.

On 22 May 1986, 1564 Flight at Mount Pleasant Airfield merged its Sea King operation with the Chinooks of 1310 Flight, re-forming 78 Squadron. The unit survived until the Chinook's withdrawal in December 2007.

84 SQUADRON

After forming at Beaulieu in January 1917, 84 Squadron trained ready to depart for France on the S.E.5a in September. It remained in Germany after the Armistice, returning to the UK in August 1919 and disbanding on 30 January 1920.

In August it re-formed on the DH.9A at Baghdad and never again returned to the UK. It soon moved to Shaibah for policing and photographic work, as well as several long-range flights, re-equipping with Wapitis and subsequently Vincents.

Shaibah remained home until September 1940, when 84 Squadron took its Blenheims into combat across Iraq, Syria, the Western Desert and Greece. Posted to Java in January 1942, the unit lost its aircraft to enemy attack on 1 March.

It re-formed in India the following month, but technical issues with its new Vultee Vengeance equipment kept it out of combat until 16 February 1944. It began transferring on to the Mosquito FBVI in July, but the wooden Mosquito was initially ill suited to the local weather and 84 Squadron was out of action for the remainder of the war. It rejoined combat in the Netherlands East Indies and Malaya, employing Mosquito FBVIs and Beaufighters, respectively, in 1946.

Returning to Iraq in February 1949, 84 Squadron re-equipped with the Bristol Brigand, a type it took into action over Malaya until disbanding in January 1953 after structural issues grounded the Brigands.

Renumbering 204 Squadron in Egypt created a new 84 Squadron in February, equipped with Valetta transports. Having moved to Aden in 1957, the unit took a number of Beverleys and flew both types until the Valettas formed 233 Squadron in 1960.

In 1967, 84 Squadron converted on to the Andover in Bahrain. It continued flying local transport missions until September 1971, when it disbanded at Muharraq. It reappeared at Akrotiri the following January as a renumbering of 1563 Flight, a Whirlwind HAR.Mk 10 SAR unit. 230 Squadron also had a Whirlwind detachment on Cyprus, and this was absorbed into the new 84 Squadron.

The unit therefore acquired SAR and utility roles, continuing them with the Wessex HAR.Mk 2 after re-equipping in 1981. On 1 April 2003, the Griffin HAR.Mk 2 replaced the Wessex, civilian company Cobham supplying and maintaining the helicopters, which are flown by military aircrew.

203 SQUADRON

Formed as a scout unit in June 1916, 3 Squadron, RNAS fought in France and became 203 Squadron, RAF on 1 April 1918. It disbanded on 21 January 1920, only to re-form, again on the Sopwith Camel, in April. In 1922 it embarked in HMS *Argus* for a visit to Constantinople, returning to Leuchars and disbandment on 1 April 1923.

Number 482 (General Reconnaissance) Flight was operating Southampton IIs from Plymouth when it renumbered as 203 Squadron on 1 January 1929. In February it set out for a new base at Basra, becoming operational in March. Later, it visited India, before taking Short Rangoons in 1931.

With these it ranged as far afield as Australia, before a 1935 re-equipment with the Short Singapore III and a move to Aden in response to Italian aggression against Abyssinia. It was back to Basra in 1936, from which station 203 Squadron visited Singapore. With war looming, the squadron relocated back to Aden for patrol and escort work. It continued after February 1940 in roughly the same role, but with Blenheims.

A 1564 Flight winchman descends towards HMS Clyde, *where the author was awaiting 'rescue', on 1 May 2013.*

On 19 August 2010, 1564 Flight despatched RESCUE 25 to evacuate a fisherman 200nm east of the Falkland Islands. Seriously ill with a suspected lacerated bowel and septicaemia, the man was stretcher-winched from the vessel Jacqueline *in heavy seas and flown to Stanley Hospital.*

Operations across the Middle East and east Africa occupied the squadron into February 1942, when it added Lockheed Hudsons and Martin Marylands to its operation, before taking the Martin Baltimore from August. The Baltimore bore the brunt of 203 Squadron's 1943 workload, which included anti-ship patrols, convoy escort, reconnaissance and regular ASR.

Already well-travelled, in November the unit changed base and continent, re-equipping with the Wellington Mk XIII and beginning operations in India. A year later, 203 Squadron exchanged its Wellingtons for Liberators. With these it flew a variety of patrol, supply-drop and transport missions, before flying back to the UK in May 1946.

Now exchanging the Liberator for the Lancaster ASR3, 203 Squadron became a maritime patrol and ASR unit at St Eval. In 1953, it moved to Topcliffe and re-equipped with the Lockheed Neptune. The US type was short-lived, however, and the squadron disbanded on 1 September 1956.

It reformed as a Shackleton MR1A unit through a renumbering of 240 Squadron at Ballykelly on 1 November 1958. Once again destined for overseas service, 203 Squadron departed for Malta in January 1969, from where it provided MR, ASW and SAR coverage for the entire Mediterranean. The mission continued with the Nimrod MR1 from 1971, until the disbandment of the unit on 31 December 1977.

Since its formation in 1916, 203 Squadron and its RNAS predecessor had proven particularly enduring and this was again the case, since although almost two decades had elapsed, the unit returned on 16 October 1996, as 203 (Reserve) Squadron, the Sea King OCU. It continued in the role until 14 September 2014.

1312 FLIGHT

Like 1563 Flight, 1312 (Transport) Flight has enjoyed multiple iterations, having first been established at Llandow on 19 April 1944. It was effectively a private airline, equipped with Ansons and tasked with moving aircrews assigned to ferry aircraft. After D-Day it took on the additional role of casevac from Normandy, before disbanding on 21 July 1944.

It returned to service as 1312 (Transport Support) Flight on 14 September 1954, flying the Hastings and subsequently the Valetta, until disbanding on 1 April 1957.

The unit's final existence to date began as 1312 (Inflight Refuelling) Flight, operating Hercules modified as C.Mk 1K tankers out of RAF Stanley from 20 August 1983. Some 13 years later, 1312 Flight took its first Vickers VC10 tanker, operated, as was the Hercules, by crews rotating out from the UK-based operating squadrons. The VC10 was accompanied by a 'straight' Hercules C1, allocated maritime patrol and SAR tasks as its primary missions, rather than transport; both aircraft could be employed for casevac to the South American mainland should the need arise.

As the VC10 force drew down, so a Lockheed TriStar K1 joined 1312 Flight on 31 August 2013, but only as a stop-gap, since the Airbus Defence and Space Voyager KC2 replaced it from the following February. Change was also afoot for the Hercules community and, with the C1 withdrawn, the new-generation C5 took its place.

Finally, the Hercules C5 was also withdrawn, leaving only the long-fuselage C4 operational. This type is less suitable for the unique Falklands mission and the Airbus Defence and Space Atlas C1 was therefore equipped with Air Sea Rescue Apparatus (ASRA) and deployed for the first time in March 2018. Number 1312 Flight continues its operations from Mount Pleasant, employing single examples of the Atlas and Voyager.

1564 FLIGHT

Number 1564 Flight formed out of 103 Squadron, at El Adem, on 31 July 1964. Equipped with the Sycamore and Whirlwind, it disbanded at the same base on 31 December 1966. Still in the SAR role, it reappeared at El Adem, on 1 May 1969, out of 'D' Flight, 22 Squadron. This new existence was short-lived, with 1564 Flight disbanding again on 31 March 1970, but not before relocating to Cyprus.

In the aftermath of the 1982 Falklands War, 202 Squadron's 'C' Flight dispatched Sea Kings to Port Stanley, where they supplied SAR and support; the detachment became 1564 (Tactical Support) Flight the following year.

On 22 May 1986, 1564 Flight merged with Chinook-operating 1310 Flight, also on the Falkland Islands, to form 78 Squadron. Both flights therefore disappeared, but the Chinook was withdrawn in December 2007, 1564 Flight having re-formed in November. It continued with two Sea Kings, latterly operating out of Mount Pleasant Airfield, until UK SAR provision on the islands was privatised, disbanding on 31 March 2016.

Organised by 203(R) Squadron, Exercise Yellow Scorpion was a training consolidation exercise. This scene occurred during its 2014 iteration.

SAC Gina Edgcumbe / © UK MoD Crown Copyright

Number 1312 Flight's Atlas on 10 June 2019.

Sgt Paul Oldfield / © UK MoD Crown Copyright

Flight Lieutenant Thomas 'Sticky' Bunn was captain on 22 Squadron's initial response to the Swanland *incident.*

SAC Faye Storer / © UK MoD Crown Copyright

Flight Lieutenant William Wales flew as 'Sticky's' co-pilot.

SAC Faye Storer / © UK MoD Crown Copyright

was plotting and reporting back on our finds, so as to help any subsequent searches.'

Wales continued the story:

We remained on scene for approximately 45 minutes longer, searching the area for survivors, but sadly none were found. We returned to base to drop the casualties off, before refuelling and returning to search new coordinates. In the meantime, helicopters from Ireland, Chivenor and Culdrose were either on scene or approaching. During our second search, another person was found, sadly not alive, by the Ireland crew. He was the last found.

It really was a tricky SAROP [SAR operation], not just because of the type of job, with the vessel sinking so fast, but with the weather. It was some of the worst I'd ever seen, even by Anglesey standards, and it was at night.

Master Aircrew Richard 'Rich T' Taylor was awarded The Queen's Commendation for Bravery in the Air for his part in the *Swanland* operation. Remarkably, it added to his Queen's Gallantry Medal…

On 31 January 2008, the ferry *Riverdance* departed Warrenpoint, Northern Ireland, on its regular course to Heysham, Lancashire.

The vessel ended its final voyage beached at Cleveleys, where it was eventually broken up, but only after attracting 100,000 visitors to the area.

Loaded with 54 trailers and four passengers, the ferry had a crew of 19. The weather was poor when it set sail, with gales, heavy rain and rough seas, but not so poor that its experienced captain should consider the conditions too bad for a safe crossing. Nonetheless, a reduction in speed became necessary to prevent overloading the engine. Two of the trailers secured on deck also became loose in their lashings and, with the ship leaning very slightly because of its shifted cargo, the captain and senior crew began speaking seriously about the worsening situation.

Then a massive wave hit the ship, rolling it from one side to the other. Before it righted naturally, a second hit, sending it far to port as most of the cargo broke free. In a series of excellent decisions, the captain took manual control, but when the port engine failed,

he called the Coastguard at 19.41 for tug assistance. Soon the call had become a Mayday.

The RAF, Royal Navy and Irish Coastguard launched helicopters, while *Steersman*, a tanker sailing in the area, acted as communications relay. Rig support vessels *Clywd Supporter* and *Highland Sprite* also moved into position to offer assistance, as a pair of RNLI lifeboats closed on *Riverdance*. Meanwhile, its crew had managed to reduce the ship's list to 20 degrees, most likely preventing it from capsizing. At 21.10, the starboard engine failed.

Up from RAF Valley's 'C' Flight, 22 Squadron, Flight Lieutenant Lee Turner and crew faced a dilemma: 'It was quite a difficult position for the aircraft. I wouldn't say it was impossible, but it did take quite a bit of head scratching.' The ferry's crew and passengers had gathered on deck in the relative safety of its starboard side, placing them in a difficult position for winching. After an initial

A still from the FLIR turret on Bunn's Sea King shows the two Russian seamen safe in a liferaft.

© UK MoD Crown Copyright

Master Aircrewman Taylor lifts the cold and frightened, but unharmed sailors safely into the helicopter. By this stage in the rescue, Taylor had already had to swim for his life.

© UK MoD Crown Copyright

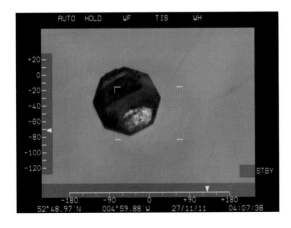

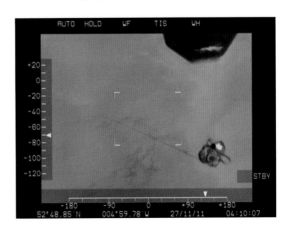

attempt failed, MACr Rich Taylor – known to his colleagues variously as Rich T or 'Biscuits' – winched down to the bridge, extracting the passengers and non-essential crew. 'It was some of the hardest flying I've ever been involved with,' he later told the press. 'I've done some big jobs before, but that was the scariest thing I've ever done.'

The Royal Navy Sea King extracted six more crew, leaving nine essential personnel on board when *Riverdance* bottomed on the sea floor as it drifted towards the beach at Cleveleys. It settled upright and the remaining crew prepared to float it off the beach at the next high tide. Their best efforts failed. The vessel again lost power and turned parallel to the beach, where it came aground listing dramatically to starboard and eventually fell on to its side. At 05.15, Jim Smith, *Riverdance*'s captain, reluctantly declared the second Mayday of his career and asked if the helicopter might come back.

Rich T again winched from the bridge, now listing at 60 degrees. The Valley crew employed a hi-line, which broke, but persisted and eventually lifted the final crewmember – the captain – to safety. MACr Taylor received the Queen's Gallantry Medal for his part in the rescue, while Flight Lieutenant Lee was awarded the Air Force Cross.

The End

On 1 April 2015, 'D' Flight, 202 Squadron at RAF Lossiemouth and 'E' Flight, 202 Squadron at Leconfield stood down. 'C' Flight, 22 Squadron at Valley followed on 1 July. It was the turn of 'B' Flight, 22 Squadron at Wattisham on 14 August and 'A' Flight, 202 Squadron at Boulmer on 30 September.

Master Aircrewman Richard 'Rich T' Taylor.

SAC Faye Storer / © UK MoD Crown Copyright

On 4 October 2015, 22 Squadron crews flying from RMB Chivenor completed the final operational RAF UK SAR Sea King sortie, after responding to a final call that had come in at 03.21. The alert aircraft was despatched to recover an unconscious man from the beach at Ilfracombe. It was on scene before 04.00 and the casualty was flown direct to Swansea Morriston Hospital. SAR Force had made its final 'rescue'.

'A' Flight, 22 Squadron flew its farewell sorties on 13 October before ceasing all operations. Wing Commander 'Sparky' Dunlop, Officer Commanding 22 Squadron was there to receive the two aircraft as they shut down, as well as the call from the UK ARCC authorising the RAF to stand down from more than 70 years of continuous SAR operations.

With the Chivenor flight stood down, Group Captain Steve Bentley, Search and Rescue Force Commander, said:

It is with enormous pride that we can reflect on the RAF's life-saving achievements since rescue operations began in 1941.

This continuous operational standby commitment has been delivered day-on-day across eight decades through the dedication, selfless commitment and the determined pursuit of the highest professional standards of our aircrew, engineers and support staff.

Today's crews reflect the ethos of the service first established by their forebearers in the RAF Directorate of Air Sea Rescue. They can take great pride in the contribution they have made in the service of the nation.

And yet, it wasn't quite the end. More than 8,000 miles to the south, RAF SAR crews were still active with 1564 Flight. On 26 November 2015, it launched a Sea King on a mission surpassing even that of April 2000. With a 1312 Flight Hercules, also launched from Mount Pleasant Airfield, providing SAR overwatch and acting as rescue co-ordinator and radio relay, the helicopter refuelled from HMS *Clyde* before recovering a British casualty from a Russian cruise ship 800nm off the Falkland Islands.

The man was aboard MV *Akademik Sergey Vavilov* when it visited South Georgia, where a fur seal bite left his arm seriously injured. With the casualty back on board, the ship steamed for the Falkland Islands while HMS *Clyde* raced to a point 200nm south of the Falklands,

LOCKHEED & LOCKHEED MARTIN HERCULES

On 2 February 1951, the US Air Force (USAF) issued a General Operational Requirement for an aircraft to replace its large fleets of Curtiss C-46, and Fairchild C-82 and C-119 piston-engined transports. Lockheed responded with its L-206 design, which the USAF chose as the winning contender on 2 July 1951, ordering two YC-130A prototypes based on the proposal. The first production C-130A Hercules entered service in December 1956.

After the Armstrong Whitworth AW681 vertical take-off transport was abandoned on the drawing board, the RAF needed to replace its piston-engined Blackburn Beverley and Handley Page Hastings transports, while augmenting the Armstrong Whitworth Argosy turboprop. Sixty-six Hercules were therefore ordered to C-130H standard, but designated C-130K for export to the UK.

Known to the RAF as Hercules C.Mk 1 (the C-130K designation only came into regular use as a differentiator after the C-130J entered service), the first aircraft completed its maiden flight on 19 October 1966. The type entered service in 1967, but defence cuts in 1975 saw 13 aircraft withdrawn.

In 1978 a conversion programme began to produce 30 Hercules C.Mk 3 aircraft by stretching the fuselage of the C1 to increase cabin capacity. Lockheed produced the initial C3, flying it for the first time on 3 December 1979, while Marshall produced the remainder at Cambridge Airport in the UK.

A December 1993 MoD requirement identified the need for a Hercules replacement and although the European Future Large Aircraft (FLA) was considered, the only substitute for a Hercules was the more powerful C-130J, a next-generation machine then under development and featuring the latest avionics systems. The December 1994 order comprised ten standard C-130J aircraft and 15 of the longer C-130J-30, with first delivery (of a J-30) in August 1998. The initial operational example reached RAF on 21 November 1999.

Designated Hercules C.Mk 4 in service, the C-130J-30 is just a little shorter than the C3, while the Hercules C.Mk 5 had the same fuselage length as the C1. Inflight refuelling probes were installed as standard (they were retrofitted on the C1 and C3), while the type's improved range enabled most sorties to be flown without the characteristic underwing fuel tanks of the legacy versions.

Working intensively on operations alongside the legacy Hercules Fleet, the C-130J rapidly accumulated flying hours. The 2010 Strategic Defence and Security Review identified it for withdrawal from service in 2022, a decade earlier than originally planned, while the C-130K was retired on 28 October 2013.

By now the A400M programme was well advanced, but the C-130J had an important tactical role to play until the new type was fully established. The 2015 Strategic Defence and Security Review reflected this thinking, with the announcement that 14 Hercules C4s will remain in service until 2030, with additional funding allocated for upgrades and life extension.

Although transport has always been the Hercules' primary role, its long range was also an advantage during a permanent Falklands detachment, 1312 Flight operating aircraft equipped with ASRA, which enabled liferafts and emergency supplies to be airdropped. The final 1312 Flight Hercules C.Mk 5 returned to RAF Brize Norton on 5 April 2018, the role passing to the A400M as the short-fuselage Hercules was withdrawn from RAF service.

•••

SPECIFICATION

LOCKHEED MARTIN C-130J HERCULES

Powerplant four 4,700shp Rolls-Royce AE2100D3 turboprop engines
Length (C.Mk 4) 112ft 9in (34.41m)
Length (C.Mk 5) 97ft 9in (29.84m)
Height 38ft 4¾in (11.70m)
Wingspan 132ft 7in (40.45m)
Wing area 1,745sq ft (162.11m^2)
Cruising speed 320kt (593km/h)
Maximum altitude 40,000ft (12,190m)

ready for a HIFR with the outgoing Sea King. With the Hercules on constant watch, the Sea King, a military doctor added to its crew, took fuel from *Clyde* as planned, then flew a further 100nm across the South Atlantic to rendezvous with *Akademik Sergey Vavilov*. The casualty was winched off into the care of the doctor and the Sea King turned for Stanley.

Remarkably, this epic long-range mission came just eight days after both Sea Kings, and 1312 Flight's Hercules and Voyager, in addition to HMS *Clyde,* had been involved in a mass rescue from the French luxury cruise ship *Le Boreal*. With the vessel drifting after a serious engine room fire, the captain gave orders to abandon ship at 02.00 on 18 November 2015.

According to *Le Boreal's* operator, all 347 passengers and crew were safely evacuated to the nearby *L'Austral*, but a Ministry of Defence press release described a rescue operation occurring in a 'north-westerly gale'. According to the release, the ship was in danger of grounding on Cape Dolphin, East Falkland, and came within three miles of land.

HMS *Clyde* was reported as having assisted 200 casualties in lifeboats, while the Sea Kings winched 79 casualties from liferafts and the ship itself, taking them directly to Mount Pleasant. Commenting on the effort next day, Commander British Forces South Atlantic Islands Commodore Darren Bone said:

We responded with everything we had yesterday to assist in what was an extremely complex and hazardous rescue operation in difficult conditions, but I am delighted that we can report all of the passengers and crew of the vessel are safe and well and the vessel itself in a stable condition. This was a huge team effort involving close liaison with the Falkland Islands Government and I am enormously impressed with the reaction by all the British forces involved, it was an exemplary performance all round.

Number 1564 Flight stood down on 31 March 2016, ending the RAF's dedicated helicopter SAR provision. At the very end, with the Falklands commitment safely passed on, more than half of the SAR Force personnel transferred to the RAF's Chinook fleet. Others transferred to Bristow

Members of 'D' Flight, 202 Squadron and their families gathered for the unit's 1 April 2015 disbandment after 43 years at RAF Lossiemouth.

SAC Robyn Stewart / © UK MoD Crown Copyright

Helicopters, where pilots initially operated on rig support missions to gain experience with a glass cockpit, before resuming SAR duties, carrying on more or less exactly where they had finished.

SAR Force itself actually continued as an entity until 18 February 2016, when it too stood down. Official statistics recording RAF SAR operations only go back to 1983, since when the six SAR flights rescued 26,853 people in 34,025 calls to action. In total, the RAF's SAR personnel had been awarded six George Medals and more than 50 AFCs, plus a plethora of other medals and commendations. Working under the control of the Aeronautical Rescue Coordination Centre at Kinloss, SARF had been responsible for rescues across 1.1 million square miles of land and sea.

But the last word ought to go to Wing Commander 'Sparky' Dunlop, 22 Squadron's final Officer Commanding. After the ultimate SAR Force mission on 4 October 2015, he said:

SAR crews are a very well-trained set of specialists who, because of their job, become used to working in dangerous conditions. As a pilot, things can get tricky, but remember I'm always in a warm cockpit seat. It's the winchmen I admire, who've to go down the wire in all conditions.

I feel sad because it has ended, but the world is full of change and the new providers have taken on some of our people, so in a sense the RAF's DNA will be passed on to the new service.

I'd say we worked hard, we trained hard, and we brought hope to people in what they thought were hopeless situations.

1

2

3

4

5

6

7

8

9

10

11

12

1 ‘E’ Flight, 202 Squadron’s final sorties come to an end back
at Leconfield.
SAC Gina Edgcumbe / © UK MoD Crown Copyright

2 ‘E’ Flight, 202 Squadron at Leconfield stood down on 1 April 2015.
SAC Gina Edgcumbe / © UK MoD Crown Copyright

3 Flight Lieutenants Rebecca Bethell and Matt Thompson on
1 April 2015, before flying ‘E’ Flight, 202 Squadron’s Sea Kings
into retirement at Valley.
SAC Gina Edgcumbe / © UK MoD Crown Copyright

4 Operations continued without respite, right to the end. On 6 April
2015, aircraft captain Flight Lieutenant Martin Jarvis, co-pilot
Flight Lieutenant Kate Simmonds, winchman Sergeant Dave
Currie and RadOp / winch operator MACr Nick Swannick flew
‘C’ Flight, 22 Squadron’s 10,000th rescue. They assisted Ogwen
Valley Mountain Rescue team, recovering a woman who had
damaged her ankle out walking in Snowdonia.
SAC Gina Edgcumbe / © UK MoD Crown Copyright

5 Represented in a 2010 image, ‘C’ Flight, 22 Squadron stood down at
Valley on 1 July 2015.
SAC Dek Traylor / © UK MoD Crown Copyright

6 Photographed here in 2012, ‘B’ Flight, 22 Squadron stood down at
Wattisham on 14 August 2015.
SAC Dek Traylor / © UK MoD Crown Copyright

7 Stationed at Boulmer, ‘A’ Flight, 202 Squadron stood its last crew
down at 09.20 on 30 September 2015.
SAC Dek Traylor / © UK MoD Crown Copyright

8 (From left to right) Wing Commander ‘Sparky’ Dunlop, captain
and OC 22 Squadron, Sergeants Dan Allanson and Russ Jenkins,
and Flight Lieutenant ‘PJ’ Howard flew the RAF’s last UK SAR
mission on 4 October 2015.
Cpl Peter Devine / © UK MoD Crown Copyright

9 Sergeants Tom Wilson and Andy Dixon wave from their ‘A’ Flight,
22 Squadron Sea King over Chivenor, on 31 October 2015.
Cpl Peter Devine / © UK MoD Crown Copyright

10 Final shutdown for ‘A’ Flight, 22 Squadron Sea King on 31 October 2015.
Sgt Neil Bryden / © UK MoD Crown Copyright

11 SAR Force disbanded on 18 February 2016 with a parade at RAF
Valley. The Duke and Duchess of Cambridge were in attendance to
hear SAR Force Commander, Group Captain Steve Bentley (at right,
on the podium) say: ‘The hallmark of search and rescue personnel,
both past and present, has been their commitment, sense of teamwork
and trust in each other, and selfless dedication to the task of saving
lives. They can take immense pride in their achievements.’
Cpl Rob Travis / © UK MoD Crown Copyright

12 The end for SAR Force, as the 18 February 2016 disbandment
parade draws to a close.
Cpl Rob Travis / © UK MoD Crown Copyright

1

2

3

4

1   *Mount Pleasant Airfield launched a Sea King and Hercules for an epic medical evacuation on 26 November 2015.*
    © UK MoD Crown Copyright

2   *The Sea King performed a HIFR with HMS* Clyde, *extending its range for the return trip to* Akademik Sergey Vavilov, *steaming
    rapidly towards the Royal Navy vessel.*
    © UK MoD Crown Copyright

3   *Far out of the inhospitable South Atlantic, the 1564 Flight Sea King approaches* Akademik Sergey Vavilov.
    © UK MoD Crown Copyright

4   *A 1564 Flight Sea King works over* Le Boreal *on 18 November 2015.*
    © UK MoD Crown Copyright

APPENDICES

APPENDIX 1: RAF SAR FLIGHT AND SAR HEADQUARTERS LOCATIONS

RAF SAR Flight Locations

Location	Flight	From	To	Aircraft
Linton-on-Ouse	A Flight, 275 Squadron	April 1953	November 1954	Sycamore HR.Mk 13
Thornaby-on-Tees	A Flight, 275 Squadron	November 1954	October 1957	Sycamore HR.Mk 13/14
North Coates	B Flight, 275 Squadron	February 1955	October 1957	Sycamore HR.Mk 14
Thorney Island	A Flight, 22 Squadron	June 1955	April 1956	Whirlwind HAR.Mk 2
	D Flight, 22 Squadron	April 1956	December 1959	Whirlwind HAR.Mk 2
	B Flight, 22 Squadron	May 1964	March 1973	Whirlwind HAR.Mk 10
Martlesham Heath	B Flight, 22 Squadron	June 1955	May 1956	Whirlwind HAR.Mk 2
Leuchars	C Flight, 275 Squadron	June 1955	September 1959	Sycamore HR.Mk 14
	C Flight, 228 Squadron	September 1959	August 1964	Whirlwind HAR.Mk 2/10
	C Flight, 202 Squadron	August 1964	May 1976	Whirlwind HAR.Mk 10
	B Flight, 22 Squadron	May 1976	April 1993	Wessex HAR.Mk 2
Horsham St Faith	D Flight, 275 Squadron	September 1955	September 1959	Sycamore HR.Mk 14
	D Flight, 228 Squadron	September 1959	April 1963	Whirlwind HAR.Mk 2/10
Valley	C Flight, 22 Squadron	September 1955	September 1977	Whirlwind HAR.Mk 2/10
		September 1977	June 1997	Wessex HAR.Mk 2
		June 1997	1 July 2015	Sea King HAR.Mk 3
St Mawgan	A Flight, 22 Squadron	April 1956	November 1958	Whirlwind HAR.Mk 2
Felixstowe	B Flight, 22 Squadron	April 1956	November 1958	Whirlwind HAR.Mk 2
Aldergrove	F Flight, 275 Squadron	June 1957	April 1959	Sycamore HR.Mk 14
Leconfield	B Flight, 275 Squadron	October 1957	September 1959	Sycamore HR.Mk 14

Location	Flight	From	To	Aircraft
	B Flight, 228 Squadron	October 1959	August 1964	Whirlwind HAR.Mk 2/10
	B Flight, 202 Squadron	August 1964	June 1979	Whirlwind HAR.Mk 10
	D Flight, 22 Squadron	October 1979	November 1988	Wessex HAR.Mk 2
	E Flight, 202 Squadron	November 1988	1 April 2015	Sea King HAR.Mk 3
Acklington	A Flight, 275 Squadron	October 1957	September 1959	Sycamore HR.Mk 14
	A Flight, 228 Squadron	September 1959	August 1964	Whirlwind HAR.Mk 2/10
	A Flight, 202 Squadron	August 1964	October 1975	Whirlwind HAR.Mk 10
Chivenor	E Flight, 275 Squadron	June 1957	November 1958	Sycamore HR.Mk 14
	A Flight, 22 Squadron	November 1958	November 1981	Whirlwind HAR.Mk 2/10
		November 1981	June 1994	Wessex HAR.Mk 2
		June 1994	May 1997	Sea King HAR.Mk 3
		May 1997	4 October 2015	Sea King HAR.Mk 3A
Tangmere	B Flight, 22 Squadron	June 1961	May 1964	Whirlwind HAR.Mk 2/10
Manston	D Flight, 22 Squadron	June 1961	May 1969	Whirlwind HAR.Mk 2/10
	Bristow	June 1971	September 1974	Whirlwind Series 3
	D Flight, 72 Squadron	October 1974	June 1976	Wessex HC.Mk 2
	E Flight, 22 Squadron	June 1976	August 1988	Wessex HAR.Mk 2
	C Flight, 202 Squadron	September 1988	July 1994	Sea King HAR.Mk 3
Coltishall	D Flight, 228 Squadron	April 1963	August 1964	Whirlwind HAR.Mk 10
	D Flight, 202 Squadron	August 1964	May 1973	Whirlwind HAR.Mk 10
	B Flight, 22 Squadron	April 1973	April 1976	Whirlwind HAR.Mk 10
	C Flight, 202 Squadron	April 1976	May 1997	Whirlwind HAR.Mk 10
		May 1979	August 1982	Sea King HAR.Mk 3
	22 Squadron detachment	August 1982	August 1983	Wessex HAR.Mk 2
	F Flight, 22 Squadron	August 1983	September 1985	Wessex HAR.Mk 2
	C Flight, 202 Squadron	September 1985	August 1988	Sea King HAR.Mk 3
	E Flight, 22 Squadron	September 1988	July 1994	Wessex HAR.Mk 2
Lossiemouth	D Flight, 202 Squadron	February 1974	August 1978	Whirlwind HAR.Mk 10
		August 1978	1 April 2015	Sea King HAR.Mk 3
Brawdy	D Flight, 22 Squadron	February 1974	October 1979	Whirlwind HAR.Mk 10
	B Flight, 202 Squadron	October 1979	July 1994	Sea King HAR.Mk 3
Boulmer	A Flight, 202 Squadron	October 1975	December 1978	Whirlwind HAR.Mk 10
		December 1978	30 September 2015	Sea King HAR.Mk 3
Wattisham	B Flight, 22 Squadron	July 1994	July 1997	Sea King HAR.Mk 3
		July 1997	14 August 2015	Sea King HAR.Mk 3A

RAF SAR Squadron Headquarters

275 Squadron

Linton-on-Ouse	15 April 1953	November 1954
Thornaby-on-Tees	November 1954	October 1957
Leconfield	October 1957	30 September 1959

228 Squadron

Leconfield	1 September 1959	31 August 1964

202 Squadron

Leconfield	1 September 1964	January 1976
Finningley	January 1976	December 1992
Boulmer	December 1992	April 2008
Valley	April 2008	4 October 2015

22 Squadron

Thorney Island	15 February 1955	June 1956
St Mawgan	June 1956	April 1974
Thorney Island	April 1974	January 1976
Finningley	January 1976	December 1992
St Mawgan	December 1992	September 1997
Chivenor	September 1997	April 2008
Valley	April 2008	1 July 2015

SAR Wing Headquarters

Finningley	January 1976	December 1992
St Mawgan	December 1992	April 2008

SAR Force Headquarters

Valley	April 2008	18 February 2016

APPENDIX 2: RAF MOUNTAIN RESCUE

High ground and poor weather proved as formidable an enemy as any Messerschmitt during World War II, regularly claiming aircraft on operational missions and training sorties. It was realised that in many cases aircrew survived the accident, only to succumb to their injuries, the weather or the hazards of wandering around a mountainside confused and most likely concussed.

During 1943, the RAF Mountain Rescue Service was established in response to this realisation – RAF MRS is therefore 25 years younger than its parent. Flight Lieutenant George Graham, the senior medical officer at RAF Llandwrog (Gwynedd) initially created a team specifically for the purpose of recovering aircrew downed in the Welsh mountains.

The Air Ministry noticed Graham's success and schemed an expansion of the service to cover all the UK's high ground. The service was voluntary and so was without full-time staff during its early years. Volunteers received mountain training, but were typically already recreational mountaineers or hill walkers, a fact that remains true in today's MRS.

Into the 1990s, the RAF maintained six teams at RAF Kinloss, Leuchars, Leeming, Valley, Stafford and St Athan, but this was subsequently reduced to three. These are currently stationed at RAF Leeming, North Yorkshire; RAF Lossiemouth, Moray; and RAF Valley, Anglesey.

For much of its existence, MRS has been closely associated with the RAF's search and rescue capability, latterly represented by SAR Force and, most obviously, by its bright yellow Sea King helicopters. With responsibility for UK helicopter SAR passing to a civilian contractor, on 1 April 2015, the MRS became a 38 Group asset.

Helicopters lent a new level of versatility to mountain rescue operations and RAF MRS has trained with them almost throughout its history. Here a team works with a Whirlwind at Lochnagar, not far from Balmoral, in 1969.

RAF MRS / © UK MoD Crown Copyright

An MRS team image from 1959 shows the team working with an old-style stretcher sledge that required two people to haul it up the mountain.

RAF MRS / © UK MoD Crown Copyright

Team members donned PPE before approaching close to the burned-out Griffin, which had caught fire during mountain flying training.

RAF MRS / © UK MoD Crown Copyright

A Mobile Air Operations Team (MAOT) prepared the Griffin's wreckage for extraction by Chinook; although the ground looks relatively easy, there was a steep drop beyond the netted load. Valley's MRS team secured themselves to the mountainside, then to the MAOT personnel, lest the Chinook's considerable downwash blew them off the hillside.

RAF MRS / © UK MoD Crown Copyright

Perhaps inevitably, questions were asked over the viability of disbanding MRS along with its SAR Force parent, but the recognition that it delivers unique, professional capability at relatively little cost assured its survival. The reality is that RAF MRS has been and still remains the UK's only all-weather SAR organisation.

Speaking to the author in 2016, Squadron Leader Si Moore, then Officer Commanding MRS, was counting down the days to retirement by planning a major mountaineering expedition. He explained the continuing importance of RAF MRS to military operations and the civilian populace. Moore said: 'We're there when a helicopter can't get into the mountains because the weather's too bad. We can get in, do any life-saving that's required and secure any crash site.' In fact, aircraft post-crash management is actually one of MRS's most important primary roles, alongside military SAR, within the UK and supporting the Military Aid to Civil Authorities (MACA) construct. It means that wherever a military aircraft may crash in the UK, RAF MRS arrives quickly to take jurisdiction and secure the site.

Compared to World War II, military flying has reduced massively and even compared to the 1990s there has been a significant drawdown in military activity. However, despite this, dramatically improved aviation safety standards and the rarity of military aircraft and mountain crashes, MRS is still held at high readiness as the RAF's first responder to any incident.

Mountain Incident

In August 2016, a 202 (Reserve) Squadron Bell Griffin helicopter suffered an incident during mountain flying training, resulting in an emergency call for the Valley MRS unit. Squadron Leader Si Moore explained:

The aircraft landed as part of a training exercise, but suffered a mechanical failure and caught fire just metres from a summit. Since it didn't crash, the normal response procedures weren't activated, but it was seen burning and a civilian mountain rescue team called us; we were off the station in response within 20 minutes.

An HM Coastguard helicopter had been training in the area and spotted the fire, so it flew in and picked up the aircrew. Then it took some civilian team members up to the crash site. For us the walk to the incident site was over quite steep ground, but we were there within 90 minutes of receiving the call. Once we'd reached it, we put our personal protection equipment (PPE) masks on to secure the wreckage, then settled in to stay up there as a crash guard. That's when the weather clamped in, with hill fog, driving rain and high winds.

We're equipped and trained to cope with those conditions – you couldn't send a station guard force into that weather, they'd all go down with hypothermia! It was a relatively minor incident that nonetheless required our unique capabilities.

First Response and Safety Assurance

Specialist equipment and training, combined with years of experience in austere environments come in to play as soon as accident reports are received. Typically deploying with the intention of remaining on site for a maximum of 72 hours, MRS locates, treats and evacuates casualties, then secures the crash site. Military aircraft wreckage is particularly dangerous for the obvious reasons that it may contain ammunition or other explosive material as well as fuel and lubricants, but also for the less apparent risks associated with burning and broken materials, especially the composites used extensively in modern airframe construction.

MRS teams are highly trained in a range of mountaineering techniques, including ice climbing.

RAF MRS / © UK MoD Crown Copyright

Cooperation with the new generation UK SAR helicopter service is a cornerstone of RAF MRS work. The aircraft here is an HM Coastguard S-92.

RAF MRS / © UK MoD Crown Copyright

There is also a tremendous MRS contribution to continued safety assurance, since a crash site, protected from members of the public who might inadvertently wander through it, perhaps fancying a souvenir or two, retains every scrap of evidence that might be important to the personnel of the Air Accident Investigation Branch or Military Air Accident Investigation Branch. Where an accident site is particularly difficult to access, there may also be a role for MRS in wreckage recovery.

The modern RAF MRS is subordinate to 85 (Expeditionary Logistics) Wing, part of 38 Group, headquartered at RAF Wittering. It means the Mountain Rescue Service HQ resides at a station situated on the A1 north-south trunk road, north-west of Peterborough, a city seldom recognised for its mountains, yet places it administratively alongside other organisations essential to aircraft post-crash management – the Joint Aircraft Recovery

Top right: The mountains are close by for RAF Valley's Mountain Rescue team. Here members are practising a technical rescue on Holyhead Mountain.
Cpl Peter Devine / © UK MoD Crown Copyright

Above right: RAF Valley's MRS team training with a 7 Squadron Chinook Mk 6.
RAF MRS / © UK MoD Crown Copyright

Above right, lower: The teams carry large amounts of kit into the mountains, so keeping bulk and weight to a minimum is essential. Applying a plastic 'wrap' to the standard MRS titanium stretcher produces an easy-gliding sledge for casualty extraction.
RAF MRS / © UK MoD Crown Copyright

Right: A large orange 'tent' attaches to the deployed C3 vehicle, making it a focal point at accident investigations. This scene followed a US Marine Corps F/A-18C crash in Cambridgeshire.
RAF MRS / © UK MoD Crown Copyright

and Transportation Squadron, 3 Mobile Catering Squadron and 2 Mechanical Transport Squadron.

MRS Construct

Each MRS team has a small cadre of full-time personnel, all of them having volunteered for a tour with the Service, but with trades elsewhere in the RAF to which they will ultimately return. Generally, they manage the training, transport, accommodation for weekend training and all administration associated with running a team.

Part-time volunteers, drawn from the team's parent station and others nearby, provide further manning. These volunteers train at weekends, when the MRS response time is reduced, partly since there is little military flying at the weekend, but also because a team training three hours away up a mountain takes time to recall, re-equip and redeploy.

Squadron Leader Moore described a typical ten-person search or accident cordon team: 'There'd be a team leader, radio operator, two party leaders, two first aid-qualified personnel, or immediate emergency care (IEC) providers, and a group to form search teams.' Each team has its own fleet of 4×4 pick-up trucks equipped with enclosed load beds. These are essentially response vehicles, equipped with sirens and blue emergency lights, which are rugged enough to get teams as close as possible to an incident before they're obliged to continue on foot. Each is equipped with sufficient equipment to rescue one person.

On-site communications are conducted from a larger command, control and communications ('C3') van. Its HF, satcom,

Above: From its RAF Akrotiri base, 84 Squadron's duties include firefighting. In April 2018, the unit assisted the Cypriot government in controlling a large wild-fire north-west of Yermasoyia, Limassol district. The fire consumed more than 1km² of natural vegetation and came close to residential houses for several hours.

Sgt Dave Rose / © UK MoD Crown Copyright

Top: This Griffin HT1 was with SARTU in 2008.

U/VHF AM/FM, Airwave, mobile and internet connectivity enables MRS personnel to speak to anyone, anywhere in the world. The vehicle generates its own electricity supply and features an extensive stowable antenna array. Inside, careful design keeps much of the comms gear out of sight, leaving space for briefings, a large monitor and map tables.

The C3 is also 'blue-lighted', while similar vehicles, without the comms fit, serve as basic load carriers. Team members are trained in emergency driving on lights and sirens, so-called 'blues and twos', and undertake recurrent training to ensure standards are maintained.

Regular helicopter training is also a prerequisite, including winching once or twice every year. With the Sea King out of service, working with the RAF's MACA standby Puma and Chinook helicopters has become increasingly important, but joint training with HM Coastguard's S-92 and AW189 SAR helicopters is also critical. Training with civilian mountain rescue teams and the emergency services is also essential.

Although 202 Squadron now operates the Jupiter at Valley, the aircraft belong to the Defence Helicopter Flying School at RAF Shawbury. This Jupiter was flying a winch-training sortie at Shawbury in 2017.

Ian Forshaw / © UK MoD Crown Copyright

APPENDIX 3: CONTINUING COMMITMENT

When SARF disbanded on 18 February 2016, it left behind a legacy of world-class helicopter rescue experience and capability. Many of the final aircrew moved into new jobs doing essentially the same work but with the civilian contractor, but others stayed on, keeping the RAF's long association with SAR alive and relevant.

Also preserving key elements of the SAR history and tradition, the Search and Rescue Training Unit at RAF Valley was redesignated as 202 (Reserve) Squadron, subsequently 202 Squadron after the 'Reserve' title was dropped from unit designations around 2018.

All UK military helicopter aircrew pass through 202 Squadron, which specialises in maritime and mountain flying, and still teaches SAR techniques, which remain relevant to all helicopter crews. In 2018 it swapped its Bell Griffin helicopters for the Airbus Helicopters H145, known as the Jupiter HT1 in service. Equipped with a modern 'glass' cockpit, the Jupiter is entirely representative of the helicopter crews will fly with their front-line units.

The 'new' 202 Squadron also provides full SAR training for 84 Squadron, still stationed at RAF Akrotiri, Cyprus, and tasked with numerous roles, including SAR. Ironically equipped with the Bell Griffin, 84 Squadron is the RAF's last remaining helicopter unit with a standing SAR commitment.

APPENDIX 4: DARK BLUE SAR

Quick to recognise the potential utility of the helicopter in a variety of embarked and land-based missions, the Fleet Air Arm, the Royal Navy's flying branch, took the Sikorsky Hoverfly Mk I for service with 771 Fleet Requirements Unit (FRU) at Portland from February 1945. The type also served 705 Naval Air Squadron (NAS), at Gosport, from May 1947, where the Hoverfly Mk II arrived to supplement it and remained from 1947 until 1950. The aircraft primarily flew in the training and communications roles, but did much to expand naval thinking on helicopters and introduced rotary-wing flying to a first generation of crews and engineers.

For the Royal Navy the Supermarine Walrus had primarily been a combat aircraft of considerable importance, catapulted off warships to direct naval gunfire and 'spotting' enemy vessels as an over-the-horizon extension of the ships' own visual and radar search. The type also gave valuable service flying maritime reconnaissance missions from coastal bases, and so air-sea rescue was a natural extension of the work.

From November 1944, the Sea Otter began replacing its illustrious predecessor as the FAA's ASR platform of choice, initially entering front-line service with 1700 NAS at Lee-on-Solent. Numbers 1701, 1702 and 1703 NAS joined it in the ASR and mine-sweeping roles, although only 1703 NAS remained UK-based, at Lee-on-Solent. Embarking on HMS *Khedive*, 1700 NAS finished its war in Ceylon. Of the others, 1701 was based at Kai Tak, Hong Kong, and 1702 in Greece, Malta and Tunisia. A multitude of second-line units also flew the Sea Otter, but with the arrival of the Westland Dragonfly with 705 NAS at Gosport in January 1950, the Sea Otter's days were numbered.

Search and rescue was a prescribed Dragonfly role from the outset and therefore a designated mission for squadrons based at Brawdy, Culdrose, Lee-on-Solent and Portland, plus one in Malta. The aircraft briefly served alongside the Sea Otter, which was withdrawn only in January 1952 and as well as its fair share of UK and overseas rescues, served with distinction during the floods that hit eastern England and the Netherlands on 31 January/1 February 1953.

Although it marked a considerable improvement over the Hoverfly, the RAF had discovered that a larger, more powerful, helicopter was still needed in order to accommodate a well-equipped SAR crew, provide lifting capacity for survivors and offer acceptable range/endurance. The Whirlwind provided that possibility for the FAA, as the piston-engined Whirlwind HAR.Mk 1 and HAR.Mk 3, joined from January 1966 by the HAR.Mk 9 turbine-engined conversion of the HAS.Mk 7 anti-submarine helicopter. Some 17 Whirlwind HAR.Mk 9s were produced, serving on until March 1977, when the Wessex Mk 5 became available.

In FAA service, the Wessex was very much a combat type, flying in anti-submarine and assault versions, the latter culminating in the HU.Mk 5. A battlefield utility helicopter with provision for AS.12 wire-guided air-to-surface missiles, the HU.Mk 5 could also be equipped for the SAR role. It remained active until March 1988, by which time the Sea King HAR.Mk 5 was available. Based on the HAS.Mk 5, but with much of its anti-submarine warfare kit removed, the HAR.Mk 5 ultimately served SAR detachments at RNAS Culdrose, Portland and Prestwick, seeing the Royal Navy out to the end of its standing SAR commitment, on 4 October 2015.

Mister Cube and Drum England

Royal Navy SAR crews were every bit as courageous, resourceful and determined as their RAF colleagues, accumulating an array of awards, commendations and medals, with five George Medals going to 771 NAS aircrew alone. Among the latter's distinguished members, winchman Petty Officer Aircrewman Laurence Slater endured a particularly challenging 11 August 1986, rescuing 29 souls from two stricken yachts, *Mister Cube* and *Drum England*.

The morning's *Mister Cube* rescue might have seemed especially perilous had Slater not been called to the assistance of *Drum England* in the afternoon. He plucked three adults and six children to safety from the first vessel and 20 crew from the second, six of them trapped beneath the hull after the vessel's keel was torn away and it capsized.

Slater's meritorious work that day could be considered only in terms of 29 lives saved, but his efforts brought particular recognition to RN SAR and UK military SAR in particular, thanks to the media interest that surrounded *Drum England* crewman and owner Simon Le Bon, lead singer of 1980s' pop sensation Duran Duran. Speaking to the BBC in 2016, Le Bon revealed: 'I am grateful to 771 Squadron for saving my life, for saving the lives of the other guys on *Drum*.' Of Slater he said: 'He knows how much I owe to him, and I know how much I owe and what these people do with their lives – the bravery and devotion. I know they have to look at it as just a job because maybe it would become something they couldn't face. But it's a hell of a job.' Slater was gazetted in the 11 March 1986 second supplement to *The London Gazette* of 10 March 1986:

GEORGE MEDAL

Petty Officer Aircrewman Laurence SLATER

Petty Officer Aircrewman Slater was the duty Diver of a Search and Rescue Wessex helicopter crew, which was scrambled at 0730 on 11th August 1985 to assist the yacht, *Mister Cube*, disabled in severe gale conditions approximately 55 miles south-east of Lizard Point.

Weather at the scene was sea state 7, with the wind gusting over 50 knots. The yacht was being pounded by 25-foot waves, its sails shredded, masts whipping violently through arcs of over 90 degrees and the hull was lurching heavily in the severe swell.

With considerable difficulty, a light line was passed from the helicopter to the yacht. This was attached to Petty Officer Slater on the end of the helicopter's rescue winch. The helicopter was thus able to hover clear to one side of the yacht, while Slater was lowered on the winch and simultaneously pulled in on the yacht. Fighting his way past sails and whipping rigging, he eventually reached the cockpit to find six children and three adults. He quickly reassured everyone and briefed them comprehensively on the rescue method.

Three older children were single lifted to safety. On two occasions, as Slater started double lifting the younger children, severe yacht movement caused the light line to part.

Above left: This was a 771 NAS SAR demonstration over Plymouth Sound during the Armed Forces Day National Event on 30 June 2012.

LA(Phot) Joel Rouse / © UK MoD Crown Copyright

Above right: A Royal Navy winchman working with an RNLI craft during a night-time exercise off Cornwall in February 2012.

POA(Phot) Paul A'Barrow / © UK MoD Crown Copyright

Top left and right: Based at RNAS Culdrose, this 771 NAS Sea King was engaged in a SAR training exercise with the civilian emergency services along the Cornish coast in 2004.

© UK MoD Crown Copyright

For the fifth time he was transferred to the deck, organising the single lift of two adults, but, as he returned for the final rescue the yacht was knocked onto its beam ends by a giant wave. Miraculously Slater and the last survivor managed to hang on long enough for the aircraft to position itself and lift them clear. Once away from the yacht, Slater calmly cut the light line and was winched with the survivor into the aircraft. The aircraft returned to R.N.A.S. Culdrose at 0925.

Later that same day, at 1510, Slater was again launched as part of a Search and Rescue crew sent to the assistance of a Fastnet Race casualty, the yacht *Drum England*, capsized off Porthscatho.

On arrival, 18 survivors were found crouching precariously on the upturned hull. They indicated that a further six persons were either missing or trapped inside. Despite a sea state 5 and wind gusting 36 knots, the immediate danger necessitated Slater jumping from the aircraft and free swimming to the vessel.

Totally fearless, and disregarding his own safety, Slater dived beneath the jerking hull. Fighting his way past alarming snarls of torn sail and a tangled array of rigging, he came upon a rope locker and a white hatch. On forcing the hatch open he swam into an accommodation space, and was pulled into an air pocket by the missing survivors.

Despite the eerie situation, his exceptional courage, professionalism and outstanding presence enabled him to swiftly reassure and efficiently brief an escape plan. Remarkably, Slater safely extricated all six, pulling them out past a maze of rigging, before returning each to the surface. Slater then remained on board supervising the winch evacuation of 20 survivors.

Throughout both of these exceptionally hazardous rescue operations Slater totally disregarded his own safety. The rescue of 29 people under the most arduous conditions in two very demanding situations on the same day was accomplished due to the great fearlessness, superb stamina and unflinching courage of Petty Officer Aircrewman Slater in the face of enormous danger.

APPENDIX 5: ANATOMY OF A SAR HELICOPTER

Whether Dragonfly, Wessex or Sea King, the basis of flight and control for all the RAF's SAR helicopters and, indeed, the majority of helicopters ever built, is similar.

A fixed-wing aircraft derives lift from the difference in pressure caused by air flowing over and under its wings at speed. A helicopter employs a main rotor comprising blades, each effectively a wing, rotated by the power of its engine or engines; it does, indeed, employ a rotary wing.

In a fixed-wing aircraft, engine thrust pushes the machine forwards and provides the means by which air flows around the wing, but since a helicopter's engine(s) move its 'wings' through the air, it has no requirement for forward speed in order to generate lift. Thus, the helicopter

is able to hover. Fundamentally, the different dynamics of fixed-wing and rotary-wing aircraft dictate that an aeroplane must employ a take-off run to gain flying speed, while a helicopter is able to lift vertically from the ground.

Altering the angle at which the rotor blades meet the air by tilting them back and forth, that is, changing their pitch, varies the amount of lift generated. In the cockpit, lift is managed via a collective control lever, not unlike a car handbrake in appearance, which the pilot moves up and down to vary the pitch of all the blades simultaneously, or collectively. Raising the collective increases the upwards angle of the blade leading edges as they meet the air, generating more lift but also increasing drag; thus, power must also be increased, otherwise the blades' rotation would slow, and lift would be lost. Helicopter pilots typically think and talk in terms of torque rather than power, however, this being the rotational force imparted on the main rotor by the engine(s). Therefore, torque must be increased, through an increase in power (usually demanded through a twist throttle on the collective lever), as collective is increased.

Physics dictates that the spinning main rotor generates a torque effect that naturally causes the helicopter itself to turn in the opposite direction to the rotor. As torque is increased to generate more lift, the helicopter's fuselage 'wants' to turn more quickly in the opposite direction. In helicopters configured similarly to the Sea King (of which, most are), a tail rotor, driven by a series of gearboxes and shafts from the main engine(s), provides horizontal thrust that counters the torque effect.

It follows that increasing tail rotor thrust will turn the helicopter against the main rotor torque effect, that is in the same direction that the main rotor turns. Reducing it will enable the helicopter to turn in the opposite direction, as it naturally 'wants to'. The tail rotor is controlled by the yaw pedals, the pilot adjusting the degree of yaw input according to collective position and the direction in which he or she wishes the helicopter to point its nose – or tail, given that the aircraft might be hovering and the tail rotor must be kept clear of obstacles.

Unlike a fixed-wing aircraft, which derives its forward motion as a reaction to the thrust provided by propellers or jet exhaust, a helicopter's direction of travel derives from the individual adjustment of the main rotor blades. Considering the spinning rotor as

a disk, if each blade's pitch is adjusted as it passes through the same point on the disk, then the disk is caused to tilt, varying lift as a component of rotor thrust is moved at an angle to the vertical. The pilot uses a cyclic control, usually mounted forward, between the knees, not unlike the control column or 'joystick' in an aeroplane, to impart movement of the blades in a cycle.

Tilting the rotor disk forwards generates a rearwards thrust component and the helicopter moves forwards. It can be seen that tilting the disk in any direction produces the opposite movement and thus the aircraft can be made to fly in any direction, hence the immense utility of helicopters in SAR and many other applications.

The skill and aptitude required just to combine the inputs of collective, cyclic, yaw and torque control are formidable. Add in the need to fly safely, often at the relatively low levels where helicopters operate, to navigate, frequently over a rough sea, at night for SAR crews, to work as a crew and perhaps to hover over a rolling, burning ship in high winds and reduced visibility, and one begins to appreciate the immense skill required for every SAR operation.

Although clearly posed for the camera, this 11 July 1956 winch-training exercise involving a 22 Squadron Whirlwind HAR.Mk 2 helicopter out of RAF Valley, demonstrates the close working relationship between the SAR and Shackleton squadrons.

APPENDIX 6: IN SUPPORT

Announcing details of a major UK SAR redeployment, a 21 October 1992 RAF press release noted that a Nimrod was permanently maintained on one-hour readiness to launch in support of civil SAR tasking. It goes without saying that the commitment would also apply to a military crisis. Indeed, four Nimrods responded to the 1979 Fastnet Race disaster,

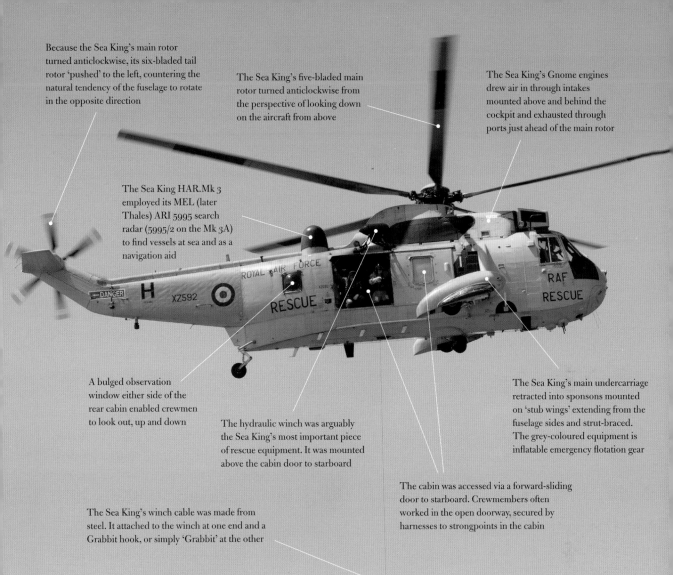

Because the Sea King's main rotor turned anticlockwise, its six-bladed tail rotor 'pushed' to the left, countering the natural tendency of the fuselage to rotate in the opposite direction

The Sea King's five-bladed main rotor turned anticlockwise from the perspective of looking down on the aircraft from above

The Sea King's Gnome engines drew air in through intakes mounted above and behind the cockpit and exhausted through ports just ahead of the main rotor

The Sea King HAR.Mk 3 employed its MEL (later Thales) ARI 5995 search radar (5995/2 on the Mk 3A) to find vessels at sea and as a navigation aid

A bulged observation window either side of the rear cabin enabled crewmen to look out, up and down

The hydraulic winch was arguably the Sea King's most important piece of rescue equipment. It was mounted above the cabin door to starboard

The Sea King's main undercarriage retracted into sponsons mounted on 'stub wings' extending from the fuselage sides and strut-braced. The grey-coloured equipment is inflatable emergency flotation gear

The cabin was accessed via a forward-sliding door to starboard. Crewmembers often worked in the open doorway, secured by harnesses to strongpoints in the cabin

The Sea King's winch cable was made from steel. It attached to the winch at one end and a Grabbit hook, or simply 'Grabbit' at the other

Introduced from 2003, the STAR-Q Multi Sensor System generated still images and video via infrared and daytime TV cameras. It was mounted to the fuselage side, under the port stub wing

Equipment attached to the Grabbit at the end of the winch cable could include more than one strop for winching casualties, or other Grabbits and lines for attaching bags or other rescue kit

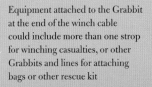

BOEING POSEIDON MRA.MK 1

Boeing announced its new Model 737 short/medium range airliner in 1964, but struggled to gain orders, so launched its development programme mostly on hope. The first 737-100 prototype completed its maiden flight on 9 April 1967, but airlines wanted greater capacity, so they sold only 30. The stretched 737-200 met this need and the 737 became a success.

The first major change in the line came with the CFM56 turbofan, which replaced the original Pratt & Whitney JT8D from 1984. In response to continuous improvements in the Airbus A320, Boeing reworked the 737 again, as the 737 Next Generation (NG) with a new wing, full-authority digital engine control (FADEC) and other improvements. Among the NG variants, Boeing selected the 737-800 as the basis of its P-8A Poseidon submission to replace the Lockheed P-3 Orion in US Navy service.

A contract for P-8 development was granted in June 2004 and first flight followed on 25 April 2009. The US Navy announced initial operating capability on 29 November 2013. By early 2020 the P-8 had been widely delivered not only to US units, but also to the Indian Navy, Royal Australian Air Force and UK; New Zealand, Norway and South Korea had also ordered Poseidons and a deal with Saudi Arabia seemed likely.

The BAE Systems Nimrod MRA.Mk 4 upgrade of existing Nimrod MR.Mk 2 airframes had been underway for some years when it was axed under the 2010 Strategic Defence and Security Review. The MR.Mk 2 was also withdrawn, leaving the UK without effective long-range, fixed-wing maritime cover. Project Seedcorn saw personnel posted into maritime patrol units with allied air arms, maintaining vital skills until the 2015 Strategic Defence and Security Review confirmed the intended purchase of nine Poseidons for the RAF.

The P-8A's comprehensive mission system features an APY-10 radar with modes for high-resolution mapping, and an acoustic sensor system including passive and multi-static sonobuoys, electro-optical/IR turret and electronic support measures (ESM). It will also be comprehensively equipped for SAR.

The P-8 will operate from RAF Lossiemouth, with 120 Squadron as the lead unit and 201 Squadron re-forming later. Crew training began in spring 2019 ready for the aircraft's arrival at the station in autumn 2020.

• •

SPECIFICATION

BOEING P-8A POSEIDON

Powerplant two 27,000lb st (120kN) CFM International CFM56-7 turbofan engines

Length 129ft 6in (39.5m)

Height 42ft 1¼in (12.83m)

Wingspan 123ft 7¼in (37.70m)

Maximum speed 490kt (907km/h)

The RAF's first Poseidon taxis in at Naval Air Station Jacksonville, Florida, after delivery on 31 October 2019.

Cpl Lee Matthews / © UK MoD Crown Copyright

supporting three RAF SAR helicopters and other airborne assets supplied by the Royal Navy and Irish Air Corps.

Withdrawal of the Lancaster ASR3/MR3 from 1951 marked the drawdown in permanent RAF fixed-wing SAR provision. No longer were fixed-wing squadrons dedicated to the ASR role, the primary mission passing to the emerging SAR helicopter. Nonetheless, the maritime squadrons maintained their SAR capabilities as secondary to their primary anti-submarine and patrol taskings, frequently launching aircraft to assist those in distress at sea.

As a stopgap type between the Lancaster and Shackleton, the Lockheed Neptune's time on RAF duty was relatively brief, but the Shackleton and its illustrious successor, the Nimrod, provided excellent service in the SAR role. The Nimrod in particular was blessed with a powerful search radar, excellent communications, a capacious weapons/equipment bay, high speed and exceptional endurance, enabling its crews not only to search for casualties, but to drop aid and remain on scene for hours, providing overwatch as the SAR helicopters plied their more intimate trade.

Several of the dedicated ASR/maritime patrol squadrons became anti-submarine/maritime patrol units with secondary SAR commitments as they progressed through aircraft types – in the case of 120 Squadron, a full progression from Lancaster, to Shackleton and then Nimrod; the squadron now has the lead for introducing the new P-8A Poseidon, an aircraft of futuristic capabilities far beyond those of the Nimrod, into service after a decade-long hiatus in maritime capability. The RAF took delivery of its first Poseidon on 31 October 2019 and the type is expected to arrive at its RAF Lossiemouth home base roughly 12 months later.

Numbers 42 and 206 Squadrons operated the Shackleton and Nimrod; 201, 204 and 205 only the Shackleton, although 201 will reappear as the second Poseidon unit.

The Nimrod's dramatic axing in all forms as a result of the 2010 Strategic Defence and Security Review left the UK with a yawning gap in its anti-submarine cover and denied its SAR community an essential tool. It also left the Falkland Islands with no dedicated maritime patrol or fixed-wing SAR platform. In the South Atlantic, the Hercules took up the mantle, permanently equipped with ASRA gear in its hold to support 1564 Flight's Sea Kings and deliver life-saving aid at range.

The subsequent drawdown in the Hercules Force saw the Hercules withdrawn from the Falklands, but the even more capable A400M Atlas has taken its place and continues the vital SAR commitment.

The Hercules has excelled on Falklands SAR operations, but also demonstrated its capability at home; 47 Squadron proving its long-range prowess in two exceptional operations in just a few weeks during 2017. It undoubtedly says as much about the adaptability and agility of RAF crews as it does about the Hercules that 47 Squadron, a unit dedicated to all manner of air mobility missions, should be able to launch crews and aircraft at short notice to effect a complex rescue.

In the evening of Thursday, 9 February 2017, a rogue wave hit the 60ft yacht *Clyde Challenger* mid-Atlantic, five days out from the Azores. The vessel lost its mast and two of three lifeboats, leaving insufficient capacity for the 14 crew to abandon ship. The UK

AVRO SHACKLETON

The ultimate development in a line of bomber, transport and maritime aircraft that began with the Avro Manchester, the Shackleton was designed postwar for essentially the role fulfilled by the US-supplied Liberator and Fortress during World War II. Avro had already produced the Lincoln on the basis of an enlarged, more powerful Lancaster. It became the mainstay of Bomber Command in the period between the withdrawal of the Lancaster and adoption of jet equipment, and Avro proposed a Lincoln Mk III ASW and MR version.

From this the Shackleton MR.Mk 1 was developed, combining a new, shorter fuselage with the Lincoln wing, which now mounted Rolls-Royce Griffon engines driving contra-rotating propellers. The prototype, designated Shackleton GR.Mk 1, completed its maiden sortie on 9 March 1949, followed on 24 March 1950 by the first production MR.Mk 1, which differed from the former through the deletion of its nose, dorsal and tail turrets. During April 1951, the MR.Mk 1 began replacing 120 Squadron's Lancaster ASR3s at Kinloss.

When it flew for the first time on 17 June 1952, the Shackleton MR.Mk 2 introduced a dramatically longer nose section, minus the undernose radome of the Mk 1 and 1A, but introducing a pair of 20mm cannon. The variant also introduced a retractable radome set into the underside of the rear fuselage. Based at St Eval, 42 Squadron was first to take MR.Mk 2s, in January 1953. Trainer conversions of the Mk 1 and 2 were produced as the T.Mk 1 and T.Mk 2, the former entering service in 1957.

But the Lancaster's development potential had yet to be exhausted and on 2 September 1955, Avro flew the radically altered Shackleton MR.Mk 3 for the first time. It featured wing tip fuel tanks for increased range and other changes, the most obvious of which was a switch to tricycle undercarriage. In service, the type was further improved in so-called 'Phases', the Phase 3 aircraft each adopting a pair of 2,500lb st (11.12kN) Bristol Siddeley Viper turbojets, helping maintain take-off performance as new equipment made the Mk 3 increasingly heavy.

The MR.Mk 3 entered service with 220 Squadron in August 1957 and remained operational until the Nimrod finally replaced it in 1971. Meanwhile, the last MR Shackletons in RAF service were the MR.Mk 2s of 204 Squadron, which disbanded on 28 April 1972.

••

SPECIFICATION
AVRO SHACKLETON MR.MK 3
Powerplant four 2,455hp Rolls-Royce Griffon 57A inline piston engines
Length 92ft 6in (28.22m)
Height 23ft 4in (7.13m)
Wingspan 119ft 10in (36.52m)
Maximum speed 302mph (486km/h)
Range (at 200mph/322km/h and 1,500ft) 3,660 miles (5,890km)
Armament two 20mm cannon in in the nose, plus up to 12,000lb of stores

Shackleton MR.Mk 2 WR960/X was on strength with 228 Squadron when it was photographed near its St Eval, Cornwall base.

AIRBUS DEFENCE AND SPACE
A400M ATLAS C.MK 1

In 1982, British Aerospace (BAe), France's Aerospatiale, West Germany's Messerschmitt-Bölkow-Blohm (MBB) and Lockheed in the US established the Future International Military Airlifter (FIMA) group to define and develop a replacement for the Lockheed C-130 Hercules and Transall C.160.

In 1989 Lockheed withdrew, to develop the C-130J, but Italy's Alenia and Spain's CASA subsequently joined Aerospatiale, BAe and Deutsche Aerospace (DASA, which had bought MBB in 1989), creating the European Future Large Aircraft (FLA) Group (Euroflag) on 17 June 1991. Work to define the FLA requirement continued as DASA became first Daimler-Benz Aerospace Airbus and then DaimlerChrysler in 1998, while Belgian and Turkish industry also joined the programme.

In 1995 it was announced that the Airbus Military Company would be established to take industrial responsibility for the FLA, but political and funding challenges meant that an international FLA request for proposals (RFP), dated from September 1997, was only issued in January 1999. An alternative Future Transport Aircraft RFP had emerged the previous July, while Airbus Military delivered the A400M design proposal in February 1999. This complex situation was resolved on 27 July 2000, when Belgium, France, Germany, Italy, Spain, Turkey and the UK announced their acceptance of the A400M.

Work proceeded under a 2003 contract, and the first A400M took the type's maiden flight on 11 December 2009 and formidable funding, political and technological challenges were subsequently overcome to bring the type into service.

By summer 2017, No. LXX Squadron was employing the A400M globally in its strategic capacity, while No. XXIV Squadron was delivering trained crews alongside its C-17 and Hercules output. Meanwhile, 206 (Reserve) Heavy Aircraft Test & Evaluation Squadron was busily extending and clearing the type's tactical capability, including natural surface runway and load-dropping trials.

Once the A400M was earmarked for the Falklands maritime patrol and SAR roles to replace the Hercules C5, the Joint Airborne Delivery Trials and Evaluation Unit (JADTEU) developed ramp-mounted launching gear for the ASRA kit; the initial aircraft deployed on 27 March 2018. The RAF expects to take the last of 22 A400Ms on order around 2021.

SPECIFICATION
AIRBUS DEFENCE AND SPACE A400M ATLAS C.MK 1

Powerplant four 11,000shp EuroProp International TP400 turboprop engines
Length 138ft 5½in (42.21m)
Height 48ft 2¾in (14.70m)
Wingspan 139ft 1¼in (42.40m)
Maximum speed 400kt (741km/h)
Maximum range 4,100nm (7,593km)
Maximum altitude 40,000ft (12,190m)

Number 1312 Flight's Atlas on 10 June 2019.

A 201 Squadron Nimrod crew ply their trade on a training sortie out of RAF Kinloss in May 2006.

Coastguard detected an emergency beacon signal at 20.00 and a number of vessels turned to the area, while US military aircraft attempted to locate the yacht.

A 47 Squadron crew launched out of Brize Norton, Oxfordshire, on the morning of 10 February, while the Type 45 destroyer HMS *Dragon* came off task and began steaming with all haste over the 500 miles to the yacht's position, 610 miles south-west of Land's End. Having found *Clyde Challenger* and established radio contact, the Hercules crew notified the ARCC of its exact location, *Dragon* steamed to that point, arriving around 14.30 on 11 February.

Realising the Royal Navy vessel might struggle to retrieve the yacht crew in the prevailing 30-knot winds and 30ft waves, the 47 Squadron personnel called an 820ft Cypriot bulk carrier to come alongside the yacht and shelter it while the crew were transferred; the ship had previously been unable to execute a safe rescue itself due to its size. Reluctant to leave *Clyde Challenger* to its predicament, the Hercules crew orbited for five hours before the need for fuel forced them back to base. *Dragon* successfully rescued all 14 men and women with minimal injuries, by around 17.00, even before the Hercules had touched down.

The second exceptional operation came during the early hours of Friday, 9 June 2017, when *Tamarind*, the vessel of a 73-year old British sailor competing in the Royal Western Yacht Club of England Original Single-handed Transatlantic Race, was severely damaged in a storm. The Canadian Coast Guard requested that the UK scramble an aircraft to coordinate the rescue mission, which aimed to have the liner *Queen Mary 2* recover the man, 1,600 miles off Newfoundland.

Launching from their Brize Norton home station, the 47 Squadron crew located the yacht wallowing in heavy seas after five hours' flying, around 1,200 miles from base. Once on station, they led *Queen Mary 2* to a successful rendezvous and the sailor was recovered without injury.

A 1312 Flight Hercules C1 at Mount Pleasant Airfield in 2009.

HAWKER SIDDELEY NIMROD

Like the Lockheed Neptune and Avro Shackleton that preceded it in RAF service, elements of the specialist kit associated with the Nimrod's maritime patrol and anti-submarine missions also equipped it for the search and rescue role. The Service's maritime aircraft had always assisted in at-sea rescues whenever called upon, but the Nimrod took a more active role as part of the UK's SAR system, employing its powerful radar to search vast tracts of ocean many miles from land.

Developed from the pioneering de Havilland Comet airliner, the Nimrod prototype flew for the first time on 23 May 1967. Some 46 MR.Mk 1 production aircraft followed from 28 June 1968, 35 of them upgraded to MR.Mk 2 standard from 1975.

Operational from summer 1979, the MR.Mk 2 was relatively new in service when it was committed to the 1982 Falklands War, for which 16 aircraft received inflight-refuelling probes and the new designation MR.Mk 2P.

Thanks in no small part to the excellence of its crews, the Nimrod gained an international reputation as perhaps the finest maritime aircraft of its era. A steadily dwindling fleet remained busy until withdrawn prematurely on 31 March 2010 without replacement, since the proposed Nimrod MRA.Mk 4 upgrade was also scrapped. One Nimrod had always been held on UK SAR alert throughout the type's career, equipped with a variety of air-droppable rescue kit in its bomb bay. Upon its withdrawal, other large aircraft, primarily the Hercules, were assigned similar duties, albeit without the Nimrod's extensive mission suite.

••

SPECIFICATION

HAWKER SIDDELEY NIMROD MR.MK 2

Powerplant four 12,140lb st (54kN) Rolls-Royce RB.168-20 Spey Mk 250 turbofan engines

Length 126ft 9in (38.68m)

Height 29ft 8½in (9.10m)

Wingspan 114ft 10in (35m)

Wing area 2,121sq ft (197.04m^2)

Maximum cruising speed at optimum altitude 547mph (880km/h)

Typical unrefuelled endurance 12 hours

Service ceiling 42,000ft (12,800m)

Armament up to 13,500lb of weapons and other stores housed in the bomb bay and/or carried on a pair of underwing pylons

The Nimrod's impressive endurance enabled it to loiter for several hours, many miles from base. This, combined with its comprehensive sensor suite, made it an excellent SAR platform as well as a fine maritime patrol and anti-submarine platform.

42 SQUADRON

From its formation at Filton on 1 April 1916, 42 Squadron worked closely with the army. Its focus remained on army cooperation and reconnaissance to the war's end and it disbanded in 1919.

Re-formed out of 'B' Flight, 22 Squadron on 14 December 1936, the new 42 Squadron was now a Vildebeest-equipped torpedo-bomber unit. Beauforts replaced the Vildebeests during 1940 and operations continued with these until the unit re-equipped with Blenheim bombers for service in the Far East. After a short period of disbandment from 31 December 1945, the squadron re-formed for barely 12 months by a renumbering of 254 Squadron, before disbanding on 15 October 1947.

It returned on 28 June 1952 as a maritime squadron operating the new Shackleton MR.Mk 1. Alongside its new primary maritime reconnaissance mission, 42 Squadron also assumed secondary ASR duties; the ASR and, later, SAR role remained important throughout the rest of the squadron's existence, through the Shackleton MR.Mk 1, 1A, 2 and 3, then the Nimrod MR.Mk 1 from April 1971, stationed throughout at St Mawgan.

In June 1983 the Nimrod MR.Mk 2 arrived to replace the MR.Mk 1, which finally departed the following June. The regular mix of patrol, anti-submarine and SAR work continued on the new model until October 1992, when it disbanded as the Nimrod force was concentrated at RAF Kinloss.

The Nimrod conversion unit, 236 OCU subsequently renumbered as 42 (Reserve) Squadron, which remained operational at Kinloss until its final Nimrod sortie on 30 March 2010. It disbanded on 26 May 2011.

120 SQUADRON

Its 1 January 1918 formation as a bomber unit came too late for it to serve in World War I, so 120 Squadron instead began mail flying between the UK and France in March 1919. It extended its reach to Germany before disbanding on 21 October.

It re-formed on 1 June 1941 at Nutts Corner, Northern Ireland, equipped with the Liberator primarily for the anti-submarine role. It continued with the type throughout the war, becoming the RAF's most successful anti-submarine squadron and establishing itself in a maritime role that it has yet to relinquish.

The wartime 120 Squadron disbanded at St Eval on 4 June 1945, but on 1 October 1946, 160 Squadron at Leuchars renumbered as a new 120. Flying continued with the previous unit's Lancaster ASR and GR3 aircraft and during May 1947, 120 Squadron made the first successful operational drop of an airborne lifeboat from a Lancaster.

Later in 1947 a detachment was sent to Palestine, while the Lancasters were used on visits to Canada and Pakistan during 1950. These were the type's swansong, however, since 120 Squadron introduced the Shackleton MR.Mk 1 into service from March 1951. Although its primary role remained anti-submarine warfare with SAR an important adjunct, the unit was involved in trooping flights to Cyprus during the 1956 Suez Crisis, by which time it was equipped with the Shackleton MR.Mk 2, before visiting Canada and the US in 1958; it began re-equipping with the MR.Mk 3 in November 1958.

In 1966, 120 Squadron detached aircraft to Changi and New Zealand, and in 1968 to Sharjah. The Nimrod MR.Mk 1 arrived from October 1970 and it was this type the unit flew during the 1970s' 'Cod War' and in subsequent patrols monitoring UK fishing grounds and oil installations.

After a move to RAF Kinloss in 1959, 120 Squadron remained at the Moray station, latterly with the Nimrod MR2, flying maritime patrol, ASW and SAR missions until the Nimrod was withdrawn in 2010, the squadron disbanding on 26 May 2011. Officially 'reinstated' during March 2018, 120 Squadron will be based at RAF Lossiemouth, where at the time of writing it was expected to arrive with the Poseidon in October 2020. Squadron personnel began training for the new type early in 2019 and first aircraft delivery took place at Naval Air Station Jacksonville, Florida, on 31 October that year.

201 SQUADRON

When the RAF was created through the amalgamation of the Royal Flying Corps (RFC) and Royal Naval Air Service (RNAS) on 1 April 1918, it absorbed both services' flying units. To avoid confusion and the need for comprehensive renumbering, the former RNAS squadrons were designated from 201, 1 Squadron, RNAS becoming 201 Squadron, RAF. Thus, 201 Squadron was originally formed as 1 Squadron, RNAS in October 1914. It quickly evolved from reconnaissance to scout duties, fighting throughout World War I and disbanding on 31 December 1919.

Contrary to many squadrons disbanded at war's end, 201 was not re-established for World War II, but as an expansion of 480 Flight, a general reconnaissance operator of the Supermarine Southampton at Calshot. Patrol and regular exercise work occupied the squadron until 1936, when it re-equipped with the Saro London. With the clouds of war gathering, 201 Squadron moved to Sullom Voe in September 1939, taking examples of the Supermarine Stranraer and Short Sunderland that same year.

The unit went to war on the London and Sunderland, having fully equipped with the latter by the time of its first definitive action against the enemy in January 1941. It fought valiantly from various British bases, searching for and striking shipping and U-boat targets, before flying Coastal Command's final wartime patrol, on 3 June 1945.

Still equipped with Sunderlands, 201 Squadron flew supplies on to Lake Havel during the Berlin Airlift, then participated in the British Greenland Expedition. It disbanded as a Sunderland unit on 28 February 1957.

On 10 October 1958 it returned as a Shackleton MR.Mk 3 operator through the renumbering of 220 Squadron, flying its traditional ASW and MR roles, with SAR as a secondary mission. In 1965, 201 Squadron transferred from St Mawgan to Kinloss, where it re-equipped with the Nimrod MR.Mk 1 in 1970. The MR.Mk 2 followed from 1982, remaining with the unit until March 2010; the squadron stood down on 26 May 2011.

In 2017, however, the MoD announced that 201 Squadron would re-form around 2021 as the second Poseidon MRA.Mk 1 unit.

Based at RAF Brize Norton as unique unit within the RAF Waddington-headquartered Air Warfare Centre, the Joint Airborne Delivery Trials and Evaluation Unit (JADTEU) worked with QinetiQ to install ASRA kit on the A400M's loading ramp. The unit's engineers designed and manufactured the system.

204 SQUADRON

On 25 March 1915, the RNAS established 4 Squadron out of the Defence Flight stationed at Dover. In August it became 4 Wing and this early element of 204 Squadron history stalled. A new 4 Squadron formed out of A Squadron, 5 Wing, RNAS, on 31 December 1916. Initially equipped for bombing, it received Sopwith Pup scouts in March 1917, later exchanging them for Camels. It remained a scout unit, latterly as 204 Squadron, until disbandment on 31 December 1919.

It re-formed less than a decade later, on 1 February 1929, operating the Southampton in the general reconnaissance role. In 1935, 204 Squadron re-equipped with the Scapa, taking the new type to Egypt as Italy threatened Abyssinia. It was back in Plymouth by August 1936, exchanging its Scapas for Londons. It departed for Australia in December 1937, returning as spring turned into summer 1938.

The squadron began re-equipping with the Sunderland in June 1939, in time for its first wartime action on 4 September. Anti-submarine warfare and patrol work from stations in the UK, Mediterranean and West Africa kept the unit busy until it disbanded on 30 June 1945. There followed a period in the transport role, employing Dakotas and Valettas in the Middle East from 1 August 1947 until 20 February 1953, when the unit renumbered as 84 Squadron.

On 1 January 1954, a new 204 Squadron stood up at Ballykelly, County Londonderry. Equipped with the Shackleton MR.Mk 2, it returned the unit to the maritime role with which it had become familiar. Remarkably, the Shackleton MR.Mk 2 (and MR.Mk 1A between April 1958 and February 1960) remained the squadron's equipment until it disbanded on 28 April 1972. By then, it had relocated to Honington, from where shipping reconnaissance and SAR were its primary duties.

205 SQUADRON

Number 205 Squadron was destined to become the RAF's final flying-boat squadron, relinquishing the Sunderland in May 1959. The unit's history goes back to 31 December 1916, when 5 Squadron, RNAS began flying day-bombing missions, before turning to photographic reconnaissance later in the war; it disbanded on 22 January 1920.

On 8 January 1929, the unit re-formed as an expansion of the Far East Flight at Seletar. Equipped with Southampton II and III flying boats, its focus was on operations throughout the Far East and ASR work. The tasking remained the same after the Short Singapore replaced the Southamptons in 1935.

While its headquarters remained at Seletar, 205 Squadron established a detachment at Koggala from April 1941, operating Catalinas. The US type fully replaced the Singapore that September, and a Catalina became the unit's first loss to enemy action, when the Imperial Japanese Navy shot it down on 6 December.

The squadron suffered badly and on 3 March 1942, just two aircraft escaped to Australia. By 23 July, when it was reconstituted back at Koggala, 205 Squadron had just one Catalina, taking two from 202 Squadron and another from 240 Squadron for anti-ship, patrol and ASR missions. The squadron continued its regular work while moving between bases and in April 1944 one of the Catalinas spotted a liferaft – the survivors on board had been adrift for 50 days.

In June 1945, the squadron converted onto the Sunderland, maintaining its ASR role and returning to Seletar, before sending a detachment to Japan for patrols off Korea. The Shackleton MR.Mk 1A arrived in May 1958 and 12 months later the squadron's final, indeed the RAF's final, Sunderland GR5 was withdrawn. The Shackleton, latterly in Mk 2 form, remained with 205 Squadron on patrol and SAR duties until the unit disbanded at Changi on 31 October 1971.

206 SQUADRON

The RNAS formed its 6 Squadron on 1 November 1916. Originally a scout unit, it disbanded in August 1917 to reappear on 1 January 1918 as a bomber squadron, subsequently redesignated as 206 Squadron, RAF. It disbanded in Egypt, by renumbering as 47 Squadron, on 1 February 1920.

On 15 June 1936, an enlarged 'C' Flight, 48 Squadron became the new 206 Squadron, tasked with pilot training. Soon the unit was employing its Avro Ansons operationally, beginning anti-shipping patrols in earnest on 1 September 1939. The hectic, dangerous work continued from several UK bases as the squadron converted onto the Hudson from March 1940. In July 1942, 206 Squadron began exchanging its Hudsons for Boeing Fortresses, with which it ranged far out over the ocean. In October it left the UK for the Azores, flying over the South Atlantic until the following April, when it re-equipped with Liberators at St Eval.

Number 206 Squadron remained on maritime operations until June 1945, when it began cargo and personnel transport. In November it took Avro York freighters, operating them during the Berlin Airlift. It disbanded on 20 February 1950, re-forming back in the maritime business on 27 September 1952.

Equipped with the Shackleton MR.Mk 1A and MR.Mk 2, it took SAR as an important secondary role, visiting New Zealand in 1956–1957 and then providing SAR cover off Christmas Island during the Operation Grapple nuclear tests. In 1958, 206 Squadron transferred to St Mawgan and the Shackleton MR.Mk 3. It changed station again in 1965, this time to Kinloss, where it remained to take the Nimrod MR.Mk 1 on strength from November 1970. The Nimrod MR.Mk 2 arrived from February 1980 and served the unit until its disbandment on 1 April 2005.

In 2009, the squadron returned as 206 (Reserve) Heavy Aircraft Test & Evaluation Squadron, an amalgamation of the Heavy Lift Test Squadron and Air Transport and Air-to-Air Refuelling Operational Evaluation Unit. The new 206 was headquartered at Boscombe Down with a detachment at Lyneham, the detachment subsequently moving to Brize Norton, to which station the entire unit moved in 2014.

Part of the Air Warfare Centre, 206 Squadron takes responsibility for trials with all the RAF's heavy aircraft, ranging from the Embraer Phenom and King Air-based Shadow, through the Hercules and Atlas, to the C-17. It will be involved in the Poseidon programme throughout the type's service career, effectively returning it to the maritime role with which it is most associated, while it also trialled ASRA equipment for the Atlas.

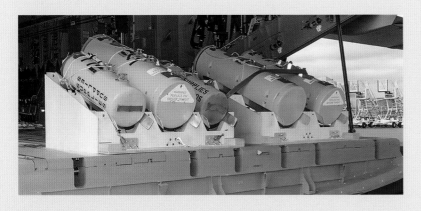

ACKNOWLEDGEMENTS

My sincere thanks go to Jay Myers at Royal Air Force Media & Communications, Headquarters Air Command, whose idea it was. Also to Lee Barton at the Air Historical Branch, whose encyclopaedic knowledge of the AHB's photographic archive made light work of sourcing many of the images used, and to the 22 Squadron Association's Paul Martin, whose work made mine so much easier. Finally, to my editor, Kate Beer, for never nagging even though I was late, and the jolly emails that kept me going.

GLOSSARY

11/18 HSU	11/18 Group Helicopter Standardisation Unit		DHFS	Defence Helicopter Flying School
18 GSU(H)	18 Group Standardisation Unit (Helicopters)		DR	Dead reckoning
3 Group HSU	3 Group Helicopter Standardisation Unit		ERS	Emergency Rescue Squadron
ACO	Air Coordination Officer		ESM	Electronic support measures
AFC	Air Force Cross		F540	RAF Operations Record Book
AFM	Air Force Medal		FAA	Fleet Air Arm
AM	Amplitude Modulation		FADEC	Full-authority digital engine control
AOC	Air Officer Commanding		FB	Fighter-bomber
ARCC	Aeronautical Rescue Coordination Centre		FLA	Future Large Aircraft
ASR	Air sea rescue		FLIR	Forward-looking infrared
ASRA	Air Sea Rescue Apparatus		FM	Frequency Modulation
ASRS	Air Sea Rescue Services		FRU	Fleet Requirements Unit
ASRU	Air/Sea Rescue Unit (surface craft)		ft	Feet
ASV	Anti-surface vessel		GM	George Medal
ASW	Anti-submarine warfare		GR	General reconnaissance
ATM	Auto-hover trim		HAR	Helicopter Airborne Rescue
AuxAF	Auxiliary Air Force		HAS	Helicopter Anti-Submarine
BIH	British International Helicopters		HC	Helicopter Transport
BS	British Standard		HF	High Frequency
C	Transport		HIFR	Helicopter inflight refuelling, or hover inflight refuelling
C3	Command, control and communications		HMAFV	His Majesty's Air Force Vessel
Casevac	Casualty evacuation		hp	Horsepower
CBI	China, Burma, India theatre of operations		HQ	Headquarters
CFS	Central Flying School		HR	Helicopter Rescue
CFS(H)	Central Flying School Helicopter		HSL	High-speed launch
CMB	Coastal motorboat		HT	Helicopter Training
DfT	Department for Transport			

HU	Helicopter Utility (transport)	QCVSA	Queen's Commendation for Valuable Service in the Air
IEC	Immediate emergency care	QGM	Queen's Gallantry Medal
in	Inch	QHCI	Qualified Helicopter Crewman Instructor
IR	Infrared	QHI	Qualified Helicopter Instructor
JADTEU	Joint Airborne Delivery Trials and Evaluation Unit	(R)	Reserve
K	Tanker	RAAF	Royal Australian Air Force
KC	Tanker Transport	RadOp	Radar Operator
kN	Kilonewton (the thrust delivered by a jet engine, expressed as a force)	RAF	Royal Air Force
kt	Knot, one nautical mile per hour	RAF MRS	RAF Mountain Rescue Service
lb	Pounds	RAF SKTU	RAF Sea King Training Unit
lb st	Pounds of thrust (delivered by a jet engine)	RAuxAF	Royal Auxiliary Air Force
LRRC	Long-range rescue craft	RCAF	Royal Canadian Air Force
m	Metre	RCC	Rescue Co-ordination Centre
m²	Square metres	RFC	Royal Flying Corps
MACA	Military Aid to Civil Authorities	RFP	Request for proposals
MAOT	Mobile Air Operations Team	RMB	Royal Marines Base
MCA	Maritime and Coastguard Agency	RNAS	Royal Naval Air Service
MCS	Marine Craft Section	RNLI	Royal National Lifeboat Institution
Met	meteorological	RTTL	Rescue and Target Towing Launch
Mk	Mark, suggesting an iteration of a design, Lysander Mk III being the third iteration of the Lysander, for example	SANA	Società Anonima di Navigazione Aerea
		SAR	Search and rescue
		SAR – H	Search and Rescue – Helicopter
MMS	Multi Sensor System	SARF	SAR Force
MoD	Ministry of Defence	SAROP	SAR operation
MR	Maritime Reconnaissance	SARTS	Search and Rescue Training Squadron
MRA	Maritime Reconnaissance and Attack	SARTU	Search and Rescue Training Unit
MRCC	Maritime Rescue Co-ordination Centre	Satcom	Satellite communications
MRR	Maritime radar reconnaissance	SOE	Special Operations Executive
MRT	Mountain rescue team	SOPs	Standard Operating Procedures
MTB	Motor torpedo boat	SOUMAR	Southern Maritime Air Region
MTO	Mediterranean Theatre of Operations	sq ft	Square feet
MU	Maintenance Unit	SRCC	Southern Rescue Co-ordination Centre
NAS	Naval Air Squadron	ST	Seaplane Tender
nm	Nautical mile	T	Trainer
No.	Number	TANS	Tactical Air Navigation System
Nos	Numbers	U-boat	Unterseeboot; 'under sea boat', a German submarine
NVGs	Night-vision goggles	UHF	Ultra High Frequency
OC	Officer Commanding	USAAF	US Army Air Force
OCU	Operational Conversion Unit	USAF	US Air Force
OEU	Operational Evaluation Unit	USAFE	US Air Forces Europe
OTU	Operational Training Unit	VHF	Very High Frequency
PFI	Private finance initiative	W/Op	Wireless Operator
PPE	Personal protection equipment	W/T	Wireless transmitter
QCBA	Queen's Commendation for Bravery in the Air	WAAF	Women's Auxiliary Air Force
QCI	Qualified Crewman Instructor		

BIBLIOGRAPHY

Royal Air Force Aircraft & Weapons (Key Publishing in association with Royal Air Force Media & Communications, Headquarters Air Command, 2017)

Royal Air Force Squadrons: The Story Behind Today's Units (Key Publishing in association with Royal Air Force Media & Communications, Headquarters Air Command, 2016)

World Air Power Journal, various volumes (Aerospace Publishing, 1990–2000)

The Official Royal Air Force Annual Review, various volumes (Key Publishing in association with Royal Air Force Media & Communications, Headquarters Air Command, 2009–2020)

Donald, David, editor, *American Warplanes of World War II* (Aerospace Publishing, 1995)

Donald, David & Lake, Jon, editors, *World Air Power Journal Encyclopedia of World Military Aircraft* (Aerospace Publishing, 1996)

Doylerush, Edward, *The Legend of Llandwrog: The story of an airfield and the birth of the RAF Mountain Rescue Service* (Midland Counties Publications, 1994)

Franks, Norman, *Another Kind of Courage: Stories of the UK-based Walrus Air-Sea Rescue Squadrons* (Patrick Stephens Limited, 1994)

Franks, Norman, *Images Of War: The RAF Air Sea Rescue Service In The Second World War* (Pen & Sword, 2016)

Jefford, CG, Wing Commander (Retired), *R.A.F Squadrons: A Comprehensive Record of the Movement and Equipment of all RAF Squadrons and their Antecedents Since 1912* (2nd Edition, Airlife, 2001)

March, Daniel J, editor, *British Warplanes of World War II* (Aerospace Publishing, 1998)

Moyes, Phillip, *Bomber Squadrons of the RAF and Their Aircraft* (New edition, MacDonald and James, 1976)

Overill, Tony, *Crash Boats of Gorleston: An Illustrated History of 24 RAF Airsea Rescue Unit Gorleston-on-Sea, Norfolk* (Woodfield, 2005)

Pitchfork, Graham, Air Commodore (Retired), *Shot Down And In The Drink: RAF and Commonwealth aircrews saved from the sea 1939–1945* (The National Archives, 2005)

Rawlings, John, *Coastal Support and Special Squadrons of the RAF and Their Aircraft* (MacDonald, 1969)

Rawlings, John, *Fighter Squadrons of the R.A.F and Their Aircraft* (Jane's, 1982)

Sturtivant, Ray & Balance, Theo, *The Squadrons of the Fleet Air Arm* (Air-Britain, 1994)

Sutherland, Jon & Canwell, Diane, *The RAF Air Sea Rescue Service 1918–1986* (Pen & Sword, 2005)

Thetford, Owen, *Aircraft of the Royal Air Force since 1918*, (Putnam, 1995)

Websites:

www.22squadronassociation.org.uk

www.rafweb.org

INDEX

Page numbers in *italics* refer to illustrations